Bryan S. Turner
A Theory of Catastrophe

De Gruyter Contemporary Social Sciences

Volume 19

Bryan S. Turner

A Theory of Catastrophe

—

DE GRUYTER

ISBN 978-3-11-162252-1
e-ISBN (PDF) 978-3-11-077236-4
e-ISBN (EPUB) 978-3-11-077244-9
ISSN 2747-5689
e-ISSN 2747-5697

Library of Congress Control Number: 2023930087

Bibliographic information published by the Deutsche Nationalbibliothek
The Deutsche Nationalbibliothek lists this publication in the Deutsche Nationalbibliografie;
detailed bibliographic data are available on the internet at http://dnb.dnb.de.

www.degruyter.com

Contents

Contents

Chapter 1
Introduction: Disasters, Crises, and Catastrophes

Angelus Novus
'The angel would like to stay, awaken the dead, and make whole what is smashed. But a
storm is blowing up from Paradise; it has got caught in his wings with such violence that
the angel can no longer close them. This storm irresistibly propels him into the future to
which his back is turned, while a pile of debris before him grows skyward. This storm is
what we call progress,'
Walter Benjamin (1973: 259–260), *Theses on the Philosophy of History*

Paul Klee's monoprint (an oil transfer with watercolour on paper) of the angel of
history is the jacket cover for this study of catastrophe. Walter Benjamin (1892–
1940) bought the monoprint in 1921 for 1,000 marks. His friend Gershom Scholem
has given an intimate account of the importance of the picture for Benjamin's life
in an essay 'Walter Benjamin and his Angel' in *Jews and Judaism in Crisis* (Dannhauser, 1976). In fact, Benjamin had intended to create a journal in the 1920s called
Angelus Novus. I dwell on this image at this stage to grasp the significance of the
tradition in Judaism of writing on Talmudic angels of which Benjamin was well
aware (Handelman, 1991). The theme of messianic hope in Judaism is an important
theme running through this account of modern catastrophes. The theme of messianism also illustrates the significant gap that existed between the secular Marxism of the Frankfurt Centre during Benjamin's involvement in the research group.
There is, as I show in subsequent chapters, an important overlap between the
secular-Marxist hope for a society based on equality and mutual respect and the
Jewish-Christian hope for a world to come.

Benjamin committed suicide, escaping from the advancing *Wehrmacht*, and
carrying the Klee painting with him, at Port Bou on the French-Spanish border.
The work of Benjamin and other members of the Frankfurt School plays an
important part in this study of catastrophes. As Jewish victims of fascism, their theories have played an important role in many critical responses to the Holocaust,
Auschwitz, modern technological, militarism, capitalist development and Enlightenment ideas on the inevitability of progress. Any theory of catastrophe will
have to take the legacy of the Frankfurt School seriously, especially Benjamin's relationship to messianic visions of time and Marxist views on revolutionary disruptions to history.

When a contemporary author announces that he or she is writing a book
about catastrophes, a common response may be to condemn all such authors as
pessimistic 'doom sayers'. In many circumstances, as a sign of hope, this may be
an apt response. However, the crises of recent years are numerous, global, and

https://doi.org/10.1515/9783110772364-001

overwhelming. We may expect to see many volumes appearing with titles referring to catastrophe. I mention two here. In *catastrophes: views from natural and human sciences*, Andreas Hoppe (2019) conflates a variety of different, if related, concepts: hazards, disasters, crises and catastrophes. One aspect of my approach is to avoid what can be regarded as conceptual promiscuity. Hazards – such as a foggy morning – are not equivalent to catastrophes. Another volume which is much closer to my project is Heinrich August Winkler (2015) *The Age of Catastrophe 1914–1945*. This volume, which was published in Germany in 2011, is volume II of a more expansive project on the history of Germany in the context of European history. Winkler is a distinguished German historian and volume II concerns the catastrophe of two world wars and their consequences for Germany. More precisely he considers the struggle between democratic and authoritarian politics in German society. His research therefore addresses the idea of political catastrophe with reference to Germany and more broadly the European continent. His research question is, to what extent democratic polities can accommodate the endless political struggles between left and right without descending into civil war.

My approach is not confined to political catastrophe. My approach to catastrophes was initially written in response to and in the context of the COVID-19 pandemic, which overshadowed my research from the early months of 2019 until the late Autumn of 2022. The WHO report in 2022 claimed that 150,000 million people had died as a result of the pandemic. Government data showed that life expectancy in the United States had declined by 2.7 years from records collected between 2019–2020, which was the lowest since 1966. As the pandemic unfolded, other catastrophes were developing. The Russian invasion of Ukraine in February 2022 and the threat of nuclear war were, by any definition, a catastrophe of tragic proportions. As I worked towards a conclusion, there was further evidence of a climate catastrophe as southern Europe suffered from drought conditions and much of Pakistan was under water.

Although writing this volume has been a depressing experience, I need to declare at the beginning my commitment to the view that the aim of life is human happiness. In making this statement, I realize that happiness is essentially difficult to define and for many difficult to achieve (Turner and Contreras-Vejar, 2018). The idea was much discussed by Aristotle and by Christian theologians like St. Augustine. It was the central notion behind the utilitarian philosophy of political theorists such as Jeremy Bentham (1748–1832), who promoted the idea that the aim of government is the 'greatest happiness of the greatest number'. Although the contexts or 'regimes' of happiness have varied over time, it remains the goal of human activity if it is understood in broad terms as including health, personal security, companionship, and longevity. The achievement of happiness is without question challenged by the diverse disasters, crises, and catastrophes I describe in this volume.

For that very reason, the quest for happiness becomes more intense for this generation and perhaps even more so for the next generation. Also, for that reason, we need to take seriously the question of inter-generational justice, which is another theme running through my account. Can we hand over a world to the next generation that is intact and does not seriously disadvantage them as a result, for example, of climate change?

A catastrophe tends to produce many additional catastrophic consequences. Perhaps I can be allowed to use the medical term 'sequelae' – the subsequent conditions that follow an original injury or infection – to describe the ways in which one catastrophe produces many subsequent crises or catastrophes. The catastrophic invasion of Ukraine has its sequelae by creating a world shortage of grain which may result in famine in the poor countries of Africa and Asia. Famines often create conditions for the spread of disease, resulting in a catastrophic loss of population, economic decline, and scarcity. The combined effect will create the conditions that contribute to civil unrest and political instability (Homer-Dixon, 1999). The multiple sequelae of catastrophe threaten to result in social and political chaos. In my conclusion, I look at the possible options between optimism and pessimism in the face of the burden of troublesome times.

There have been various influential publications on state failure such as *Why Nations Fail* (Acemoglu and Robinson, 2012) and others on why nations collapse (Diamond, 2005). There has also been a growing literature on the potential risks that could bring about the extinction of the human species (Bostrom and Cirkovic, 2008; Leslie, 1996; Ord, 2020; Reese, 2003). These studies, that are primarily by natural scientists rather than by social scientists, have considered a range of potential threats that might presage the end of humans: natural catastrophes, thermonuclear war, terrorism, biological weapons, totalitarianism, advanced nanotechnology, artificial intelligence, and social collapse. Their broad conclusion is that the threat of natural disasters, while real, is unlikely to bring about a sustained crisis, let alone human extinction. They also assume that the other threats, such as social, technological, biological, and military ones, are clearly troublesome, but unlikely to constitute conditions that cannot be managed and contained at some level. These volumes on extinction were based on research or publication dates before the COVID-19 pandemic began in 2019 and the invasion of Ukraine in 2022. Alongside these catastrophes, there has been growing authoritarianism in modern politics. This combination – pandemic, war, famine – has historically been the basis for disease. A combination of catastrophes in 2022–2023 may well produce a deeper global crisis that was not fully anticipated by earlier studies of catastrophe that in retrospect look overly optimistic.

A more comprehensive, but equally pessimistic appraisal of our future, was explored by Vaclav Smil (2008) in *Global Catastrophes and Trends*. Smil sought to avoid a static analysis of catastrophe by looking at a projection of fifty years. His basic argument proposed that critical discontinuities often occur as low probabilities, while there are recurrent or persistent issues such as earthquakes or pandemics. In both cases, scientific understanding can assist in reversing or reducing the risks they present. His list includes events that have not occurred before, such as a global nuclear war or new manifestations of climate change. While human intervention can reduce risks, there may be no easy answer to growing resistance to antibiotics for common pathogenic bacteria. The natural resources necessary for human survival are already seriously depleted. Writing at the beginning of this century, he anticipated a new pandemic to occur every half-century with devastating consequences for the third world. COVID-19 is the perfect illustration of his analysis. His predictions also included the mass exodus of populations fleeing from wars, famines, and poverty.

Premonitions about human extinction and the fatal flaws of human societies are often associated with warfare. Oswald Spengler (1880–1936) was one of the most influential authors of his generation, especially in the context of the Weimar Republic. Popular understanding of his work regards him as a 'prophet of doom' in his analysis of the western crisis resulting in disintegration and collapse. He published *The Decline of the West* (Spengler, 1928). It was conceived before 1914 and completed by 1918, thereby covering the time of WWI. It appeared in Germany in two volumes beginning in July 1918 with the title *Untergang des Abendlandes*. Some 90,000 copies were printed in anticipation of robust sales. The German title is perhaps more interesting than the English translation, because *Untergang* is 'setting' or 'sinking'. Figuratively, it can mean 'ruin'. *Abendlandes* is literally the 'lands of the evening' or the Occident. The title then can mean the setting of the West and its ruin. A civilization for Spengler was what a culture becomes once its capacity for creativity is in decline. In this sense a vital culture is always in a state of development. He identified various philosophers and religious leaders who marked these transitions into decline. For example, Jean-Jacques Rousseau (1712–1778) stood at the apex of Western culture before its descent into decay. One further aspect of this erosion is the growing dominance of technical rationality over spiritual creativity and depth.

Spengler, an obscure and unknown author, became instantly famous, partly because the book matched the pessimistic mood of the period, especially in Germany as the War came to an end. Spengler claimed that the work was inspired by both Johann Goethe (1749–1832) and Friedrich Nietzsche (1844–1900), who were inspirational figures in western culture and underpinned Spengler's understanding of western culture. For Goethe, in the story of *Faust*, humans are also confronted by sensations of nothingness. However, by accepting our own limitations, there is the possibility of creating new values that will allow us to triumph finally over nihilism. Nietzsche died in 1900, but his account of western nihilism was also foundational in the century that was to witness two world wars. For Nietzsche, with the death of God, human life in modern societies was characterized by its emptiness. Nevertheless, he struggled against nihilism and came to regard it as merely a transitional stage in *The Will to Power* (Nietzsche, 2017). In the future, he anticipated a counter-movement and declared that he was not a 'no-saying' spirit. In short, two authors, associated with modern nihilism, saw its limitations. The problem of nihilism for any philosopher would be the question: why write a book about it? Is a book a yes-saying affirmation that we are rejecting nihilism? I confront this question in my final chapter.

Despite its severe limitations, Spengler's publication has enjoyed a remarkable long *durée*, because it captured the mood of the period and its aftermath (Rojek, 2018). The basic model was that cultures pass through a cycle of birth, maturity, and decline. Metaphorically, the cycle was also understood in terms of spring, summer, autumn and winter. As a model of historical change, it has few supporters among professional historians. Northrop Frye (1974) recommended that we should not attempt to read this as world history, but as a poetic analogy. In the changing seasons, the West had arrived at its 'winter' in which its accomplishments in the arts and philosophy are exhausted. Its defining energies are now in technology which becomes the basis of wars, dictatorships, and annihilation. The era of individualism, humanitarianism, intellectual inquiry, and scepticism was drawing to an end. In the emerging cultural winter, there would be greater restrictions on freedom, a revival of religious faith and an increasing use of force. Faced with post-war defeat and humiliation, 'the German-speaking public could find in Spengler's work a tidy explanation of the calamities that had overwhelmed them – and that were about to befall their neighbours' (Hughes, 1959: 378).

Spengler is important for my conceptual framework in that the decline of culture and its transformation into an otiose civilization cannot be understand as a routine disaster. It must be understood within the larger debate about the catastrophic finale of cultures. We need to distinguish between crisis as an actual social or political crisis and the use of 'crisis' as a rhetorical strategy. Spengler in 1919 anticipated the struggle for a different social order in his overlooked pamphlet on *Prussianism and Socialism*. The pamphlet serves as both a warning to Germany in defeat and as a challenge. The German nation must come together as it did in the war effort of 1914. It needs to create a genuine organic community to overcome class divisions and the culture of individualism. If it can create what Spengler called the Prussian socialist spirit, then the German people will not be subordinated to the rule of the English banks. The rallying cry for this Prussian socialism was heard across the political spectrum. For conservatives such as Ernst Jünger, the pamphlet created an opportunity after the disarmament of Germany for a Conservative Revolution to avoid both liberalism and communism.

While Spengler's view of historical change may be flawed, any large-scale vision of historical change finds it necessary to address Spengler. Arnold Toynbee (1972) in his *Study of History* felt it necessary to criticize Spengler's 'fatalism'. Similarly, Samuel Huntington in his *The Clash of Civilizations* recognized that 'the "decline of the West" has been a central theme in twentieth-century history' (Huntington, 1997: 83). The theme of three stages of history was also repeated by Philip Rieff (2006) in *My Life among the Deathworks*. The first age was the pagan age stretching from ancient Athens to aboriginal Australia. Its major theme was fate, and its vertical authority system was dominated by non-negotiable taboos. The first world has disappeared. The second world was dominated by the monotheistic religions. Faith rather than fate was its major motif. The third world negates the culture of the second world through its radical scepticism. It works on the fictions of power. It is the age of postmodernism in which 'deathworks' are deployed to destroy any established culture and the dominant institutions become the battlegrounds of the culture wars. For Rieff, Andres Serrano's *Piss Christ* was part of the relentless effort 'to make the second world identity repulsive, untenable' (Rieff, 2006: 98). In Nietzsche's terms, the third world is catastrophic (Rieff, 2006: 178–179). Although Rieff does not discuss Spengler, the parallel treatment of three stages of human history or at least the history of the West is remarkable.

Spengler was concerned primarily with the West, indeed with the problems of post-war Germany. In writing about contemporary catastrophes, we need to pay attention to globalization. The rapid spread of COVID-19 from 2019 to appear in every part of the world is an important reminder of the essential interconnected nature of modern societies. While this global context is especially evident in the case of infectious disease, it applies to the various catastrophes I discuss in this volume, such as the global economic 'contamination' that followed the collapse of Lehman Brothers in 2008 (Calhoun and Derluguian, 2011). Populist politics have opposed globalization insofar as it is seen as a major aspect of migration and the changing ethnic and cultural composition of the West. Demographic decline has become a major feature of populist politics in the West (Torpey and Turner, 2017).

An issue that arises throughout my attempt to develop a theory of catastrophes is the question as to whether there can be positive or beneficial outcomes to catastrophes. Many sociologists have argued that disasters and catastrophes can increase community awareness and enhance the resilience of institutions. Roland Robertson (1992) wrote about 'globality' as the awareness of existing in a common world or the world as a single place. One can argue that COVID-19 created the sense of a common global problem, but is it a fractured 'globality'? Whereas a cosmopolitan ethic was perceived as an inevitable development of globalization, these optimistic interpretations have given way to concerns about growing authoritarianism in western politics.

There is a tradition in sociology that has addressed civilizational change, system collapse and social break-down. In this respect, one can refer to the work of Pitirim A. Sorokin in such publications as *Man and Society in Calamity* (Sorokin, 1968). Although he referred to 'calamities' rather than catastrophes, Sorokin could claim to have invented a sociology of catastrophes (Alalykin-Izvekov, 2020). Unfortunately, his work was ignored by his generation, possibly because of his combative style and his stinging criticisms of colleagues. In the most influential work on social theory by Talcott Parsons in 1951, there is one reference to Sorokin (Parsons, 1991: 490). These early approaches to large-scale social breakdown are more the exception than the rule and are contrasted with the legacy of Talcott Parsons on functionalism in the study of the social system.

The modern study of ancient civilizations has been stimulated by the legacy of Karl Jaspers on the so-called 'Axial Age' in the period 800 – 400 bc. Its growth and decline were conceived within an evolutionary framework that spoke mostly about 'transitions' rather than radical disruptions (Bellah and Joas, 2012). There is, however, a well-established sociology of revolutions that draws on the Marxist tradition. It is perhaps best illustrated in contemporary publications by Theda Skocpol (1979) in her *States and Social Revolutions*. One suspects that the numerous crises currently confronting the global order will produce a revival of interest in how catastrophes change societies and their global connections. Unsurprisingly, there has already been a flurry of sociological studies of COVID-19 and how it is radically transforming societies and to some extent repeating the experiences of previous pandemics (Delanty, 2021). Perhaps what is remarkable is that most publications on the sociology of social change do not routinely include plagues, famine, and war.

The global scale and widespread consequences of these events – both known and unknown – prompted me to describe them as 'catastrophes' and to think about the historical sociology of catastrophes. I examine a range of catastrophes that typically have global implications and consequences. Chapter 4 is devoted to plagues, involving discussion of the nature of the zoonotic disease, namely diseases that spread from animals to humans, such as SARS and COVID-19. Other chapters consider wars, colonial history, economic collapse, and famines. These chapters also include a theoretical analysis of a range of concepts: crisis, catastrophe, calamity, disaster, and utopia. We need to recognize COVID-19 as a catastrophe that is global and transformative with consequences bearing significantly on human welfare, wealth, happiness, and political stability. Few analyses of COVID-19 have in fact described it as a 'catastrophe'. However, two recent volumes come to mind that have seen COVID-19 as unambiguously a catastrophe. Richard Horton's *The Covid-19 Catastrophe* (2020) in which he criticized governments for failing to take early and effective action based exclusively on science. He made important comparisons between the Spanish Flu of 1919–1920 and COVID-19 in terms of the high number of deaths and government inaction. Daniel Fierstein's *Social and Political Representations of the Covid-19 Crisis* (2019) argued that regardless of its biological origin, the COVID-19 pandemic was primarily a social phenomenon. Understanding state policies, civil responses, outcomes, and long-term consequences requires sociological and political analysis. Politicians of all political stripes failed to fully grasp the social character of the problem facing them. COVID-19 has involved a continuous struggle between economic and political interests on the one hand and the social needs of ordinary citizens on the other. Working on three levels, epistemological, emotional, and ethical-moral, Fierstein's analysis of the failed policies of Argentina is described as a catastrophe, providing an important lesson for societies facing a legacy of both individualism and distrust of state power. At the psycho-analytical dimension, the many responses involving fear of the catastrophe have resulted in denial, projection, and scapegoating. Government inaction or at least a slow response to 'monkeypox' in the United States has been criticized. San Francisco declared an emergency in August 2022 with some 300 known cases.

In contemporary sociology much attention has been devoted to industrialization, modernization, postmodernity, and globalization. However, little or no attention has been specifically given to catastrophes, even though sociology evolved during the 20th century amid many catastrophes, including two world wars. The Korean War and the Vietnamese War were equally catastrophic in their scale and consequences.

There is an extensive literature on risk, hazard, danger, and disaster. Some aspects of economics and political economy have argued that capitalism is crisis-prone. There is a long tradition of analysis of speculative crises, chronic unemployment, class conflict and eventual breakdown from David Ricardo to Karl Marx to Thomas Piketty. Many of these issues are explored in chapter 7 in which I consider the inevitable exhaustion or entropy of the natural resources of the earth in the 'bioeconomics' of the Romanian economist Nicholas Georgescu-Roegen.

Classical economic theory has of course focused on various forms of risk. Economics does not treat the business cycle or business collapse as catastrophic. The collapse of Lehman Brothers and the economic down-turn of 2008–2011 were not seen as a catastrophe, but rather as a weakness in regulation relating to the subprime mortgage strategy, the over-heated housing market, and false expectations of the 'trickledown effect'. The collapse of Lehman Brothers can be said to have had catastrophic consequences in the European Union where the austerity strategy magnified the negative consequences of de-regulation.

The concept of risk has been dominant in economics with the emergence of sea-faring nations, where piracy was one obvious risk to emerging global trade. The word 'risk' comes from the Italian root *risica, risco,* and *rischio* and became a common term for describing the hazards involved in international trade. The growth of trading companies to conduct international trade such as the English East India Company of 1600, became the driving force behind early calculations of risk. In contemporary sociology, there is some agreement that 'risk' is a 'catch-all' concept that covers diverse and different conditions (Battistelli and Galantino, 2019). In the absence of a clear idea of catastrophe, in everyday language 'catastrophe' and 'disaster' are often used interchangeably. One aim of this study is to clarify the differences between risks, disasters, and catastrophes. Taking two contrasted examples, while a train crash is a disaster, a nuclear fall-out is a catastrophe. We need, however, to say more about catastrophe other than drawing attention to its size and scope.

Catastrophe theory in biology is based on a simple distinction between continuous and discontinuous processes. Catastrophes are seen as discontinuous processes. Mathematical models were originally developed by the French mathematician René Thom in the 1960s to create a mathematical tool known simply as 'catastrophe theory'. Thom employed this approach to study and make predictions of sudden discontinuous processes. In the 1970s his theory was taken up by mathematicians and scientists in several fields. These ideas have been applied, for example, in theories of international relations to study wars that are seen as discontinuous eruptions and those that emerge slowly in a continuous process (Holt, Job, and Markus, 1978). The attempt to develop mathematical models of the outbreak of wars contrasts sharply with the so-called English School of International Relations that was dominated by historians under the leadership of Martin Wight in the late 1950s at the London School of Economics. Wight was struck by the fortuitous character of political events and opposed any optimistic view of progress, but the focus of the group was the comparative approach to state-systems in world history.

For societies that have both long-standing internal religio-ethnic conflicts and an unfavorable external environment, the prospects for national sovereignty and political stability are limited. One example is Lebanon which has divisive internal conflicts between Druze, Christian and Muslim communities, a history of civil wars, unstable relationships with its neighbours especially Israel and Syria. Lebanon suffered from a long civil war from 1975 to 1990. The conflict involved a range of militia groups including Maronite Catholics, Sunni Muslims, Shi'ite populists, and the Palestinian Liberation Organization. It is estimated that there were 120,000 fatalities. The resulting peace did not result in a satisfactory solution or the election of an effective government (Ghosn and Koury, 2011). It has been subject to continuous external interventions from France, America, Syria, and Israel.

In recent history, there is also the growing influence of Hezbollah with the backing of Shiite supporters from Iran. It has been described as the 'battle ground of the Middle East' (Hirst, 2010). These diverse political problems are compounded by the contemporary failure to appoint a competent government with popular support. Lebanon may be said to be a political catastrophe without a denouement or ending.

Despite the sophistication of the mathematics, catastrophe theory lost favour after numerous criticisms were raised against it (Ekeland, 1988; Horgan, 1996). The conclusion was that catastrophe theory may be relevant to the 'exact sciences' (engineering), but not to the 'inexact sciences' (social sciences). The mathematical approaches often considered individual human responses involving fear and anger resulting in aggression (Zeeman, 1976). These assumptions are not obviously helpful in studying large-scale wars lasting for decades. Mathematical approaches are helpful in studying natural catastrophes in considering their sudden or continuous nature. Both sudden and continuous dimensions are present, for example, in earthquakes. They are experienced as sudden eruptions, but their causes may have been evolving over 1000s of years.

The Sociology of Disaster

Perhaps the most developed area of research falls under disaster studies and related areas such as security studies. I am not critical of disaster studies. They have contributed important research on the causes and consequences of disasters. Their research often includes the perspectives of sociology and political science. My argument in this volume is that there are important contrasts to be drawn between disasters and catastrophes. In disaster studies, there is the idea of 'megadisasters' which might conceivably stand in for 'catastrophe'. Hurricane Katrina has been described as a catastrophe in *The Sociology of Katrina: Perspectives on a Modern* catastrophe (Brunsma, Overfelt and Picon, 2008). There is also significant research on Katrina's impact on children within the perspective of disaster research (Fotheringil and Peak, 2015).

The sociology of disasters is thus a well-established area of research. Sociologists played a central role in building the University of Chicago's National Opinion Research Center which examined human responses to disasters. Subsequently, sociologists were involved in research projects at the National Academy of Sciences National Research Council's Disaster Research Group, the Disaster Research Center, the Natural Hazards Center, the Hazard Reduction and Recovery Center, and the International Hurricane Center (Webb, 2002). There is a Research Committee within the International Sociological Association on disasters. In Robert Merton and

Robert Nisbet's *Contemporary Social Problems,* Charles Fitz (1961: 655) wrote the chapter on 'Disasters' which he defined as occurring when 'the social structure is disrupted and the fulfilment of all or some of the essential functions of the society, or its subdivision, is prevented'. Sociology was not overly concerned with the actual fatalities, or the physical destruction involved in disasters. Rather what interested sociologists was how these disasters have differential effects on social groups, many of which are already powerless. Sociologists typically raise questions about whether disasters produce more social solidarity or result in deeper social divisions and civil unrest.

Disasters frequently have natural causes such as earthquakes, but they can also be related to modern technology such as nuclear disasters. Disasters can have both political causes and political consequences. While 'disaster mythology' predicted societies would collapse into disorder and anarchy, actual research found that after a disaster, societies can experience positive social responses. Altruistic behaviour is often common as societies pull together to confront a shared crisis. Over the last twenty-five years, many of these positive outcomes have been documented in *Facing the Unexpected: Disaster Preparedness and Response in the United States* (Tierney, Lindell, and Perry, 2001). Based on decades of research, the sociology of disaster has emerged as a recognized area within the discipline (Drabek, 2017). However, in *Disasters A sociological approach* Tierney (2019) has argued that the sociology of disasters should move to become part of mainstream of sociology. The principal conclusion is that after disasters there are often positive outcomes as societies experience greater social cohesion following a shared crisis. My argument is that catastrophes typically have the opposite outcomes.

Various studies of disasters such as earthquakes have made important contributions to the study of civil unrest following large-scale destruction of property and the death of their inhabitants. Earthquakes often expose the depth of existing inequalities and the difficulties the poor may experience in receiving material support such as food and shelter. The 2005 earthquake that struck Northeast Pakistan and Pakistan – controlled Azad Kashmir killed 70,000 people and left three million homeless. The difficulties of distributing relief were complicated by Kashmir's relationship to the Pakistan central government, where Kashmir citizens lack formal representation. Despite the difficulties, a new sense of purpose developed among the poor enabling them to claim rights as 'disaster citizens' (Schild, 2022).

The development of 'political ecology' has made valuable contributions to research on the impact of natural disasters on social systems (Brown, 2001). Earthquakes can have multiple effects on agriculture, the economy, and institutions, especially the state. Research in this field has focused on the idea of scarcity following major disruptions to all sectors of society. The consequences of natural disasters often include famine and disease. These negative consequences are the trigger for significant social unrest and political violence (Nel and Righarts, 2008). From a sociological perspective, disaster research has identified the 'youth bulge'– a significant section of the population in the age group 15–24 years – as an important factor in civil unrest (Urdal, 2006). In many developing societies with limited employment opportunities, natural disasters increase the sense of helplessness among young cohorts of the population who often respond violently to further economic decline. These findings support the arguments of Amartya Sen that democracy provides the best protection against civil unrest after disaster (Dreze and Sen, 1989; Sen, 2009: 342–354). Democracies are generally better prepared to cope with social and political disruption, and they can respond more openly to criticism and enjoy a higher level of trust in the population. These examples in disaster research also illustrate the fact that there is no such thing as a natural disaster, only political and social disasters. Disasters are political, because governments have not made the necessary social and technical preparations to respond effectively to the demands placed on them by disaster.

There has been a separate development in German sociology on disasters which is known as *Katastrophen-Soziologie* (Schorr, 1987). Unfortunately, it has remained relatively unknown outside Germany. Its development is interesting, because it was specifically critical of the American sociology of disasters, which was seen as a particular aspect of functionalism, namely the dominant trend in American sociology through the first half of the 20th century. German sociologists complained that the American tradition saw disasters as having primarily or exclusively external natural causes. *Katastrophen Soziologie*, which was influenced by Marxist social theory, wanted to look at the social and political causes of disasters, namely arising from the failures and negative effects of capitalism. Rather than stressing the ways in which external disasters can create new communities or revive existing communities, the German tradition saw the social and economic inequalities that typically accompany natural disasters as reflecting and intensifying existing class conflicts.

There are various reasons for drawing a distinction between disaster studies and a fully developed sociology of catastrophes. Confronted by climate change, famine, wars, soil erosion, economic collapse, and zoonotic disease such as COVID-19 and monkeypox, I raise questions relating to the meaning of such events, including their cultural and religious significance. After a catastrophe, people typically ask: 'why me, why now, why here and what for?' These questions raise problems about the meaning and significance of catastrophic events that have no scientific answers, or at least not convincing scientific answers or still less. I also consider catastrophes that typically fall outside disaster studies such as war, colonialism, economic collapse, plagues, population decline and genocide.

In approaching this legacy of doom, we must balance such visions with the optimistic legacy of utopian thought, namely hopeful aspirations for the future and the positive philosophies of the Enlightenment legacy. Any analysis of catastrophes will also raise questions about optimism and pessimism, utopias and dystopias, and questions about whether humans have any future or at best a problematic future on this planet. I consider whether technology can in fact solve some of the problems of survival by recycling waste, growing food in laboratories, creating adequate means to harness wind, sea, and sun power to limit the effects of fossil fuel. In chapter 7, I consider whether there is an entropic limit to resources which cannot be restored or produced by new technologies.

Catastrophe, Eucatastrophe and Apocalypse

The work of J.R.R. Tolkien would not normally feature in disaster research and yet we can read his work as an imaginative account of war and evil in political catastrophes. *Lord of the Rings* told the story of the heroic struggle of the hobbits to defend their society against evil forces that threatened the Shire. It is assumed that the hidden influence behind story was the grim experience of the catastrophe of trench warfare in WWI and the survival of ordinary people against overwhelming odds. The set of three volumes sold 150 million copies.

Can catastrophes have good outcomes? Tolkien developed the idea of good outcomes of catastrophe in his 'On Fairy Stories' (Tolkien, 2008) which reflected the Christian framework of his fiction. The Gospel as an account of the struggle of good and evil can be read as a Christian perspective on Eucatastrophes (Wood, 2007). Tolkien's discussion of fairy stories, in which he coined the idea of the 'Eucatastrophe', was written in 1939 and published in a collection in 2008. For Tolkien, fairy stories are not necessarily or only about fairies in children's stories. The theological background to Tolkien's stories was the New Testament account of the death and resurrection of Christ as the foundation of Christianity. With his Roman Catholic background, Tolkien understood the resurrection and the universalism of St. Paul's letters to the young Church as a eucatastrophe emerging from out of the defeat of the crucifixion. However, Tolkien also said that a eucatastrophe does not rule out what he called 'dyscatastrophe' (Bergen, 2017: 112). The idea of a Messiah at the end of history does, however, have a much longer history in Judaism in which the coming of the Messiah brings human history to an end. In developing this theory of catastrophe, one must consider the messianic themes of Judaism and Christianity, the history of utopian thought and human hope in the face of tragedy.

It has been Jewish and Christian theology which over time has produced the richest foundations for human reflection on catastrophe in the West. We should, however, also include Islamic eschatology and the belief in a Mahdi who will appear in times of crisis and irreligion. Perhaps we should refer more broadly to the idea of the 'biblical imagination' to include various traditions relating to the apocalypse. In this regard John Hall's *Apocalypse: From Antiquity to the Empire of Modernity* (2009) has been an influential source. The biblical imagination has contributed much to the religious and mythical understanding of catastrophe. The idea of apocalypse has an obvious relation to catastrophe and has been analysed in various historical publications such as *The Four Horsemen of the Apocalypse* (Grell, 2000). The apocalypse includes a revelation that uncovers the hidden meaning though the passage of time. John of Patmos, reflecting on the dramatic disappearance of his world with, among other calamities, the fall of Jerusalem, composed the Apocalypse in the Book of Revelation. The idea of 'apocalypse' has influenced various political-theologies that anticipate the dramatic end of times. In Islam the memory of the Messenger of God evolved ino the messianic figure of the Mahdi. The myth of the Mahdi offered an 'inexhaustible resource for subsequent generations' to challenge the routinization of the everyday world with revolutionary fervour (Arjomand, 2022: 10).

The most enduring and tragic vision of catastrophic modernity is associated with the legacy of Walter Benjamin (1829–1940), who combined Jewish and Marxist themes on the end of history in his *Theological-Political Fragment* (1968) and, as I have already indicated, in his *Theses on the Philosophy of History* (1973). For Benjamin, from the standpoint of history, the Kingdom of God 'is not the goal of history, it is the end' (Benjamin, 1968: 312). Benjamin's critique was a blend of Marxism and kabalistic mysticism that was based in his religious opposition to money, consumerism, and secular power, but it was in this respect far removed from the political economy of Marx and Engels (Scholem, 1981). Benjamin's messianic view of history continues to influence modern philosophers such as Jacques Derrida (1989) whose *Specters of Marx* combines Marxism and messianism. Benjamin is important in my study insofar as modernity is seen to be a primary cause of modern catastrophes. In this regard, he argued that there was little difference between fascism and social democracy in that they were both committed to the idea of historical progress. He argued that both political movements saw progress as irresistible and boundless, embracing the perfectability of the whole of mankind.

My approach is from the perspective of historical sociology in which I attempt to examine catastrophes from a long historical period starting with the ancient Greek analysis of earthquakes. The ancient world suffered from massive earthquakes and, given the nature of the building materials available in the ancient world, the collapse of buildings resulted in a considerable loss of life and on a regular basis. There is consequently a well-established tradition of historical research on catastrophes in ancient Greece (Meier, 2007). While natural catastrophes preoccupied Greek philosophers, war as a catastrophe was recognized during the leadership of Thucydides (Furley, 1990). While the Ancients recognized and responded to the destruction caused by natural catastrophes, they also recognized that earthquakes could bring benefits, for example, by opening new springs as sources of drinking water.

Genocide as Catastrophe

I include the history of genocide as a history of catastrophes in which the notion of 'disaster' can play no meaningful role. To call genocide a disaster would be morally offensive. The Holocaust of the Jews was described as the *Sho'ah* or 'calamity'. However, when in 1934 Chaim Weizmann described Hitler's rise to power as 'an unforeseen catastrophe', *Katastrophe* was translated as *Sho'ah*. Similarly, the *an-Nakbah* or Palestinian catastrophe refers to the 1948 conflict with Israel when 78% of Palestine was acquired by Israel and 700,000 Palestinians were displaced as a consequence of war. The period of German history from the rise of Hitler to the final fall of the Third Reich was also described as a 'catastrophe' (Meineke, 1946). Tragedies, and human suffering on this scale, merit 'catastrophe' rather than mere 'disaster'. A sociology of catastrophe calls for a moral and sociological understanding of the long history of human suffering (Wilkinson, 2005). I devote a chapter to colonialism and genocide, but it is useful at this stage to signal the later discussion.

I include a discussion of genocide in the history of colonialism in Chapter 5. The colonial settlement of North America brought disease, the relocation of whole communities, confiscation of the land and colonial wars. The destruction of aboriginal cultures globally must be understood as a colonial catastrophe. Inevitably therefore the sociology of catastrophe raises questions about values. The settlement of Protestant communities in North-East America was for them an obvious blessing as they escaped persecution. After the American Revolution, the wars against and displacement of native communities intensified, ending eventually with the creation of reservations and the establishment of so-called 'Indian Territory'. The cultures and economies of the nomadic communities of the Great Plains were over.

In demography, there is the idea of a 'Malthusian catastrophe', where population growth outstrips agricultural production, resulting in poverty, famine, and the possibility of war. While Malthusianism has been the topic of extensive criticism, historians of North America have generally accepted the idea of a Malthusian demographic catastrophe in the destruction of aboriginal communities between the end of the 15th century and the massacre at Wounded Knee in 1890. David E.

Stanford's history of the conquest of North America describes it as the 'American holocaust' (Stanford, 1992). He estimates that a total of 100 million people were killed through disease, starvation, dispossession, and military activity. A similar historical account of the decimation of native peoples in Canada is presented in *Clearing the Plains* (Daschuk, 2013) which records the history of how diseases such as smallpox and policies of starvation subdued and then destroyed native communities in Canada. One cannot describe the destruction and displacement of people in the Americas, Africa, and the Pacific as simply a 'disaster'. Many native communities are still surviving in the Americas. There are many accounts of heroic survival such as *Holding Our World Together: Ojibwe Women and the Survival of Community* (Child, 2012), but their land has been confiscated, their means of survival destroyed, and their way of life undermined. Many tribes may be present on reserves, but their culture and way of life were destroyed by colonialism. At the height of their power, the Lakota controlled the Great Plains to the Mexican border (Hamalainen, 2019). The Lakota Indians, who appeared in circus performances with Buffalo Bill (alias William Cody) did not sustain their traditional culture; they participated in a commercial farce (Bridger, 2002).

In the literature, there is broad agreement that genocide constitutes a human catastrophe. One influential historical example is the study of the attack on the Greek community of Istanbul and other cities in Asia Minor by Spiros Vryonis (2005) in *The Mechanism of Catastrophe*. He claimed that the pogrom on 6–7 September 1955 was orchestrated by the state. The Turkish attack was primarily against the Greek bourgeoisie in Istanbul. His publication includes numerous photographs of the crimes against Greek citizens and ample documentary evidence of the destruction of property. The background to the attack was the crisis over Cyprus and the reluctance of either the British or the American authorities to intervene in the conflict. The provisions of the Treaty of Lausanne of 1923, offering protection to both Greek and Muslim minorities in Turkey and Western Thrace, were ignored. The ethnic conflict also included a religious conflict between Islam and Greek Orthodoxy. The word *pogrom* is borrowed from the Russian, meaning 'devastation' or 'riot to destroy' following attacks on Jewish communities in southern and western provinces of the Russian Empire. Its official meaning is any organized attack on a community or group that is tolerated or ignored by the authorities. As with the idea of genocide, the use of *pogrom* gives rise to legal and political dispute. Governments and their political elites will not openly admit to genocide. The Arminian genocide involved the destruction of the Arminian people at the end of WWI as the Ottoman Empire began to fall apart. No government will admit that such a genocide occurred.

My interest in these definitions and these examples is, however, neither an exercise in etymology nor in historical research. It is rather to develop a more precise sociological approach to the different, but related crises that currently confront us. I examine various examples, such as genocide associated with colonialism and warfare, on the one hand, and natural catastrophes, such as earthquakes and volcanic eruptions, on the other. The plagues of the 17th century had natural causes, but the widespread infections were consequences of expanding trade. The causes of COVID-19 are at present contested, but zoonotic diseases are certainly associated with environmental degradation and human contact with animals. The infections rapidly become global. It may, in that regard, be seen as a natural catastrophe. If it was caused by human error in an experimental laboratory, then it may be regarded as a social and political catastrophe.

From these limited examples, we can begin to distinguish different causes and characters of catastrophe: natural (earthquakes), political-economic (colonial genocide) and catastrophes that appear to have multiple and often ambiguous causation. The Spanish Flu of 1918–19 of avian origin (H1N1) infected 500 million people globally. The pandemic had high infection rates, because both the civilian population and the combatants from an industrial war were exhausted by devastating wartime deprivations. It had high fatality rates among younger age groups. However, the causes and consequences of catastrophes are perhaps inevitably ambiguous. The nuclear bombs that were dropped on Hiroshima and Nagasaki in 1945 were catastrophic. They brought the war in the Pacific to an end, but traditional Japanese society did not survive. The Japanese military surrender was the first military defeat experienced by Japan. The United States' occupation resulted in a restructuring of the society and economy. Contemporary Japan is a thriving and successful society, but in what sense did Japan survive?

My view of catastrophe is that there are no unambiguously good outcomes, because there is no complete recovery. In this respect, catastrophe theory is distinct from early theories of utopia and dystopia. Catastrophic denouements are events that disrupt social institutions and bring traditional values and patterns of life to an end. The consequences of catastrophes are typically on a large scale, such as the collapse of empires or plagues that undermine whole economies. There was no recovery from Pompei as an example of a natural catastrophe or from Nazi Germany as a political and military disaster. Pompei has admittedly become a popular tourist destination, but one would not want to classify that outcome as an example of the cultural survival of the Roman city of Pompei. Modern-day Germany is a highly successful society, but with the fall of the Berlin Wall it struggled to integrate communist East Germany. How much of Germany survived? Did European Jewry survive the *unvorhergesehene Katastrophe* – the unforeseen catastrophe?

Catastrophe and the Search for Meaning

At this stage in my argument, it is therefore important to grapple with the complex concept of catastrophe. *The Shorter Oxford Dictionary* defines catastrophe as 'a final event; a conclusion generally unhappy' and 'an event producing a subversion of the order or a system of things'. The concept of catastrophe is derived from Aristotle's account of tragedy in his *Poetics* in which the final act or denouement was the *cata-strophe*. We can, following Aristotle, define a catastrophe as a general and systematic breakdown of social or political institutions. We might make a common-sense distinction between natural catastrophes, such as earthquakes and volcanic eruptions, such as the eruption of Mount Vesuvius that destroyed Pompeii in 79 ce or socio-political catastrophes, such as the fall of Constantinople or the break-up of the Ottoman Empire. However, in most examples both natural and social causes and consequences are present. Catastrophes typically have global consequences. WWI and WWII changed the map of the system of nation states, began the final unravelling of the British Empire, and broke up various European and Asian empires. The collapse of the Ottoman Empire was in many respects the most dramatic and comprehensive. It is, however, difficult to conclude confidently that these wars had no positive or beneficial outcomes. While I am tempted to define catastrophe as having only bad outcomes and to rule out good 'unintended consequences', we need to pay attention to ancient Greek understanding of earthquakes as catastrophes. The ancient Greeks identified various beneficial consequences of earthquakes such as opening new sources of drinking water.

My final addition is to focus on the meaning of catastrophes. Sociology is a science that seeks to understand the meanings that are ascribed to social actions and institutions. What meaning if any can we ascribe to catastrophes? Historically humans have invented theodicies to make sense of gross misfortune, but in a secular age we struggle to make any sense of catastrophes. Does COVID-19 have any meaning and does the science of zoonotic disease provide us with any ethical or spiritual insight into the global catastrophe?

We need therefore to attend to the meanings that are given to catastrophes. In all ages, catastrophes have called forth meaning systems. Historically these were often theodicies, which explained human relations to God in seeking to reconcile God's benevolence with human misery. Of course, some catastrophes are on such a scale and involve unimaginable suffering such as the Holocaust that they defy any attribution of meaning. Hannah Arendt, reporting on the famous trial of Adolf Eichmann, in one sense said his bureaucratic behaviour, in contributing his services to the Final Solution, had no meaning; it could only be described in terms of its monotonous 'banality' (Arendt, 1994).

Catastrophes such as the Great Depression typically create specific generations that are defined by a transformative experience, such as long-term unemployment and poverty (Elder, 1999). Such generations are defined by a common experience of immense suffering, resulting, among other things, in what we may call a catastrophe consciousness (Edmunds and Turner, 2002). While creating new generations, catastrophes typically bring things to an end. The word *strophe* in Greek tragedy was the 'turning' point in the structure of the drama when the chorus moved from right to left of the stage. The catastrophe is the final turning and is connected to the idea of endings or the final act. After a flood hits a river system, people continue to use the river and the society does not come to an end or stop river travel to transport people and goods. My underlying assumption therefore is that a catastrophe is a crisis from which there is no clear recovery because it is an act of turning and thus a post-catastrophe typically brings to an end existing institutions. Successful societies may be defined as surviving societies that have the capacity to build a new, but obviously different, social world.

Conclusion: Vulnerability and Suffering

Catastrophe has attended human societies through out the existence of humans. We continue to confront the catastrophes that humans have always experienced throughout their existence: earthquakes, volcanic eruptions, pandemics, starvation, and warfare. In any discussion of catastrophe, we need to bring in another dimension to the discussion, namely the vulnerability of human beings and the inevitable suffering that attends human life. The word 'vulnerability' comes from the Latin for 'wound' indicating that humans are prone to physical or mental wounding (Turner, 2009a; 2022). In my approach to the idea of vulnerability, I introduce ideas from philosophical anthropology and especially from the work of Arnold Gehlen (1904–1976). He was a controversial German conservative, but his ideas have been influential, especially with the English translation of his major work as *Man: His Nature and Place in the World* (1988). His basic argument was that humans have limited instincts and must create institutions to survive. Human infants are not only extremely vulnerable in the early weeks of their existence, but they remain dependent on their parents for years. Humans are relatively slow-moving, have no thick fur for warmth, or large fangs, and have no venom by which to neutralize attackers. Humans have survived by developing technology – the knife and the spear – and by forming social institutions – the tribe. We will need to consider whether medical science has radically reduced our ancestral vulnerability. Vaccination, in reducing our vulnerability, during the COVID-19 pandemic is one obvious example. However, the ageing of humans has yet to be dramatically reduced. To what extent can 'rejuvenative medicine' reduce or eliminate the ageing of the body to extend human life indefinitely (Dumas and Turner, 2007)? In chapter 7 on the economics of survival, I consider arguments to the contrary that an extension of life is a threat to the environment and that we can consider the proposal by Josef Popper-Lynkeus, that while there is a right to live, there is also an obligation to die in the interests of inter-generational justice and the protection of shared resources.

Attention to vulnerability forces us to consider the issue of suffering in relation to catastrophes. Diana Harvey (2012) argues that sociology, unlike many other social sciences, has a definite focus on suffering. A specific focus can be found in Iain Wilkinson (2005), in his study of *Suffering*. Although suffering is implied in disaster studies, it must occupy a major space in catastrophe studies. Our suffering is associated with our vulnerability as human beings. My aim in this volume is to combine the basic idea of human vulnerability with the catastrophes people face in earthquakes, volcanic eruptions, plagues, and war, and with the meanings that are ascribed to catastrophic events, including the idea of evil.

Despite advances in science and technology, natural crises contribute to the modern sense of human vulnerability. One recent example was the dramatic image of the volcanic eruption in the Spanish Canary Island of La Palma in September 2021, from which over 5000 people were evacuated. Contemporary catastrophic conditions have a magnified impact on communities that are already vulnerable and at risk. Droughts occur in both developed and developing countries with significant impacts and are currently growing in frequency, and severity. Over-use of water resources, changing weather conditions and climate change are key factors in the rising level of risk. Underdeveloped countries are the most affected by these environmental changes owing to social, political, and economic conditions, including differences in available scientific knowledge and skill levels in local health care services. These circumstances in Asia are resulting in serious food insecurity, and as a result are undermining human health. Growing threats from pests, disease and famine are consequences of contemporary droughts.

The COVID-19 crisis is clearly not a one-issue threat to the global order, and it is certainly not the last of the zoonotic infections. We were in 2022 confronted by four inter-connected catastrophic threats – political instability, natural disasters, climate change, war, famine, and zoonotic disease. The political crises are all too obvious: Chinese expansion into the Pacific; political paralysis in the United States between Democrats and Republicans; political tensions in Europe after Brexit; the rise of authoritarianism especially in Eastern Europe, and the invasion of Ukraine. The natural disasters are equally daunting. Earthquakes and volcanic eruptions have destroyed whole communities and major fires in California and Australia have burnt out of control. Other parts of the world suffer from devastating droughts. COVID-19 has caused countless fatalities and destroyed whole communities. Will this century be the age of catastrophes? In these multiple catastrophes, there is little evidence of a community of risk and scant indication of collective hope. How we come to view COVID-19 from either a pessimistic or optimistic perspective may depend on whether we side with Voltaire or Rousseau on the axiom 'All is well' as a hopeful response to catastrophe.

Chapter 2
Risk Society and Liquid Modernity

Introduction: Modernity?

Does modernity contain within itself the seeds of its own inevitable destruction? A theory of catastrophe is also a theory of the character of modernity, because the sociological perspective suggests that modernization has amplified the conditions that produce catastrophes. Advances in technology, such as nuclear energy, can magnify the scale of accidents leading to catastrophe. Critiques of modernity, especially with respect to the unintended consequences of scientific progress, find support from intellectuals across every political persuasion. Martin Heidegger (1977), who embraced a conservative view of the dangers of technology in his *The Question Concerning Technology,* played an important role in identifying modern technology as a threat to human existence. I focus here on Heidegger, because his sense of alienation in modernity was shared by a whole generation of western intellectuals, many of whom have influenced this study of catastrophe. Heidegger is important for this volume, because the problematic nature of technology is a theme running through my account of the origins and consequences of modernization. The problem, briefly described, is whether technology is the cause of many problems facing modern societies or our only solution to the enormous difficulties facing our catastrophic world or indeed whether it is both source and solution. To take a simple example, the petrol-driven vehicle has caused air pollution, urban congestion, and environmental degradation. However, vehicles driven by electric engines as pioneered by Elon Musk and the Tesla Corporation might reduce some but not all the risks.

Despite widespread criticism of his politics, *Being and Time* (1962), which was published in Germany in 1927, is often regarded as the most influential philosophical work of the 20th century. It was written against a background of rapid social and economic change in Germany, such as industrialization, urbanization, new transport systems, and advances in military technology. It was also a Germany recovering from WW1 and the problematic Versailles Treaty. These developments convinced Heidegger that there was a crisis facing the European world. The modern debate, perhaps unwittingly rehearsing Heidegger's criticism of technology and its underling rationality, continues to influence responses to catastrophes such as climate change. Despite his sustained critique of post-war Europe as a derelict society, Heidegger had no practical suggestions as to how this situation might be remedied. In his engagement with national socialism, he saw the rise of fascism

https://doi.org/10.1515/9783110772364-002

as a German antidote to the pervasive crisis. In a speech to German students in 1933, he urged them to embrace the Führer, because 'he and he alone is the future German reality and its law'. Heidegger's relationship to fascism has generated a long-running debate about the extent and duration of his commitment to national socialism (Rockmore and Margolis, 1992). While unsurprisingly Heidegger's character, his attachment to the Nazi Party and the actual meaning of his philosophy have deeply engaged German intellectuals, the ambiguities of his legacy have been even more decisive in French intellectual culture (Ferry and Renaut, 1990).

Heidegger's basic question was 'what is man?' which he translated into the more comprehensive question 'what is being?' In many respects, this question came from the work emerging from Max Scheler (1874–1928) in the development of philosophical anthropology in the late 1920s. The original inspiration came from Scheler who believed that philosophical research had to take into consideration the developments and findings of the emerging disciplines in the humanities, namely anthropology, history, biology, and sociology. His major publication was *Die Stellung der Menschen im Kosmos* in 1927 which was translated in 1958 as *Man's Place in Nature*. He was driven by a puzzle. Given all these scientific developments, the irony is that philosophy has not answered the basic question: what is 'Man'? This basic question became the driving force behind Heidegger's philosophical inquiry into 'being'. Arnold Gehlen's *Der Mensch, seine Natur und Stellung in der Welt* in 1940 was directly inspired by Scheler. In the English translation as *Man: His Nature and Place in the World* (Gehlen, 1988), his basic view was that humans are by their nature vulnerable, and they can only survive by collective arrangements based on institutions including legal provisions. We can summarize Gehlen's philosophy in one sentence, which is in turn the basis for my understanding of human vulnerability: 'Simply staying alive is man's ultimate challenge' (Gehlen, 1988: 55).

Heidegger's sense of alienation was constantly repeated in his sense of homelessness (*Unheimlichkeit*). In fact, nostalgia for the peasant life that was fast disappearing occupied his thought (Magill, 1985). His nostalgia involved a personal reflection of his own provincial background and was also expressed in his attire, including leather trousers and his devotion to his rural hut in later life. Pierre Bourdieu (1991: 47) has argued that Heidegger's discomfort with the academic culture of prestigious German universities such as Heidelberg was a consequence of his humble origins in 'the lesser rural petty bourgeoisie'. The inauthenticity of modern urban life was a crucial aspect of what Heidegger regarded as the crisis. Nostalgia, narrowly defined as an escape from the present, is a theme I have tried to avoid in this study of catastrophes and human responses. In his famous *Der Spiegel* interview in 1976, he declared 'only a God can save us'. This was not intended to be understood as a recipe for hope.

We must be careful in approaching Heidegger's version of technology. By 'technology' he referred to technological thought or modes of calculative thinking which have become the dominant mode for understanding the world. While Heidegger was associated with German fascism during the rise of Hitler to power, his critique of modernity has been influential across the political spectrum. Heidegger's philosophy, especially *Being and Time,* had a complex relationship with the critical theories of the Frankfurt School. Herbert Marcuse (1898–1979), who was influential on the Left, was a former student of Heidegger's. The 'Left Heideggerians' retained Heidegger's vision that modern society or 'one-dimensional society' was fundamentally inauthentic. Modern technological advances in the shape of the automobile, hi-fi set, split-level home, and general kitchen equipment represent the domestic space of this 'one-dimensional society'. In this respect, Marcuse combined Heidegger's idea of inauthentic everydayness and Marx's theory of alienation (Marcuse, 1964). Similarly, Theodor Adorno (1903–1969), one of the leading intellectual figures of post-war Germany, had a life-long engagement with the legacy of Heidegger. His *Jargon of Authenticity* (1964) was a sustained critique of Heidegger. Nevertheless, Adorno recognized the widespread appeal of Heidegger among German intellectuals and described Heidegger's influence as *Heidegerri* (Müller-Doohm, 2005: 326).

The other figure in this long reaction to Heidegger in post-war Germany is the philosopher-sociologist Jürgen Habermas (1929-), who was critical of Heidegger's impact on the critical understanding of objectivity and truth. In an early article in 1959 with the title 'The Great Influence', Habermas (1983) argued that 'Criticism has always been opposed to metaphysics... However, as a counterpoise to crisis and a notion to counter metaphysics, Heidegger names not criticism but mythos.' In his debate with Marcuse over the basic characteristics of modernity and technology, Habermas's defence of modernity became the more prevalent view in social sciences. However, public anxieties about climate change and environmental pollution have influenced a more critical response to modernization or at least to its technological foundations.

Habermas, as he is the first to admit, has been influenced by the work of Reinhart Koselleck on the history of the idea of 'crisis' in his *Critique and Crisis: Enlightenment and the Pathogenesis of Modern Society* (Koselleck, 1959). Koselleck and his generation were a product of the crisis consciousness after two world wars, but especially of post-war Germany in the 1950s when he submitted his doctoral dissertation in 1954. Habermas's reading of Koselleck was especially important in shaping his views on the general problems of modernity. Koselleck traced the history of the concept of crisis from Greek philosophy and medicine to its use in the analysis of revolutions, to a theory of history, to economics and finally to its generality, if not its erosion, in contemporary thought. In Greek medicine, crisis was a turning or breaking point in the course of an illness in which the patient would either die or survive. In revolutions, it was also a hinge or turning point in social and political history. In economic thought it came to characterize Marx's view of the instability of the capitalist system which lurched from one crisis to another before the final collapse of the system and its replacement by communism. For Marx and Engels, crisis had a positive glow in presaging the eruption of communism from the ruins of the capitalist system. From WWI, the Great Depression and WWII, cultural critiques and global interpretations of crisis have proliferated. In 1918 Paul Valéry identified three overlapping crises: the military, economic, and intellectual. Husserl spoke of the crisis of European sciences. Huizinga thought that crisis would lead towards a more progressive conclusion. The principal transformation, however, was from confronting a set of harsh and unavoidable alternatives with a choice to several alternatives that might be possible at any given moment. By contrast, the early history of crisis involved inescapably the question of making a judgement which might be either right or wrong. This issue also brings into focus the theological background to the history of crisis, namely The Day of Judgement.

Habermas's views on modernity have also evolved as he came to consider the role of religion in the public domain (Calhoun, Mendieta and Van Antwerpen, 2013) and promoted the idea of 'post-secularism' to mean that western societies had moved into a new era. Habermas supported tolerance of religion in the public domain as a critical basis for the general canopy of rights in a democracy. The main theories of modernity in classical sociology had simply assumed that modernization would also result inevitably in secularization, but this basic assumption has been challenged by contemporary sociologists who argue that religions in fact continue to play a significant role in public life, and not least in the United States (Casanova, 1994).

In classical sociology, Max Weber (1864–1920) is most clearly identified with theories of modernity. For Weber, rational bureaucracy was the dominant characteristic of modern societies. In fact, 'Bureaucracy is, however, distinguished from other historical bearers of the modern, a rational way of ordering life by the fact of its greater *inescapability*' (Weber, 1994: 156). His lectures from 1918 until his death in 1921 were full of pessimistic observations on the crisis in German politics. In two lectures towards the end of his life – *Politics as a Vocation* and *Science as a Vocation* – he presented a bleak overview of modernity as the consequence of a rationalization process ending in an 'iron cage' of bureaucracy (Gerth and Mills, 2009). In addition, Weber, as with many of his contemporaries, saw the Treaty of Versailles as a political failure with respect to the causes and consequences of the War. In retrospect, we can see that the terms of the Treaty laid the foundations for the rise of fascism and allowed Adolf Hitler and his generation to see the terms of surrender as a betrayal of the German army and the German people. It gave rise to a 'stab in the back' view of the terms of peace. Unsurprisingly, many Germans came to see the outcome of the two world wars as yet another catastrophe for the German society, as described in Friedrich Meinecke's *Deutsche Katastrophe* (1946) and Wilhelm Hoffman's *Nach der Katastrophe* (1946). These volumes identified multiple conditions behind the rise of German nationalism, fascism, and Hitler's role in German militarism, many of which were in place long before the Treaty. The causes of the catastrophe were as much cultural as economic and political, such as the Prussian military legacy, the notion of *preussische Tugenden* or the Prussian ethic and the ensemble of ideas about efficiency, power, and the superiority of the Kingdom of Prussia. It goes without saying that Weber's sociology was deeply influenced by the legacy of Bismarck, the place of Prussia in German affairs, the role of the military in social life and the outcome of WWI. This context was the social and historical framework for his views on bureaucracy, the state and power. Bureaucratic rationality shaped his general view of modernity.

Risk Society and Liquid Modernity

Modern sociology has taken a different view of the development of modernity as resulting in a state of post-modernity and *post-histoire*. These contrasted views of what for convenience we can call 'early' and 'late modernity' also preoccupied Ulrich Beck (1944–2015) and Zygmunt Bauman (1925–2017). Their different approaches to modernity shared a common understanding of the new challenges of modernity in terms of uncertainty and ambiguity. Anthony Giddens (1990) in *The Consequences of Modernity* developed a range of ideas about risk, trust and expert systems that built on Beck's sociology and, like Beck, Giddens was not pessimistic about the condition of modernity. He defended the credibility of the notion of 'utopian realism'. One example of the prospects for realistic utopianism was offered by the role of emancipatory social movements such as ecological protest movements.

Ulrich Beck's *Risk Society* (1992) can be considered as a major work on modernization and risk that touches on catastrophes as well as how early modernity had evolved into risk society. *Risk Society* appeared in its German version in 1986 only weeks before the Chernobyl nuclear power plant crisis. The book gained instant recognition, because the nuclear catastrophe was the perfect example of his argument that a new type of society had emerged out of modernization. *Risk Society* in fact was an attempt to develop a general theory of social change and the emergence of a new type of society creating both new dangers and opportunities (Burges, Wardman and Mythen, 2018). Although Beck's sociology of risk was embraced as an important development in the study of modernity, we should note that Frank Knight, who was a student of Max Weber, is celebrated in economic theory for his *Risk, Uncertainty and Profit* (Knight, 1921). Knight was particularly interested in the uncertainties of our knowledge of the future. For Knight, profit was the reward for bearing the uncertainties of investment and hence the burden of uninsurable hazards (Brooke, 2010).

Beck's quest was to revitalize sociology by analyzing the development of a radical modernity through a process of 'reflexive modernization'. Beck's aim was to re-direct sociology to take account of major developments that were not adequately covered or explained by existing sociological approaches to modernity. Alongside Beck, there is also the work of Zygmunt Bauman who developed a perspective on new forms of modernity in *Liquid Modernity* (2000). For Bauman, the early development of modernity produced a solid or static society which was eventually replaced by a society in perpetual motion and change. In this phase, nothing is stable, everything is in perpetual motion.

While both Beck and Bauman saw a radical break between early and late forms of modernity, their vision of society was different. Beck offered an optimistic view that risk society presents both risks and opportunities. Bauman's view was far more dystopian in concentrating on the limited opportunities for progressive change out of liquid modernity. Liquid modernity did not necessarily result in greater equality or break-down of the barriers between insiders and outsiders. Bauman nevertheless had faith in the capacity of dialogue to forge solutions to our social and political ills, thereby creating opportunities to repair what he called our 'life in fragments' (Bauman, 1995).

Beck and Catastrophism

Beck's underlying theme was that, as technology becomes more complex and intrusive, the consequences create greater and more frequent risks. For Beck, the first industrial revolution produced a 'society of scarcity', but that was eventually replaced by a new 'reflexive modernization' that exploited nuclear, chemical, and genetic technologies. Whereas the first stages of modernization involved the unequal distribution of wealth, risk society is based on an unequal risk allocation. These new destructive forces develop beyond existing control mechanisms and the unintended consequences are disastrous and sometimes catastrophic. As a result, modern societies are driven into a 'radicalized modernity'. Whereas risk was a fully developed notion in earlier forms of modernity, in a risk society risks have become incalculable. We are confronted by a situation of 'nonknowledge'(-

Nichtwissen) giving rise to the political struggle of experts to define what is reliable knowledge (Beck, 2009). Beck combines this perspective on the 'unintended consequences' of the new modernity with his existing approach to the idea of individualization to describe the loss of community and the hollowing out of the nation state by globalization, resulting in a 'world risk society' (Beck, 1996). Given the profound impact of globalization on human societies, sociology required a new approach that Beck called a 'cosmopolitan methodology'.

While some critics such as Simon Cottle (1998) have spoken about Beck's 'catastrophic view', this interpretation misrepresents Beck's actual position. He was, in fact, critical of doom-laden 'preachers of catastrophe', and rejected the view that catastrophes always have uniformly negative outcomes. Beck was in general terms critical of what he called 'catastrophism'. His view of how technology might replace labour is a good example of his rejection of public talk about 'crisis' and 'catastrophe' in the German debate about employment trends. Mass unemployment for Beck is not an unmitigated 'crisis, because the replacement of labour with partly or fully automated production could, if properly applied, bring epochal opportunities for an expansion of human freedom' (Beck, 2000: 125). A fluctuation in the business cycle might not amount to a catastrophe or even a crisis. Beck recognized that technological change does destroy existing jobs relating to out-of-date technology, but it also creates new jobs and employment opportunities.

The distinction between risk and catastrophe is important for political reasons. His ultimately optimistic view of risk and crisis was most clearly expressed in an article on 'Emancipatory Catastrophism' (Beck, 2015) in which he developed his position through three propositions. The first is that the threat of climate change gives rise to expectations about a transformation that disrupts any assumptions about sacred norms governing human existence. Secondly, it produces an anthropological shock to society, that we may call an 'ontological wake-up call', and thirdly it generates a social catharsis, resulting in a collective hope for regeneration. In the face of a global crisis, 'emancipatory catastrophism' releases collective efforts to prepare for and prevent pending catastrophe. Risk society is both an effect and a cause of increasing global interconnectedness, which is not the traditional normative cosmopolitanism, but rather the 'side-effect cosmopolitanism' of global risk. In other words, catastrophe has a beneficial outcome in social healing. Beck appears to assume that there are no completely bad unintended consequences. Therefore, Beck's sociology of risk was ultimately optimistic by giving a central place for hope.

One key aspect of Beck's theory is that disasters and catastrophes create a global community of risk that allows people to respond creatively and effectively because of massive social and political dislocations. Beck (2011) referred to new forms of cosmopolitanism that would emerge from societies at global risk. These global events in the new modernity create communities of risk that pull people together and give expression to their hope for a better or at least a different future. This is a common theme in much disaster research. In the Tohoku earthquake and tsunami that struck Japan in 2011, there is some indication of a post-crisis reconstruction that supports Beck's argument about communities of risk. The earthquake resulted in 19,747 fatalities, 2,556 people reported missing, and 121,777 buildings destroyed. Nevertheless, after the earthquake and its many tragedies, there was a sense of *seise* (regeneration) and *kizuna* (bonds of community) among the survivors (Morris-Suzuki, 2017).

Are there no bad endings to such catastrophic events in Beck's risk society? At the end of his life, Beck (2014) published 'How might climate change save the world?' in response to debates and approaches to climate change. Here again he opposed 'catastrophism' and offered instead an expectation that the crisis of climate change might produce beneficial political outcomes. For Beck, major developments such as climate change create an 'anthropological shock' that transforms society, politics, and culture. As a result, citizens begin to initiate new ideas for cultural, political, and social transformations, and this emancipatory catastrophe then liberates people from old values, norms and structures that are in fact no longer relevant.

Beck (2014: 169) contrasted two questions: what is climate change *bad* for? What is it *good* for? In response to these opposed positions, he developed a range of theses that gave expression to his optimism regarding globalization in the face of crises and provided an answer to what is good about climate change. The first is that it re-opens the debate about the failures of industrial capitalism to deliver wealth and stability, and hence the environmental issue presents us with opportunities to identify the failures of neo-liberalism, and to organize to develop new economic policies. Secondly, risk is not catastrophe but rather the opportunity to avoid catastrophe. Thirdly it sets in motion a range of cosmopolitan dynamics.

Beck saw an affinity between the theory of risk society and the principle of hope in the work of Ernst Bloch (1885–1977). First published in Germany in 1959, Bloch was critical of Marxist understanding of the peasantry. For Bloch (2000), their radicalism was fuelled by the hope they derived from the tradition of Christian millenarianism. The sociology of hope was further developed by Henri Desroche (1914–1994) in his *Sociologie de L'espérance* and translated in 1979. The presence of hope motivates people to act even when their world has been destroyed by war or natural disasters. We can only grasp these opportunities for political action on a global scale. Hence the fourth thesis, the crisis forces us to grasp the fact that one cannot consider domestic politics without its global context. The fifth thesis, although a consensus is always problematic, we can achieve a negative consensus regarding what is to be avoided. The sixth thesis is that we need to recognize how national politics and international competition both obscure the opportunities for cosmopolitanism. The seventh thesis is that cosmopolitanization is irreversible, and highly developed. In this final thesis, Beck believes that the global city is already driving the cosmopolitan agenda in creating new openings and new beginnings.

Beck's sociology of risk society had its origins in a major catastrophe, namely the Chernobyl nuclear explosion on April 26, 1986 – often described as an 'accident'. It is not possible to calculate how many people in the long run died from cancers arising from nuclear radiation. Beck died in 2015 thereby not being able to develop his theory with respect to the COVID-19 pandemic or the war in Ukraine. I consider the COVID-19 pandemic in chapter 8 and discuss the war in Ukraine in chapter 6. I describe both pandemics and wars as catastrophes and argue that they rarely confirm either Beck's theory of global cosmopolitanism or his optimistic view of risk. With respect to the COVID-19 pandemic, there was little evidence of global sharing of resources. Many poor African and Asian societies did not receive vaccines on time or in sufficient quantities to combat the infections. Nations closed their borders and imposed lockdowns that were often the occasion for violent protests from right-wing movements. The Chinese government either rejected or controlled external scientific investigation of the origins of the virus in Wuhan. The spread of fake and false information produced a general distrust in governments and the various measures to contain and control the virus. There was little evidence of 'emancipatory catastrophism'. It is too early to make any sound judgments about the long-term consequences of the war in Ukraine. However, with respect to the devastation of Ukraine, the least appropriate response would be, what is it *good* for? In these multiple catastrophes of climate change, war and the emerging breakdown of a global order, there is little evidence of a community of risk and scant indication of collective hope.

Modernity, Family and Reproduction

Another dimension of modernity and globalization includes major changes to courtship, marriage, and family life. Beck and Beck-Gernsheim have produced two volumes which offer further reflections on modernity and cosmopolitan globalization. Family life in the West has changed dramatically with the availability of contraception, reforms in the divorce laws, late marriage, and new forms of cohabitation. These are all components of a revolution in family life which they describe in *The Normal Chaos of Love* (1995). The process of 'individualization' means the men and women meet on more equal terms. Marriage is no longer the accepted route to respectability. The basis of becoming a couple is romantic attachment and love perhaps provides a haven from the work demands of late capitalism. However, modern romanticism may never escape the pressures of consumerism (Illouz, 1997). Love as the rationale for long-term relationships does not provide a stable platform for coupledom and love is complicated by the demand from women for equality, respect, and especially equal opportunities. Marriages based on romantic love are necessarily fragile. Despite their recognition of the fragile nature of romance, their approach fails to consider how class, status and race influence the durability of love. However, their study remains optimistic in believing that the new patterns of love, cohabitation and marriage offer new possibilities for developing individual identities outside the confines of the traditional patriarchal family. The collapse of the traditional family has its upside in the space to explore new identities.

Their next major publication was *Distant Love* (2014) which explored the impact of globalization on couples, marriage, and family life. These are the new 'world families' whose composition transcends national borders and national cultures. These world families include families that are connected by communication technology if the partners live in different societies separated by time and space, or couples from separate parts of the world who now live together. Globalization, new patterns of citizenship and advanced technologies are all changing the shape, not only of the family, but of love itself. These world families give additional expression to Beck's concern for 'cosmopolitanization' in that these families undermine any rigid distinction, for example, between East and West. In short, the chaos of love and the growth of distant love are further aspects of Beck's general view that radical modernization can have positive outcomes. Chaos is not the same as catastrophe.

If we begin to look at the demographic changes that are, so to speak, the material basis of family chaos, we can also see some negative aspects of familial modernization. The first and second demographic transitions are well known. They involved a transition from high birth rates, and death rates, to low birth and death rates. These changes were brought about by improvements in child-care, contraception, late marriage, and improvements in the status of women through educational opportunities. The result was a significant decline in the Total Fertility Rate or the hypothetical number of children a woman would have if she completed her reproductive life between, for example 15 to 49 years of age. The TFR gives us an estimate of whether a population is being replaced, namely a TFR around 2.1. Many societies in both the West and Asia have TFRs below population replacement, for example, South Korea 0.9, Singapore 1.1, Spain 1.2, Italy 1.3, France 1.9, and Norway 1.5. In this context, demographers also refer to a third demographic transition where many societies have low fertility resulting in falling total population that cannot be easily reversed. These trends are not easily reversed, because women in the labour force who now have considerable independence from men do not necessarily welcome the opportunity to exchange employment for motherhood. While populations are declining, they are also ageing and this trend has serious implications for welfare services, provision of elder care facilities, medical investments, and pensions. Consequently, many societies must depend either on inward migration or improvements in technology to replace their labour force in combination with new social policies such as removing the compulsory retirement age. These developments are often connected to populist opposition to immigration and assertive forms of masculinity including such groups as InCel (Involuntary Celibacy).

One might argue that population decline is beneficial because it reduces the pressure on our fragile environment thereby reducing the impact of the human population on the survival of the planet. There is, however, another more sinister aspect of this decline in populations concerning human health. Another more hidden aspect of low fertility rates is the decline in male sperm counts. In *Countdown* (2022) Shanna Swan and Stacey Colins, based on extensive empirical research in 2017, report that the sperm count in males primarily in western societies has declined by 59% between the 1970s and modern times. This decline in the quantity of sperm is also accompanied by changes in the shape and mobility of sperm. In addition, women's reproductive health has also been damaged as women now produce fewer eggs and of declining quality. These physical changes in men and women would further disrupt and undermine traditional notions of gender difference, but at considerable cost to the reproductive health of both men and women.

These changes are associated with EDCs (endocrine disruptive chemicals) in our environment such as plastics in our kitchens and items of personal hygiene including make-up. Our dependence on these items in our everyday lives could be reversed – with considerable government intervention and legislative regulation. Without radical changes to our domestic and work environments, the male sperm count could drop to zero by 2050 in the developed world. As with attempts to reduce the rate of damage to our physical environment, these changes require considerable and persistent political, legislative, and economic change. If the long-term collapse of human reproductive capacity can count as reproductive catastrophe, it would be difficult to describe these outcomes as a eu-catastrophe.

Bauman on Bureaucratic Rationality and the Holocaust

Bauman's general project in sociology was two-fold: to offer insights into our fluid contemporary society as well as work out a way to a future of a truly public life including the rediscovery of the common good through our capacity for 'civility', or, as Bauman might argue, through constructive 'dialogue'. In this search for an engaged sociology that could contribute to a more equal society, he would need to offer alternatives to our contemporary consumer society. Bauman unexpectedly found some prospect for hope in Pope Francis who has been a lone voice often in welcoming refugees and embracing the social outcast. In attempting to engage with the vision of the Pope, Bauman also found hope in the promise of dialogue. In *Liquid Modernity* (2000), Bauman retained his dystopian view of modern individualism, isolation, the weakness of social bonds and the decline of civility. However, he recognized the importance of dialogue in breaking down barriers between isolated individuals and allowing otherwise opposed social groups to find some common ground.

Bauman's vision of modernity is not unlike that of Beck's understanding. Bauman calls the first stage of modernization 'solid modernity' as a description of its attempts to impose stability and uniformity on society by bureaucratic means. In the second stage, we arrive at 'liquid modernity'. In this stage, nothing is firm or fixed and everything is temporary. In some respects, Bauman's view of the flux of a hyper-consumer world was anticipated by Marshall Berman's *All that is Solid Melts into Air: The Experience of Modernity* (Berman, 1982). Both Berman and Bauman follow Marx and Engel's own vision of capitalism as endlessly changing and endlessly destructive social and economic system (Beilharz, 2016). In chapter 1 of The *Manifesto of the Communist Party* in 1848, Marx and Engels (1969) laid the basis for ideas about risk, uncertainty, and liquidity:

> Constant revolutionising of production, uninterrupted disturbance of all social conditions, everlasting uncertainty and agitation distinguishes the bourgeois epoch from all earlier ones. All fixed, fast-frozen relations, with their train of ancient and venerable prejudices and opinions, are swept away, all new-formed ones become antiquated before they can ossify. All that is solid melts into air, all that is holy is profaned, and man is at last compelled to face with sober senses his real conditions of life, and his relations with his kind.

There is much in common between Berman, Beck, and Bauman. However, Bauman paints a darker picture of both stages of modernization. Bauman's world is darker because, as a Polish migrant intellectual, he saw the social world from the perspective of an outsider. The figure of the outsider and the outcast occupied his thinking throughout his life from the early *Modernity and Ambivalence* (Bauman, 1991) to 'Strangers at our door' (Bauman, 2016), in which Bauman reflects on the anxieties underlying the European response to the growing refugee crisis. For Bauman, the real crisis in Europe is the refusal to engage in dialogue. The silence over the refugee problem is the product of indifference. Pope Francis is one of the few public figures to speak out about the moral and political dangers of ignoring the global refugee problem. The British decision in April 2022 to send young African refugees to Rwanda is a morally bankrupt strategy and has little in common with any cosmopolitan ethic.

Bauman saw the Lisbon earthquake of 1755, which I discuss in chapter 3, as the beginning of modern secularization. It brought into question any confidence or optimism about progress in human society. The earthquake was an important stage in the evolution of Enlightenment rationalism in the debate between François-Marie Voltaire (1698–1778) and Jean-Jacques Rousseau (1712–1778). In his critical response to Voltaire's despair, Rousseau maintained hope for the future (Dynes, 2000; Havens, 1944; Voltaire, 1912). While Bauman is critical of the Enlightenment vision of the steady march of progress, he believes in the possibility of dialogue, moral concern, and civility.

While Bauman clung to the hope for a future where civility would still be possible, the Holocaust remains a stumbling block to any confidence in a civilizing progress. His analysis of the Holocaust and the rationality of the Nazi bureaucratic machine follows Weber's perspective on 'the iron cage' of rational, bureaucratic modernity. He rejected the attempt of Theodor Adorno and the Frankfurt School to locate the Holocaust in the individual psychology of the Nazis. It is not possible to explain the rise of Nazi Germany in terms of the cruel disposition of fascists or by arguing that they were irrational. For Bauman the Nazis who planned and managed the concentration camps were perfectly rational. The Holocaust catastrophe was consistent with Enlightenment rationality – at least as seen through Weber's analysis of bureaucracy. Rejecting the idea of a civilizing process, he argued that 'At no point of its long and tortuous execution did the Holocaust come in conflict with the principles of rationality' (Bauman, 1989: 17).

Bauman's approach to the issue of rationality openly follows the earlier work of Hannah Arendt in *The Origins of Totalitarianism* (1951) and *Eichmann in Jerusalem* (1965) in which she also analyzed the origins of the Holocaust in bureaucratic rationalism. For Arendt, the Final Solution was made possible by administrative rationality. Arendt, however, had introduced a new dimension to the debate by introducing the controversial notion of the 'banality of evil' to describe the character of Adolf Eichmann who believed that his duty to the state was based on Kantian ethics. Eichmann believed he was innocent of any wrong-doing and that he had faithfully fulfilled his duties to the state. For Arendt, the problem of evil was not confined to the Eichmann trial. For Arendt, in a book review of Denis de Rougemont's *The Devil's Share*, 'The problem of evil will be the fundamental question of post-war intellectual life in Europe' (Arendt, 1945: 259). Constructing a memory of the Holocaust such as a museum raised difficult questions about who owns the memory and the question as to whether a Jewish Holocaust museum could stand in for other holocausts or mass killings as in Bosnia (Linenthal, 1995). Arendt's more general reflections on ethical issues raised by monstrous crimes against humanity appeared as *Responsibility and Judgment* (Kohn, 2003).

Bauman also saw the attempt to exterminate the Jews as part of a more general policy of removing individuals or whole groups of people who did not fit the Nazi dream of biological purity. Thus 'well before they built the gas chambers, the Nazis, on Hitler's orders, attempted to exterminate their own mentally insane or bodily impaired compatriots through "mercy killing" (falsely named "euthanasia"), and to breed a superior race through the organized fertilization of racially pure by racially superior men (eugenics)' (Bauman, 1989: 72). These attempts to regulate the population through the application of science constituted nothing less than 'the rational management of society' (Bauman, 1989: 72). This view of the Nazi racial policy that was aimed at removing the misfit may have been the basis for Bauman's life-long interest in the outsider, the refugee, and the migrant.

Beck and Bauman were not directly concerned with natural catastrophes and their connections to political instability, because their attention was directed to social and political catastrophes. However, natural crises are adding to the modern sense of human vulnerability. One contemporary example is the dramatic image of the volcanic eruption in the Spanish Canary Island of La Palma in September 2021 from which over 5000 people were evacuated. Contemporary catastrophic conditions have a magnified impact on communities that are already vulnerable and at risk. Droughts occur in both developed and developing countries with significant impacts and are currently growing in frequency, and severity. Excessive exploitation of water resources, changing weather conditions and climate change are key factors in the rising level of risk. Underdeveloped countries are the most affected by these environmental changes owing to social, political, and economic conditions including differences in available scientific knowledge and skill levels in health care services. These circumstances in Asia are resulting in serious food insecurity, and as a result are undermining human health. Growing threats from pests, disease and famine are consequences of many modern developments: deforestation, urbanization, soil degradation and droughts.

Retrotopia: the Escape into Nostalgia

In *Retrotopia* (2017), Bauman complained that, in the face of modern problems, nostalgia becomes a regressive attitude. As a term that began to emerge in 16th-century medical ideas, nostalgia comes from the Greek *nostos* (to return home) and *algos* (pain). *Retrotopia* thus takes up themes that were already present in *Liquid Modernity*. Whereas Beck saw risk society as future-oriented, Bauman believes that in the contemporary world the utopian imagination is directed towards the past rather than the future. The utopian dream is projected towards the return to an ideal past more than towards the construction of a better future, in response to a dark world of growing insecurity and violence. With the contemporary instability of our increasingly complex world and the insecurities and anxieties of our profoundly fragmented and individualized liquid life, the return to a tribal attitude and an acceptance of indifference toward inequality, the outsider and the stranger seem increasingly 'rational' or at least 'practical'. The retrospective vision might thus be compared to nostalgia, in which there is often a desire to return in time and space to the origins of individuals or social groups (Frow, 1997).

However, the tide can still be turned, and Bauman seeks to reorient the contemporary gaze toward the future. With *Retrotopia*, Bauman opens a window on the problems of contemporary society and points to a future in which public life, civility and the common good might be restored through open dialogue. His aim was once more to make sociology more relevant to understanding persistent problems of inequality, injustice and the world of the socially excluded. Especially towards the end of his career, these themes are illustrated by major publications such as *Work, Consumption, and the New Poor* (Bauman, 1998), *Wasted Lives: Modernity and its Outcasts* (Bauman, 2004) and *Collateral Damage* (2011a). These publications were underpinned by his engagement with ethical questions about modernity, but they are perhaps less engaged with his idea of liquidity and more directed to the traditional concerns of sociology into social stratification.

Hope and Catastrophe

Ideas about hope and survival form part of the background to this study of catastrophes. The formative idea is associated with Thomas More (1478–1535). More's *Utopia* (1961) was published in 1516 in the context of a political and religious crisis. More was executed in 1535 for treason, having denied that Henry VIII was the head of the Church of England. The broader background was the Protestant Revolution and the effects of the changes to English culture. The other issue was the question of succession which lasted all the way to James I after Elizabeth I eventually refused to marry and assumed the title of the Virgin Queen.

At the time of its publication, *Utopia* was seen to be either a political manifesto or it was a Catholic tract. Was it a manifesto for social change or merely a moral allegory? More conceived of an island that was either a 'Utopia' or 'Nowhere'. He considered yet another title of 'Eutopie' or a land of felicity. The more serious theme in the island was the absence of private property and hence there would be no propertied class. The needs of the population would be taken care of by arrangements that resemble an early welfare state.

It envisaged a lifestyle of sobriety and simplicity and therefore for some interpretations it described monasticism. More's work invented the word to describe an ideal existence and the work took its place in the English fictional tradition (Davis, 1983). More's description of a society without inequality or private property and social harmony has been identified as an early form of socialism, but in the modern age of global crisis, even socialism now looks like a utopian dream of the past.

More's analysis of the ideal state starts with an account of barbarity of hanging for theft. The punishment is 'unjust and socially undesirable' and moreover it doesn't have the desired effect of reducing theft (More, 1961: 44). Hanging is like 'teachers caning their students rather than teaching them' (More, 1961: 44). He continued 'it would be far more to the point to provide everyone with the means of livelihood so they don't need to steal' (More, 1961: 44).

'With everybody doing useful work and with such work reduced to a minimum, they build up such large reserves of everything that from time to time they can release a huge labour force to mend any roads which are in bad condition' (More, 1961: 79). If there are no such tasks needing attention, 'the authorities announce a shorter working day' (More, 1961: 79). More also anticipated pacifism in that war is rejected by the Utopians. 'Fighting is a thing they absolutely loathe. They say it is quite subhuman form of activity' (More, 1961: 109). They fail to see anything glorious in war.

While the end of private property and the construction of a welfare state might be described as a version of communism, the island also depended on domestic slavery. More's utopia was full of unsolved contradictions. However, it may well be the case that utopian dreams are inevitably burdened with ambiguity and contradiction. Utopian dreams may be just that – powerful, but unrealized dreams. Perhaps they end in tragedy and dystopia.

Although utopia emerged in the wishful thinking of alternatives to poverty and human misery from medieval times onwards, it has occupied the thought of critics of modernity and finds a contemporary expression in the desire to return to the simple lifestyle of the countryside and village life. As an English example, we might turn to the nostalgic reminiscences of the philosopher Roger Scruton in his *Our Church* (2012) in which he constructs a picture of the Church of England, which most of his reviewers claim never existed.

By contrast, I argue that utopia has the potential to be a forward-looking time frame that we can consider via a sociology of generations, where again we find a key reference in Karl Mannheim (1951), who argued that the consciousness of generations is typically forged by major historical events that continue to determine the consciousness of the different time frames of different generations. Bloch's *The Principle of Hope* (1986) was partly addressed to correcting the authoritarian socialism of East Germany. In a similar framework, Zygmunt Bauman's sociology can be interpreted as an unfolding engagement with utopian ideas especially in his *Socialism: The Active Utopia* (2011b).

Conclusion: Resilience and Dialogue

In this chapter I have been concerned to examine responses to modernity, especially in the work of two sociologists who captured the public imagination through two essentially simple concepts: risk and liquidity. Both men were engaged with social changes that were in many respects threatening and with times when the actual survival of human societies was at stake, especially through developments in advanced technology. These consequences of advanced technological changes were what sociologists often refer to as the unanticipated consequences of social action (Merton, 1936). While unanticipated consequences often turn out to be negative, Beck and Bauman saw opportunities for positive change. Beck essentially saw opportunities for re-building communities and resilient institutions out of catastrophe. Baumann saw dialogue as offering a route to restoring the virtues of civility and understanding. While humans should not give up on hope, we will need radical change to offset the worst outcomes of climate change and the destruction of our environment, such as wilding, deindustrialization, dmilitarization, and significant international co-operation.

Chapter 3
Enlightenment and Catastrophe

Enlightenment Optimism

In a study of catastrophe, it is important to include an inquiry into the nature and consequences of the Enlightenment. One feature of this inquiry is to ask to what extent the modern fascination with and dependence on technology come from the Enlightenment celebration of reason, rationality, and science. The contemporary ambition is to develop our scientific understanding of the world to prevent or at least to manage the physical and social damage arising from natural catastrophes. There is, however, a second reason which in some respects is more central than science to a sociology of catastrophe. The Enlightenment believed in human progress and had an optimistic view of the future. The modern optimistic ethos of scientific work on disasters has all the hallmarks of the legacy of the 18th-century Enlightenment (Guggenheim, 2014). The explosion of ideas in the Enlightenment period is seen as the dawn of modernity. The many intellectuals who are critical of contemporary applications of technology are also critical of the Enlightenment and its version of modernity.

What we might call the 'Enlightenment Agenda' included science, secularism, optimism, confidence in human progress, and happiness. The positive ideas that have emerged in response to contemporary disasters such as COVID-19 – resilience, community building, unforeseen opportunities, scientific success, human fortitude, and global co-operation – continue to promote, at least implicitly, Enlightenment values and sentiments. Although I am here referring to the dominant ideas and sentiments of the Enlightenment, we should avoid treating the movement as completely coherent and unified. We need to keep in mind the emphasis on humanitarianism among Enlightenment intellectuals. For example, the sentimental notion of 'humanity' was important in their enlightened views regarding the abolition of slavery and prison reform (Gay, 1969: 29 – 45).

The debate about the value of the Enlightenment and its legacy continues to rage. In *The Philosophy of the Enlightenment: The Christian Burgess and the Enlightenment*, Lucien Goldmann (1973) argued that the basic Enlightenment values – freedom, equality, and respect for the individual – were the product of an emerging free market and the growth of a bourgeois class. They challenged the power of the nobility and brought into question the teaching and social influence of the Church. He concluded that those values are still important, although they have been challenged by modern developments such as socialism. For example,

https://doi.org/10.1515/9783110772364-003

Goldmann (1973: 91) claimed that 'an economy entirely planned by the central authority poses a most serious threat' to the values of the Enlightenment.

This understanding of the Enlightenment legacy continues to enjoy a general endorsement. This tradition sustains the view that western culture has nourished individual liberty, belief in progress, constitutionalism, secularism in the separation of church and state, and confidence in scientific rationality. Stephen Pinker (2018) gave a spirited defence of Enlightenment values in his *Enlightenment Now: The Case for Reason, Science, Humanism, and Progress* in which the concluding three chapters defend 'reason, science and humanism'. In his view, those critical of the Enlightenment suffer from 'progressophobia'. Following the Enlightenment tradition, religion is incompatible with reason or at least the deism of some Enlightenment thinkers did not embrace an anthropomorphic God. Thus 'few appealed to the law-giving, miracle-conjuring, son-begetting God of scripture' (Pinker, 2018: 8). In the modern world, a 'theistic morality' cannot be supported by the usual appeals to faith, revelation, scripture and so forth (Pinker, 2018: 421). Against Pinker's secularism, it is obvious in the United States that Christian values about the sanctity of life have had a significant impact on voting behaviour and the values of the Supreme Court.

The Enlightenment was carried along as much by political revolutions as by revolutions in thought. The American Revolution in 1778 and the French Revolution in 1789 promoted ideas about citizenship and the rights of man that challenged existing forms of privilege. Insofar as sociology was itself a product of the Scottish Enlightenment, it too was a conduit of Enlightenment science and values (Swingewood, 1970). Enlightenment sociology rejected any reference to God as no longer relevant to explaining social institutions and it embraced the idea that society was moving in an evolutionary progression from barbarity to a civilized society based on scientific rationality. Secularism involved not just the separation of church and state, it challenged the basic theological notion that God was the ultimate cause of all social institutions and relationships. Peter Gay (1966) accurately described the Enlightenment as 'the rise of modern paganism'. While classical sociology took an extensive interest in religion, it was to inquire what society would look like once it was no longer based on religious beliefs and values. In other words, it wanted to understand the consequences of a society without religion. This conventional view of Enlightenment opposition to religion needs some qualification to note that their principal target of criticism was the Roman Catholic Church. The *philosophes* were critical of celibacy, ritual, and the oversupply of religious holidays. By contrast, they thought Protestantism was less irrational and more conducive to civil virtue (Rosenblatt, 2008: 16–24).

The Enlightenment was in many respects the turning-point in the emergence of modern secularism. Denise Diderot (1713–1784) developed a view of evolution, sexuality, pleasure, and gender that was strikingly modern. One of his philosophical fragments recalls a conversation in which the question was 'are there any real atheists?' His reply was to ask whether there are any 'real Christians?' Diderot's witty response underlined the fact that the age of Enlightenment produced a bourgeoisie that had not just lost its faith, but rather a social class, whose very lifestyle was inimical to traditional forms of faith. The Enlightenment philosophers were especially hostile to the monastic life, because one of their basic assumptions was that humans are sociable and gregarious. Monks and nuns were seen to be alienated not only from society, but from their bodies and themselves (Hulliung, 1994: 15). Diderot placed a significant emphasis on the body over mind, celebrated sexual satisfaction and regarded the mortification of the flesh as pointless (Gooden, 2001). It is important to dwell on the explicit secularism of the Enlightenment to understand the character of western modernity as a project in secularity.

The foundations of the modern social sciences were laid during the Enlightenment, when the view that it was possible to know the world through reason and experience without any theological presuppositions became widely held. The ideas of Immanuel Kant (1724–1804) played a special role in this development, but his contribution has often been neglected. In 1798 Kant published his *Anthropology from a Pragmatic Point of View* (Kant, 2006) in which he presented anthropology as an empirical discipline, the aim of which was to provide important factual 'knowledge of the world'. Kant's anthropology represents an attempt to develop a social science to examine the social and moral cultivation of humans. In a brief note on 'What is Enlightenment?', Kant claimed that

> Enlightenment is man's leaving his self-caused immaturity. Immaturity is the incapacity to use one's intelligence without the guidance of another. Such immaturity is self-caused if it is not caused by lack of intelligence, but by lack of determination and courage to use one's intelligence without being guided by another. *Sapere Aude!* [Dare to know!] Have the courage to use your own intelligence is therefore the motto of the enlightenment (Kant, 2014: 60–61).

In this spirit of education, Enlightenment philosophers sought not only to promote new ideas through their debating societies and academic associations, but they attempted to catalogue and expand human knowledge through the *Encyclopedia*. The attempt to summarize and then expand knowledge was inaugurated by Pierre Bayle's *Historical and Critical Dictionary* of 1697. Ephraim Chambers (1680–1740) published his *Cyclopedia* by subscription in 1728. The subtitle was *Universal Dictionary of Arts and Sciences*. The comprehensive ambition was to make museums redundant by developing modern encyclopedic knowledge and to challenge the established and elitist universities by providing knowledge to a general audience (Yeo, 2001). The *Cyclopedia* was the model for the more famous publication of the *Encyclopedie* in 1751 with Denis Diderot and Jean le Rond d'Alembert (1718–

1783) as chief editors. It contained skeptical contributions about religion including false ideas about miracles. It was banned by the Catholic Church in 1758.

A basic theme of the Enlightenment and its famous *Encyclopedia* was an account of the rise of civilization from barbarity. This historical view was challenged by two historical catastrophes, namely the collapse of the Roman Empire and the fall of Constantinople. If Rome could fall, was it possible that an enlightened Europe could be confronted by a similar fate? The critical publication was Edward Gibbon's six-volume *The Decline and Fall of the Roman Empire* between 1776 and 1781 (Gibbon, 2017). Despite the scale and complexity of Gibbon's analysis of Rome, his thesis was simple and consistent. He declared, in his incomplete *Autobiography* (Gibbon, 1978) that was published after his death, that he continued to believe that the triumph of the Church was inseparably connected to the decline of Rome. The fragile character of human societies, including its greatest empires, presented Enlightenment rationality and optimism with a serious challenge. Nevertheless, the mood of the early Enlightenment was optimistic about human progress. The Marquis de Condorcet (1743–1794) in his *Sketch for a Historical Picture of the Progress of the Human Spirit* argued that there was abundant evidence of human progress and material affluence based on advances in both natural and social sciences. Humanity had evolved from savagery to civilization.

We often think therefore that the Enlightenment project was dominated almost exclusively by its praise for the role of science and reason in the progress of human societies. However, a neglected feature of the Enlightenment was the idea that human happiness was the goal of all human endeavour. This aspect of the Enlightenment has been emphasized in a recent publication by Ritchie Robertson (2021) on *The Enlightenment: the pursuit of happiness 1680–1790*. We can illustrate this theme of happiness by considering two prominent examples: Alexander Pope's *Essay on Man* and Condorcet's famous *Sketch* that was published posthumously in 1795.

Pope's *Essay on Man*, published in 1733–1734, was described by Voltaire as a 'beautiful poem' in 1736. Pope's essay was frequently translated into French, where it was well received. The poem in Epistle II of the *Essay* famously starts with a plea for a humanistic knowledge of the world: 'Know then thyself, presume not God to scan; The proper study of Mankind is Man'.

In Epistle IV of the *Essay* on *Of the Nature and State of Man, with Respect to Happiness*, Pope (2018) declared that happiness:

> is the end of all men, and attainable by all. God intends Happiness to be equal; and to be so, it must be social, since all particular Happiness depends on general, and since he governs by general, not particular laws. As it is necessary for order, and the peace and welfare of Society, that external goods should be unequal, Happiness is not made to consist in these. But notwith-

standing that inequality, the balance of Happiness among mankind is kept even by Providence, by the two passions of Hope and Fear.

In many respects the Marquis de Condorcet was the leading intellectual of the Enlightenment. He argued that truth, happiness, and virtue were held together in an 'indissoluble chain'. Condorcet claimed that there was ample evidence of human progress and material affluence based on advances in natural and social sciences. Humanity had moved from barbarism to civilization. He also argued that population growth was a clear indication of growing prosperity and happiness. It was this brief commentary on population growth that provoked Thomas Malthus (1766–1834) into publishing the *Essay on Population* (Malthus, 2004) in 1798 against Condorcet's optimism. Malthus's solution to overpopulation was to promote delayed marriage, contraception, and small families. His demographic arguments were uniformly condemned by Charles Dickens, Percy Shelly, Samuel Taylor Coleridge, Willian Godwin, William Hazlitt and not least by Karl Marx (Macfarlane, 2018).

However, the event that fundamentally challenged both Enlightenment optimism and Christian faith was a natural catastrophe in 1755 when Lisbon was destroyed by an earthquake and tsunami that, in its cultural and religious consequences, ushered in the modern age. This event is an important basis to my argument that modernity starts with a catastrophe.

Lisbon Earthquake of 1755

We might argue that catastrophe defined the origins of modernity, and much of its early history and character. My starting point therefore is the Lisbon earthquake and tsunami which brought to an end the possibility of theodicy as a credible religious response to catastrophe and represented a challenge to the confident optimism of the European Enlightenment. The German philosopher Gottfried Leibniz (1646–1716) who published *Theodicy* (Leibniz, 2005) in 1710 argued that we live in the best of all possible worlds, including plagues and earthquakes, and therefore we should be optimistic. The aim was to justify Christian belief that God was wise, all powerful, and benevolent despite the evidence of natural disasters, famine, and warfare, and the obvious extent of evil in human affairs. Leibniz had died in 1716, but his philosophy had many followers. However, for many observers his theodicy was fatally undermined by the Lisbon earthquake in 1755, which destroyed much of Lisbon and affected the whole of the Iberian Peninsula, North Africa, and southern Ireland, killing some 20,000 inhabitants. For many philosophers, this catastrophe falsified Leibniz's view of God's providential care for mankind and questioned human optimism in the face of catastrophic events. Immanuel Kant offered a rational view of natural events. He was interested in the science of earthquakes writing three short scientific articles on the earthquake for the Königsberg local newspaper in 1756. He also produced a defence of optimism in 1759 in *Versuch einiger Betrachtungen über den Optimismus* (*An Attempt at Some Reflections on Optimism*) (Kant, 1990).

Voltaire was sceptical regarding any religious response that could reconcile the Lisbon earthquake with a divine plan. He pointed out in his *Poem on the Lisbon Disaster – or the examination of the axiom – all is well* in 1755 that many capital cities such as Paris and London were hotbeds of vice and corruption (Voltaire, 1912). Why didn't God destroy them as well? The poem provoked a decade – long correspondence between Jean-Jacques Rousseau and Voltaire over the appropriate response to the earthquake (Bridgeman, 1919). Rousseau argued that the real problem at Lisbon was that the houses had not been built appropriately. They were too tall and too close together. Based on these observations, Rousseau is plausibly credited with the first attempt at a social science perspective on the catastrophe (Dynes, 2000). Rousseau's response was optimistic in that with better social organization, including better social planning, European cities could avoid the worst consequences of future earthquakes. Rousseau in many respects anticipated the contemporary response of disaster research to natural disasters, that argues there is no such thing as a natural disaster (Bankoff, 2003). The real problem rests with inappropriate building materials, poorly designed urban spaces, misconceived location of human habitat, inadequate emergency services and unreliable warning systems. Natural disasters, according to disaster research, are hedged about with a history of inadequate political and social responses. Although this argument is convincing, the Lisbon tsunami was a catastrophe on such a scale that advanced planning and preparation of the citizens may not have made a significant difference. The Lisbon tsunami might be better described as the 'Iberian Catastrophe'.

Adorno and the Dialectic of Enlightenment

In contemporary philosophy and sociology, the most serious and consistent critique of Enlightenment assumptions was undertaken by the Frankfurt School (Institute for Social Research) and within the Frankfurt tradition it was Theodor Adorno (1903–1969), who was and remains the dominant figure. A majority of its leading members were Jewish survivors of the Nazi regime and the Holocaust. Adorno spent WW II in the United States in a condition he called 'hibernating with dignity'. Their critique was directed at the basic assumptions of western rationality, technological efficiency, and the idea of the historical unfolding of social progress. They argued that the basic, but disguised, theme of the Enlightenment was domination to be achieved through rationality. Hence the critique of modernity had to be a critique of Enlightenment.

The key members were Theodor Adorno, Max Horkheimer, Herbert Marcuse, and Eric Fromm. In their critical theory, they rejected the standard positivism of social science, but they were also critical of Marxism. They sought to create a new approach based on the idea of 'dialectics'. The history of the Frankfurt School cannot be understood outside the European catastrophe of the 1930s and 1940s. Their critical thinking was driven by their experience of fascism and the rise of Nazi Germany. Their critical philosophy argued that the rationality of the Enlightenment was embedded in 'late capitalism' on the one hand and by the concentration camps of the Holocaust on the other. Technological rationalism had produced the totally 'administered society'.

Theodor Adorno caused ongoing controversy in his frequently misquoted statement that 'after Auschwitz' there can be no poetry. As Michael Rothberg (1997) points out, we need to see this idea of 'never again' within the broader context of Adorno's work. In particular, the attempt to exterminate the whole Jewish community was a clear and brutal demonstration that the Enlightenment view of endless progress from barbarism to civilization was a comforting myth. Adorno remained convinced that the Germany that emerged after the war with its 'economic miracle' had, for the majority of Germans, buried the memory of war crimes. The target of much of his work was Germany under fascism, but his time in America also laid the foundations for his criticisms of consumerism and the emerging mass culture as illustrated in the film industry. The key texts were *Negative Dialectics* (Adorno, 1973), *Dialectic of Enlightenment* (Adorno and Horkheimer, 2002) and *Minima Moralia* (Adorno, 2005). These publications were the critical texts in which Adorno examined various dimensions of the catastrophe that had overwhelmed European civilization.

While I argue here that the Frankfurt School developed a radical critique of the Enlightenment, the intermediary figure between the Enlightenment optimism and Frankfurt pessimism was Georg Wilhelm Friedrich Hegel (1770–1831). For my narrative of the end of the Enlightenment, Hegel is important because his view of history was the foundation of Karl Marx's interpretation of the revolutionary – indeed, catastrophic – transitions from feudalism to capitalism and finally to socialism. Following Leszek Kolakowski (1978) we can, however, regard the Frankfurt School as part of the historical 'breakdown' of the foundations of Marxism. The breakdown was illustrated by the fact that the leading figures of post-war Marxism and specifically the members of the *Institute* had no vital connection to working-class politics and uniformly came from the bourgeois elite of pre-war Germany. The ambition of this cohort did not include a revolutionary overthrow of post-war European states. The mood of this generation, again in contrast to the Enlightenment philosophers, was captured by Perry Anderson (1976: 88–89) in his *Considerations on Western Marxism*, when he observed that 'they shared one fundamental emblem: a common and latent *pessimism*' and a 'pervasive melancholy'.

Hegel's relationship to the Enlightenment was ambiguous (Giovanni, 1995). He was sceptical towards the mechanistic view of the universe and the materialism that underpinned the Enlightenment perspective. Hegel's philosophy was connected to Romanticism which was associated with a more holistic and less mechanical view of reality and the unfolding of history. Whereas Enlightenment thinkers were, in broad terms, secular, Hegel recognized the importance of religion as the expression of the consciousness of a people and its culture. Marx followed Hegel in seeing history as a dialectical progression from feudalism to capitalism, resulting eventually in the collapse of capitalism through revolutionary struggle. While Hegel was critical of the abuses of the French Revolution, he nevertheless saw it as the major turning point in history in terms of a growing awareness of the unfolding of the consciousness of freedom (Ritter, 1982).

It is important to recognize that Adorno was not offering a blanket criticism of the European Enlightenment. The problem, according to Leszek Kolakowski (1978: 373), was that the Enlightenment had inadvertently 'created a positivist, pragmatist, utilitarian ideology and, by reducing the world to its purely quantitative aspects, had annihilated meaning, barbarized the arts and sciences, and increasingly subjected mankind to "commodity fetishism"'. By giving humans control over nature, Enlightenment ideas about progress had resulted in the general alienation of humanity from nature. In many respects, Adorno followed Max Weber's sociology of western modernity as a system of rational bureaucratic management. For Weber, the world of rational bureaucracies was a world of disenchantment (Roth and Schluchter, 1979). In the *Dialectic of Enlightenment* (Adorno and Horkheimer, 1973), Adorno and Horkheimer had argued that Enlightenment assumptions gave rise to totalitarian systems in society and politics. Thinking of his experience of emigration to the United States, Adorno argued that with the erosion of reason, subjectivity and feeling had resulted in a degradation of culture, most powerfully illustrated in the mass entertainment industry. As a distinguished music critic, Adorno was also critical of modern jazz. Kolakowski in *Main Currents of Marxism. The Breakdown* (1978) saw the Frankfurt School as a key element in the unravelling of Marxism as the principal framework for understanding the historical collapse of capitalism. He was predictably critical of the elitist assumptions behind Adorno's critique of popular culture.

One can argue that the Frankfurt School included capitalism under a broader attack on modernity. In turn, the driving force behind their criticisms of modernity was German fascism. Adorno and colleagues undertook an empirical study of the psychological roots of fascism in *The Authoritarian Personality* (Adorno et al., 1993) in which they argued that an authoritarian, clinging and exploitative parent-child relationship produced an authoritarian clinging type that sought a powerful figure as a leader. Although this project was influential, the research has been criticized for its methodological failings. The naïve explanation of the growth of fascism had a negative effect on the plausibility of political psychology more broadly. The research also became the topic of an academic joke – there are two types of people in the world, those that divide people into two groups and those that don't. Zygmunt Bauman (1989) in *Modernity and the Holocaust* was equally critical. He argued that Adorno's thesis was circular: Fascism was cruel because the Nazis were cruel, and cruel people tend to become Nazis. Bauman's counter-argument rested on Weber's views of bureaucracy. For Bauman, there was no conflict between rationality and the Holocaust. Rejecting any idea of a civilizing process in which we moderns have left barbarism behind, Bauman claimed that the victims of Hitler's Germany and Stalin's Russia were killed because 'they did not fit...They were eliminated so that an objectively better world could be established' (Bauman, 1989: 92). Bureaucracy has the effect of creating a distance between the officials and the victims, who could be killed without ire. Bauman also rejects the standard argument that antisemitism was a key factor in the genocide. The concentration camps illustrated an efficient killing system that operated beyond human sentiment or morality. The result was a cruel catastrophe that had repercussions well beyond WWII.

Walter Benjamin and the Angel of History

Walter Benjamin (1892–1940) was close to Adorno and their correspondence stretched from 1928 to 1940 (Lonitz, 1999), but their relationship was complex, because Adorno had problems accepting Benjamin's theological interests and perspective. Furthermore, Benjamin was only an associate member of the Frankfurt School from 1935. His work is important in this study of catastrophe because Benjamin had a powerful sense of the catastrophic character of modernity and his analysis of history developed a profound criticism of any claims regarding human progress. The key texts are *Theses on the Philosophy of History* which is available in *Illuminations* (Benjamin, 1973) and edited by Hannah Arendt and the *Theological-Political Fragment* (Benjamin, 1986) in *Reflections*. The title 'Fragment' was given to the small publication by Adorno in the first edition of Benjamin's work in 1955. The *Fragment* was thus seen as a late publication in response to post-war totalitarianism in the Soviet Union and East Germany. A more authoritative interpretation was given by Gershom Scholem, a close friend of Benjamin, who claimed the 'fragment' was written in 1920–1921, responding to the aftermath of WWI when Benjamin was developing a 'philosophy of Judaism'. The point of this dispute is that the 'fragment' is important in understanding Benjamin's thoughts on the Messiah and history. In the *Fragment*, Benjamin drew a sharp line between the religious and the political. He claimed the Kingdom of God 'is not the *telos* of the historical dynamic, it cannot be set as a goal. From the standpoint of history, it is not the goal, but the end. Therefore, the order of the profane cannot be built up on the idea of the Divine Kingdom, and therefore theocracy has no political, but only a religious meaning' (Benjamin, 1978: 312).

He then praised Bloch's *Spirit of Utopia* for clearly establishing the separation of the political and the religious. Bloch wrote the book in 1915–1916 but it was not published until 1923. Bloch's understanding of hope and utopia had a profound effect on Benjamin's 'philosophy of Judaism'. Bloch's philosophy was a combination of Marxism and Messianism. He was disillusioned by the authoritarian development of the communist regimes, embraced the idea of hope as a fundamental characteristic of human societies and their historical development. Benjamin's own critique of progressive modern history also combined elements of historical Marxism and Jewish theological understanding of the role of the Messiah. Benjamin described his method as 'dialectic at a standstill' (*Dialektik im Stillstand*), which provided him with a decisive break with the Enlightenment as well as with Social Democratic notions of historical progress, which only recognizes an infinite series of empty, quantitative transitions, or the homogeneous time of the 'always-the-same' and whose defining characteristic is the piling up of 'ruins upon ruins'.

The importance of the *Theses* for this interpretation of Benjamin's philosophy of history and for this volume on catastrophe concerns his reflections on Paul Klee's painting of the *Angelus Novus* which Benjamin interpreted as the angel of history in *Thesis IX*. The conclusion is that 'The Storm is what we call progress' (Benjamin, 1973: 259–260). Towards the end of his theory of history, he focused on catastrophic ruptures. For Benjamin in *Thesis VIII*, 'the state of emergency' was not the exception but the rule. In particular, the rise of fascism requires the rejection of the idea of ongoing progress in the Marxist view of history. Christine Buci-Glucksmann (1994: 98) provides a useful summary of Benjamin's historical vision. For Benjamin's 'overcoming of the illusion of totality, system and unicity in history makes it necessary to recognize an inescapable truth of catastrophist utopianism: namely the eternal recurrence of barbarism, fragmentation, and destruction as a critical force'.

Conclusion: post-Enlightenment

I began this chapter by claiming that contemporary disaster theory is based on the legacy of the Enlightenment's view of history as a narrative of human progress. Disasters do not bring an end to progress; they are simply disruptions to ongoing human development. The Frankfurt School's negative view of any claims about progress and modernity was part of the early foundation of postmodern theory that also proclaimed the end of history. Post-modernism became a wide-spread fashion in sociology beginning with the English translation of *The Postmodern Condition* (Lyotard, 1984). In fact, the idea of postmodernism pre-dates Lyotard's intervention. The idea of post-history or *post-histoire* was associated with Arnold Gehlen, who also had close connections to Adorno, and who introduced the idea to German sociology in 1952. However, the idea also takes us back to Hegel who had a notion of the end of history in *Phenomenology of the Spirit* (Hegel, 1977: 443). There are thus many claimants to the idea that we are living at the end of history. Gehlen however attributed the idea to Antoine Augustin Cournot, who had in 1861 argued that the dynamic of history was coming to an end with the perfection of civil society. The idea became popular, but under the notion of post-modernity. With the increasing popularity of the debate about the postmodern and end of history, Jürgen Habermas was critical of its mere repetition and re-cycling of earlier ideas by writers such as Fukuyama. Habermas complained that 'I already read most of this in Arnold Gehlen when I was a student' (Habermas, 1994: 79–80).

Post-war German intellectual and cultural life is associated with a generation of intellectuals – the so-called forty-fivers – who grappled with the legacy of fascism, the War, and the division of Germany. They were unsurprisingly unimpressed by theories of progress, rationality, and the endless advance of science. One key figure here was Reinhart Koselleck who influenced Habermas among others and who was also critical of the legacy of the Enlightenment. He was particularly interested, not in catastrophe, but with the history of the idea of crisis (Koselleck, 1988). It was the subject of his dissertation thesis and reference to his work on crisis and Enlightenment appears at various stages in this study of the idea of catastrophe. For Koselleck, the Weimer Republic was a turning point in the history of the concept of crisis, but it was also the starting point in the unfolding of world war.

In Gehlen's version, post-histoire was the global process of capitalist industrialization coming to fruition, but also entering into stagnation. Global industrialization created a universalization of work, living conditions, consumption, lifestyles, and leisure. The experience of death became standardized as dying in hospital was increasingly the norm. With post-modernity, there emerged a generalized normality and uniformity. Uniqueness and difference are pushed to the margins of society. With modernization, the fundamental contradiction is between the maintenance of instrumental rationality and 'non-similarity' (*Ungleichzeitigkeit*). Although Gehlen had emerged as a leading conservative figure in post-war Germany, his ideas had a remarkable resonance with the Frankfurt School. Gehlen was on friendly terms with Adorno, who apparently regarded Gehlen as an ideal debating partner on various radio talks (Müller-Doohm, 2005: 379). In their radio debate in 1965, Gehlen accused him of 'irresponsible idealism', while Adorno criticized his 'pessimistic anthropology'. The institutions that Gehlen supported as necessary for the survival of human beings were regarded by members of the Frankfurt school as oppressive.

For Gehlen, the evolution of modern art had come to a conclusion with the development of 'conceptual art' in which the concept was more significant than the work of art itself. The point of conceptual art was to ask the unanswerable question 'But is it art?' As a result, commentaries on modern art became more important than the objects of art themselves, such as an unmade bed or a random collection of chairs or a blank canvas. Given the importance of commentary, in the world of modern conceptual art, the art dealers became as significant as the artists. The same argument applies to literature, for example, to the work of Samuel Beckett (1956), especially his *Waiting for Godot*. The richness of the play lies in the question: what is it about? For Gehlen, the apparent closure of art in the growth of art commentary reflected modern society with its energetic immobility. The Enlightenment had entered the age of postmodern stagnation.

Chapter 4
Plagues, Famines and Population

Introduction: *Fortuna imperatrix mundi*

Human societies are often disrupted and devastated simultaneously by a plurality of catastrophes rather than a singular catastrophe. The classic story from *Exodus* 7 in the Old Testament recalls how, when the Pharoah refused to release the children of Israel from captivity, the Lord sent ten plagues to destroy Egypt. These plagues represented the many ways by which a community could be destroyed and became a source of many subsequent representations of human suffering. Similarly, the Four Horsemen of the Apocalypse provide a dramatic representation of death and famine. It also remained a constant theme of popular imagery.

Because the food supply of most pre-modern communities was precarious, famines were all too common. If a plague devasted a small community, there was an immediate loss of labour power bringing with it a threat of famine. These threats to life were obviously unevenly distributed between lords and peasants, depending on the system of land distribution. While a plague of locusts can destroy an entire harvest, the extent of the suffering will also be influenced by the social structure and by responses to famines, labour shortages and how markets operate. With disruptions to the food supply, communities were often then confronted by a loss of births and rising child mortality, in turn resulting in demographic stagnation. Unstable markets and declining populations were in fact the common experiences of early European societies (Ewert, Roehl, and Uhrmacher, 2007).

The precarious character of human societies was captured by Thomas Malthus in 1798 in his bleak analysis of the relationship between the extent of arable land and the growth of the population in *An Essay on the Principle of Population*. With no obvious prospect of increasing available land for food production, periodic starvation was the inevitable fate of the laboring poor. Malthus was an Anglican priest, and his language was unsurprisingly biblical regarding the consequences of any rapid population growth that remains unchecked: 'sickly seasons, epidemics, pestilence, and plague, advance in terrific array, and sweep off their thousands and tens of thousands. Should success be still incomplete, gigantic famine stalks in the rear' (Malthus, 2004: 61). The debate between Thomas Malthus and David Ricardo over the effects of the Corn Laws captured the conundrum of how, if at all, markets could be successfully regulated. For Ricardo, the price of corn was determined, not by fortune, but by the demand for profit by rich landlords. These brief

https://doi.org/10.1515/9783110772364-004

comments on the economic background to plagues and famines once more raise a question about the actual character of 'natural' catastrophes. Are catastrophes merely fortuitous?

The idea of fortune or fate is closely associated with catastrophe, because catastrophes are typically experienced as unusual, unexpected, and damaging events. Human history has been shaped by catastrophes in which plagues, wars, famines, and earthquakes have been the primary contenders. Whereas wars may have predictable causes such as the quest for land, earthquakes and plagues are experienced as fateful. Earthquakes have been a persistent problem for urban settlements, especially when appropriate building materials were not available or because relevant building techniques had not been invented. Before the development of basic scientific understanding, human communities often had little or no warning of an imminent earthquake. With modern-day equipment such as seismometers, it is possible to predict and measure earthquake activity and prepare for future crises. While earthquakes are experienced as unanticipated and untoward events, in fact, catastrophic earthquakes may take thousands of years to develop. The earthquake and tsunami that struck Tonga on 14 January 2022 caused significant damage. The previous Tongan earthquake of 1865 also caused widespread damage and death, but earthquakes along the Tongan archipelago are not uncommon. Many of these earthquakes do not in fact cause significant damage or loss of human life. However, because catastrophes are *experienced* as unpredicted, they have historically been associated with the idea of fate as a vengeful goddess known as *Fortuna.*

A comprehensive theory of catastrophes needs to examine the ways in which societies construct meaningful accounts of the suffering that attend any catastrophe. Such radical transformations of daily life call out for interpretation that is not simply a factual or scientific analysis and report. Understanding tragic events often involves ethical, religious, or cultural accounts that do not necessarily rest on scientific evidence. Understanding is not necessarily the same as explanation. In fact, these two – understanding and explanation – are typically regarded as quite separate and distinctive (Schutz, 1967). Understanding is particularly attentive to the subjective meanings that are attached to social actions and the social world. Explanation can be conceived as the quest for the objective facts as seen by the outside observer.

Catastrophic events, where there is a significant loss of human life, inevitably confront religious belief in a benevolent and all-powerful God with the extent of human suffering that appears to be meaningless. In the long run, the quest for a meaningful religious interpretation of human suffering breaks down when confronted by the contradiction between divine benevolence and human misery. Peter Berger (1969: 7) concluded 'The social theodicy of Christianity (that is its justification of the iniquities of society) has been collapsing along with the over-all plausibility of the Christian theodicy.' For many, the horror of the trenches in WWI was the death knell of any plausible religious theodicy. The lack of significant religious interpretations of COVID-19 in terms of a convincing theodicy does suggest that modern societies are indeed secular.

Anticipating the conclusions that I draw in this study, in the absence of any meaningful and coherent response to COVID-19, we can accept that, in a highly secular society, only scientific factual explanations are preponderant, but they are characteristically descriptive and analytical without being meaningful (Turner, 2021). In the absence of a full-blown theodicy, perhaps disaster studies, with its characteristically optimistic view of recovery and resilience in the face of catastrophe, function as a pseudo-system of meaning. By contrast, an examination of the past offers us plentiful historical evidence of catastrophic plagues, on the basis of which, we can identify numerous mythical or religious systems that offered humans some form of meaning. However, in a context of the plague, even the Church, as an authoritative source of meaning, was challenged by popular understanding of the origins of their suffering. The Book of Job is conventionally regarded as an early example of a theodicy which presents a religious interpretation of calamity. However, Job confronts God with the fundamental question: why do the innocent suffer?

The Black Death was the context in which one can discern various attempts to construct a theodicy, some of which rested on Christian belief. It was typically regarded as a punishment for human sins, for which regular confession was recommended by the bishops of the Church. By contrast, the Flagellants, a sect that attracted large numbers in northern Europe in 1349, gathered in groups and paraded in white gowns striking themselves with three-pronged whips. The Black Death or the Pestilence from 1346 to 1353 had a devastating impact on the European population and gave rise to dramatic representations of suffering. There were no satisfactory explanations to account for the twenty million people who died from the plague (Benedictow, 2004; Ziegler, 1969). An early reference to the gruesome idea of the *danse macabre* came from the poet Jean Le Fevre in 1376. The *danse macabre* portrayed the plague as a hideous attack on the human population regardless of rank, wealth, or gender (Huizinga, 1996: 156–172). There were many literary responses that included Geoffrey Chaucer's 'The Pardoner's Tale' in *The Canterbury Tales* which were written between 1382 and 1400, and Giovanni Boccaccio's *The Decameron*, which was composed between 1348 and 1353. Johann Goethe's *Faust*, first performed in 1829, was based on the *Book of Job* and includes a plague episode. The story is basically a theodicy involving a struggle between good and evil in the maturation of Faust and the figure of Faust represents a serious challenge to any notion of a benevolent God (Hoelzel, 1979).

Ferdinand Braudel (1981) in *The Structures of Everyday Life* offers a compelling historical vision of the suffering of the ordinary people of Europe during the plagues and famines from the 14th century to the 17th century. He notes that famines and plagues tend to go together. There were significant food shortages in Europe in 1308 and 1318. Famine was a regular catastrophe in Europe up to the end of the 18th century. The famine in Finland of 1696–1697 was one of the worst in European history. These famines drove people to extreme solutions such as the people of Lorraine who were forced, to eat grass in 1652. Famines regularly drove peasants off the land leaving them with no options other than to migrate to the crowded towns to beg for food. The authorities feared sedition. Michel Foucault (1977) in *Discipline and Punish: The Birth of the Prison* has described the rise of institutions to house and control the 'surplus population' of the poor, destitute and insane. For example, *The Grand Hospital* of Paris was founded in 1656 and opened to take in the population of beggars and the insane.

Catastrophes came in clusters: 'Famine was never an isolated event. Sooner or later, it opened the door to pandemics' (Braudel, 1981: 78). Another problem was the spread of syphilis, which reappeared after the discovery of pre-Columbian America. By the end of the 16th century, it had attacked every level of society. However, the rich could always escape to their country estates to avoid unrest and rebellion in the towns. Samuel Pepys, who wrote regularly in his diary between 1660 and 1669, complained that no one cares for the other. Braudel drew inspiration from William McNeil's *Plagues and People* (1976), which considered three catastrophes – the smallpox epidemic in Mexico, the bubonic plague in China and the European typhoid epidemic. An important conclusion of McNeil's study is that, as humans came in their economic development to exercise domination through *macroparasitism,* so eventually the natural world came to exercise *microparasitism* in the form of germs, bacilli, and viruses.

Turning to the idea of *Fortuna imperatrix mundi* (Fortuna Empress of the World), the goddess *Fortuna* was an important figure in Roman mythology and in early modern representations she appeared as a woman in blindfold and spinning a large wheel. Human beings were depicted as mere recipients of either good or bad luck irrespective of their status, gender, or virtue. *Fortuna* expresses the idea of the ultimate powerlessness of humans in the face of the intangible forces that control our lives. The idea of humans as the mere objects of blind fortune was celebrated in the 254 poems that constitute what came to be known as *Carmina Burana*. These poems, many critical of the greed of the Catholic Church, include mockery, love and drinking songs. *Carmina Burana* refers to the name *Cucania* and describes an abbot of Cockaigne, who presides over drinking and gambling, thereby inverting the formal norms of the religious life. The poems are relatively well known because of the famous musical adaptation by Carl Orff in 1937.

This consciousness of fatefulness is associated with earthquakes and plagues, but what of wars and political catastrophes? Here again the rise and fall of empires, the collapse of kingdoms or the outbreak of wars often appear to be unpredictable and unexpected events, at least before political science emerged to analyse the cause and consequences of such major events. Before the rise of political science, the arrival of meteors might be seen to presage political turmoil. Revolutions are potentially catastrophic transformations of society, and their consequences are unpredictable, and often long-lasting.

These various examples suggest that the distinction between socio-political and natural catastrophes is somewhat arbitrary; political disasters often attend or follow natural disasters. Civil disturbances have regularly followed catastrophic disruptions of normal life. What they have in common is the human response, namely that humans often want some meaningful interpretation over and above the factual description of a catastrophe. Theodicies have been part of the human repertoire of cultural responses to disastrous episodes with the ambition of clothing them with a meaning system and offering some grounds for hope in a future free from catastrophe. Perhaps utopia can be seen as yet another aspect of theodicy as an expression of hope or at least the fantasy of an existence free from pain and want. In that regard, Cockaigne or the Land of Plenty was a common theme of medieval art and literature, depicting a land of plenty in contrast to the harsh and laborious lives of the peasantry. Cockaigne was not exactly a theodicy. but it expressed the hope for a better, richer, and safer world beyond the harsh conditions of the peasantry under feudalism. Such utopian responses may aim to provide intellectual and emotional comfort, and possibly hope for a better future. As I will indicate, Christianity, with its belief in a Second Coming and the promise of salvation for the pure at heart, has been a rich source of narratives of hope. By contrast, theodicies in the modern world, especially after Auschwitz, have typically been theodicies of despair and rage. The suspicion must be that, as with Auschwitz, such catastrophic events are more likely to be followed by confusion and anger.

The Plagues, Trade and Rats

The standard explanation for the cause of these pre-modern plagues was the presence of *Yersinian Pestis* – a virus carried, for example, with the black rat which traveled on board ships with the early growth of trade, especially along the Mediterranean. The cause and transmission of the disease were established by Alexandre Yersin (1863–1943) and Paul-Louis Simond (1858–1947) at the end of the 19th century as the bacterium carried by the flea (*Xenopsylla Cheopsis*). It is also assumed to have caused the Justinian Plague of 541–544. This plague has been called a catastrophe, because it allegedly killed some 50 million people and has also been seen as influential in the collapse of Rome or at least the collapse of the Eastern Empire.

This view was challenged by Lee Mordechai and Merle Eisengerg (2019) who claimed that existing approaches to this plague of antiquity cannot be supported by the evidence. They considered a range of research findings from various disciplines and concluded that the Justinian Plague did not spell the end of Antiquity. It did not cause widespread demographic decline and did not keep the Mediterranean population low. They concluded that the so-called Justinian Plague was an 'inconsequential epidemic'. In short, it cannot be described as a 'catastrophe'. Their analysis has been disputed (Sarris, 2021). Perhaps what is more interesting sociologically is how far the plague spread rapidly from the eastern Mediterranean to Anglo-Saxon villages such as Edix Hill in Cambridgeshire. Modern DNA examination of buried remains in Cambridgeshire found evidence of *Yersinian Pestis* that had originated in the eastern Empire. The plague was a catastrophe, but it did not cause the Fall of Rome. The Roman Empire did eventually collapse, but its internal coherence was eventually compromised by its size and the growing power of its provinces over the imperial core. Peter Sarris (2011) argued that fiscal and other reforms of the Empire in the face of the pandemic stabilized the Roman institutions. The Western Empire collapsed in the long run because of the ascendency of new militarized elites (the rule of the notables) which made the running of the empire increasingly difficult – especially in the face of barbarian invasions.

It has been assumed that rats played a crucial role in the spread of the bubonic plague, because they are associated with the transmission of *Y. pestis* to humans. When the bacteria that caused the plague outbreaks in the late 19th century was fully understood, it was taken for granted that the model of rat-flea-human transmission accounted for the Black Death. Many historians at the time also accepted this view. However, more recently, historical research has suggested that this assumption is unfounded. There are two issues of significance, namely a lack of evidence of the involvement of rats or fleas in the Black Death and a much faster speed of transmission in medieval communities compared with modern epidemics (Hufthammer and Walløe, 2013). The rat population in Europe in the medieval and early modern period was not large enough to cause such extensive outbreaks of plague. Accounts of plague outbreaks in warmer countries noted that rats were often prevalent alongside dead and dying rats before an outbreak of the plague and yet sources from more temperate countries rarely mention rats when describing the outbreak of plagues.

In addition, the climate in northern Europe at the time of the Black Death was not conducive to large rat or flea populations. McCormick (2003) has argued that a lack of written sources may just demonstrate a lack of interest in rats, possibly because they were so prevalent – therefore this cannot be used as substantive evidence that rats were rare or absent. It was thought to be an efficient medium to sustain large plague epidemics, however, these epidemics would have spread slowly, around 12–15 km each year. Conversely the Black Death spread very quickly, sweeping across England within a few months.

Several alternative theories have been presented to explain these differences in the Black Death and plague outbreaks in the 19th and early 20th centuries. A different type of insect vector may have been responsible, namely the *Pulex irritans* (human flea) or *Pediculus humanus* (human body louse), neither of which require the rat host to be able to transmit *Y. pestis* bacteria. Other scientists have concluded, however, that the flea has poor 'vector competence' (Lorange, Race, Sebbane, and Hinnebusch, 2005). Other research has considered whether other rodents, such as gerbils, might played a part in the persistence of the plague in European countries. This would explain why it could spread so prolifically, even without large rat populations. In his re-examination of the historical and epidemiological evidence of the Black Death outbreaks, Samuel Cohn argues that the Black Death was not bubonic plague, but another disease epidemic. He suggests that 'without argument, historians and scientists have taken the epidemiology of the modern plague and imposed it on the past, ignoring, denying, even changing contemporary testimony, both narrative and quantitative, when it conflicts with notions of how modern bubonic plague should behave' (Cohn, 2002: 1).

I have dwelt on these conflicting scientific theories to underline the differences between scientific explanation and cultural interpretation. We also have to accept that the scientific debate is inconclusive especially for societies without adequate means of collecting and recording evidence. Despite the conflicting evidence, the association between plague and rats is so pervasive that it is difficult to look at rodent-borne diseases, such as plagues, through an alternative lens and imagine a time when rats were not recognized as the principal carrier of disease to humans. Despite the persistent popular view that rats spread infections, rats have also featured as household pets (Robin, 2018).

Although much of the evidence does not result in a scientific consensus, much of the debate has overlooked one important issue, namely the impact of rodents on food supplies. Where rats consume large quantities of grain and compromise the food supply, they reduce the capacity of a human population to resist infections (McCormack, 2003). The economic effects place a further burden on agricultural communities that are already struggling with disease. In focusing on the actual plague, it is easy to forget the economics of the plague (Hatcher, 1977). The economic effects of the plague played an important role in the extent of fatalities. In addition to consuming grain, rats and mice also polluted food supplies making them effectively inedible.

Here again there is an obvious gap between the human need for meaningful understanding and the scientific need for adequate information to develop explanations. Plagues become shrouded in mythical and religious interpretations. Plague is one of the diseases that has had the most cultural impact on human civilization (Burt, 2006), and because the rat is so deeply associated with these devastating epidemics, it is evident why rats have become so powerfully connected to human attitudes and emotional responses towards the disease. The tale of the Pied Piper of Hamelin is one such example. In the story, dating from around 1300, the Piper was a rat catcher, but when he had finished removing the rats from the town of Hamelin, the citizens refused to pay him. In retaliation, he blew his magic pipe and the children of the hamlet followed him.

Unsurprisingly such catastrophes, in early and early modern Europe, had significant social and political consequences. There was widespread violence against Jewish communities. Many Jewish communities were destroyed, causing the eastward movement of Jews out of their traditional homelands. One other consequence of plagues was the Peasant Revolt of 1351 which was also known as Wat Tyler's Rebellion. With the decimation of the working population, wages and prices were rising. To control wage inflation, the *Ordinance of Labourers* fixed wages and introduced price controls. The revolt was in response to these economic restrictions. This political and economic crisis was also influential in the work of John Wycliffe (1320–1384), who was critical of the ruling elites and the wealth of the Roman Catholic Church. His translations of the Bible into the vernacular inspired his followers at the University of Oxford who became known as the Lollards. It was his attack on the eucharistic doctrine of transubstantiation that forced him to retreat to his rural rectory. He came to be regarded, because of his criticism of the Church, as a predecessor of the Protestant Reformation. The division of Christianity with Martin Luther's theses in 1517, the translation of the Bible into vernacular German and the rise of Lutheranism can be traced back to the catastrophic circumstances of 1346–1351.

The Black Death had long-term effects with additional outbreaks through the 14th century. Restrictions were introduced to limit its progress. Quarantine was used in Venice and Milan to control infections from ships entering the city. The word comes from *quarantena* or 'forty days'. The most systematic response to outbreaks occurred in Ragusa (modern-day Dubrovnik) when ships were held outside the harbour on local islands for 40 days. Precautions were taken about unloading and handling cargo from boats that had suffered infections among the crew. The authorities limited contacts between new arrivals and a quarantine hospital was built. There was a similar response to plagues in England when quarantine was also used in various English villages such as the village of Eyam in 1665 to contain infections. There was also evidence of social inequalities as the nobility left plague-infected London to escape to their country estates. Plagues produced instability rather than shared responses to catastrophe. We can summarize these diverse developments as spelling the end of feudalism in northern Europe as the traditional pattern of land ownership and religio-political authority collapsed.

The Irish Famine, 1849

Famine was a regular occurrence in the 16th century, often because of war. However, although famine has been a continuous threat to human populations and continues to threaten societies in the modern world, I focus on the Irish famine of 1849, because it is often described as the worst famine ever to engulf a society. By comparison with other major famines, the Great Irish Famine was the most significant and devastating demographic tragedy of the 19th century when judged in terms of the mortality rate.

It also raises in an acute form the question of natural and/or political causes of catastrophes. Consequently, the history of the famine is overburdened by political considerations – who, if anybody, was to blame for the catastrophe? Was it the potato itself, was it the Irish landlords, or was it the British government and its underlying racial attitudes towards the Irish? And are the lingering consequences of a divided Ireland an effect of famine and English colonialism?

The *Great Famine* or the *Irish Potato Famine* lasted from 1845 to 1849 although its consequences have shaped Irish history long after the famine came to an end. A mysterious blight, the *Phytophthora infestans*, destroyed the potato harvest. By the time of the worst year of 1847, the Irish population had declined by as much as a quarter and by 1855 some two million people had left Ireland in waves of migration. Millions of people left the country as the population of Ireland was falling from around nine million in 1845 to just over six million in 1851. The tide of emigration continued to grow well after the harvest failures.

The famine is politically controversial for the simple reason that the British Isles, at the time, was the most economically advanced nation in the West. In Ireland, at that time part of the United Kingdom following the Act of Union in 1801, one million people perished in what became known in Ireland as *An Gorta Mór* or The Great Hunger. In fact, there was not one food crisis but several as a consequence of a series of potato crop failures in 1845, 1846, 1848 and 1849. The rural Irish poor, many of whom were subsistence farmers on small plots of ground, were reliant on the potato for their staple diet. By 1841, two-thirds of the Irish population were dependent on small-scale agriculture to survive. This agrarian development had been intensified by the growth of British industry which had undermined Irish industrial development. Despite the stagnation of the economy, the Irish population had continued to grow. Between 1800 and 1841, the population grew from five million to over eight million. In effect, this was the classic Malthusian dilemma of an expanding population existing on fixed arable land. One response was migration (Martin, 1994).

One authority I shall consult as regards cause and blame is Amartya Sen, who has worked primarily on the history of famines in India. His view, admittedly about more recent famines, is that the causality of famine is almost invariably political. His basic argument is that 'no major famine has ever occurred in a functioning democracy with regular elections, opposition parties, basic freedom of speech and a relatively free media' (Sen, 2009: 342). Authoritarian governments, that are not regulated by elections or legal scrutiny, can afford to ignore, and neglect communities that are exposed to famines or other catastrophes. The parliamentary government of Britain in the 19th century could not be reasonably described as authoritarian. However, the English elite was geographically remote, and it was inclined to blame the Irish for their dependence on the potato. In addition, the British elite has also been accused of racism in its attitude towards the Irish, whom they regarded as backward. Sen (2009: 47) also claims that 'famines are easy to prevent, partly because they affect only a small proportion of the population, rarely more than 5 per cent and hardly ever more than 10 per cent'. Clearly, that was not the case in Ireland, where the fatalities were much higher. The famine also had more profound long-lasting results in terms of the migration of a large number of people, mainly to the United States. It may have been that migration was an alternative to revolution.

The debate about the causes of the famine has divided historians between those who blame the English elite for the famine and revisionists who believe that some of the blame falls on the shoulders of the Irish landlords. Karl Marx blamed the English elite and drew attention to the loss of population through famine and migration in volume 1 of *Capital*, 'England, a country with fully developed capitalist production, and eminently industrial, would have bled to death with such a drain of population as Ireland has suffered. Ireland is at present only an agricultural district of England, marked off by a wide channel from the country to which it yields corn, wool, cattle and 'industrial and military recruits' (Marx, 1970: 657). Whichever side of the dispute is valid, it illustrates the argument that the catastrophe had natural causes, namely the contamination of the potato crop, but it also had social and political causes such as the chasm between the lives of the peasantry and the landowning elites on both sides of the Irish Sea.

The 'Proneness' of Africa to Famine

While the Irish Famine is now a historical catastrophe, famine is still a problem of many contemporary societies. Let us consider famine in modern-day Africa. Research on African famines was radically transformed by the publications of Michael Watts (Watts, 1983) and Watts and Bohle (1993). His interventions continue to influence debate about the alleged 'proneness' of Africa to famine and the origins of political economy. Watts' early interest was in the poverty that was characteristic of the modern history of northern Nigeria. His research focus was on the pastoral societies of the Caliphate of Hausaland and more generally on the Sahelian region. More specifically he wanted to understand the impact of capitalism on the peasantry of Hausaland that has been prone to droughts and famines. His scope was general, including food and production systems, the peasant response to food scarcity and the resulting famines. In line with much of the political economy of underdevelopment in Latin America, he argued that the root problem was the impact of capitalism on a pre-capitalist peasant society and its economy from the middle of the 19th century to his research in the 1980s. The failure of the food system gives rise perhaps unsurprisingly to a number of social crises that sit, so to speak, on top of the famines.

Watts rejected a range of existing explanations for the Hausaland social crises such as the climate, state failure or even Malthusian population theory. Watts placed the blame on the rupture between the peasant economy and the intensification of commodity production. The blame for the 'silent violence' includes Marxist analysis and the socialist historians, such as E. P. Thompson, and Eric Hobsbawm. However, Watts does make use of the Marxist idea of 'modes of production'. This approach allows him to study the early evolution of the unique forms of production that developed in rural colonial Nigeria. This period involved upland millet-sorghum production and livestock which was in the care of Fulani herdsmen. In this early period there were regular episodes of local food scarcity, but not the catastrophic famines that were characteristic of the 20th century that had an impact on the entire region.

On the basis of his historical research, Watts concluded that, while drought is a climatic issue, famines are caused by politics and economics. The world of the Hausa peasantry was eventually shattered by the British colonial system, which undermined the peasant ability to manage food scarcity and recover from episodes of famine. In fact. the introduction of taxation encouraged cash cropping of cotton and groundnuts to the neglect of basic food production. With British colonialism there was also the development of new credit and credit arrangements that served the interests of urban elites over the rural sector. Watts concluded that the colonial capitalist system only served the 'reproduction of famine'.

The result of these economic developments has been to jeopardize the subsistence security of the Hausa peasants who remained dependent on traditional agricultural technology, where food and social relationships were tied to exchange values. The peasant world found itself overwhelmed by the cycle of drought and indebtedness. Watts concluded by describing the basic contradiction of the colonial state that impoverished the agrarian population that provides food for the society. One other development in this transformation of the rural economy has been the increasingly violent conflicts between the Hausa peasants and the Fulani herdsmen. In drought conditions, the cattle under Fulani control stray onto Hausa land in search of food and consume the crops being produced by Hausa peasants. While the majority of Fulani are Muslims, there is no clear religious division between Fulani herders and Hausa farmers.

In 1991, Watts published an article on 'Entitlements and Empowerment' in the *Review of African Political Economy* in which he noted the irony that, while famine had come to be recognized as 'man-made', for example, by *The Report for the Independent Commission on International Humanitarian Issues*, we fail to recognize the onset of the 'man-made' crisis. He quotes approvingly Amrita Randasmai (1985: 1747), who complained that the problem remains 'the inability to recognize the political, economic and social determinants that mark the onset of the process'. There was a more profound and depressing irony that, according to Watts, more people will die of famine and resulting exposure to disease than in any previous century according to the Feinstein Hunger Program. It is also an era in which famine is preventable. These food-poor, impoverished households are primarily in Africa and South Asia and their number has almost certainly grown.

Watts (2004) published an equally compelling analysis of 'petro-capitalism' and its impact on the Nigerian social structure. The consequence of oil exploration and development was 'Slowly, the subversion of royal authority, the strategic alliance between youth and Chiefs, and the growing (and armed) conflict between youth groups for access to Shell resulted in the ascendency of a highly militant *Isongoforo* (House of Lords) (Watts, 2004: 206). Although these developments affected the whole of Nigeria, Watts gives one dramatic example, namely Ogoniland which by the 1970s had 56 oil wells and accounted for 15% of Nigerian oil production. Despite this oil wealth, few Ogoni households have electricity, child mortality rates are the highest in Nigeria, there is one doctor per 100,000 of the population and 80% are illiterate (Watts, 2004: 208).

We might conclude this discussion by returning to Amartya Sen as Watts (1991: 20) does in his own work, observing that 'Amartya Sen's *Poverty and Famine* (1981) has done more than any other single publication to prompt debate and discussion on theories of famine causation'. Watts throughout his work describes the famines in terms of the 'crisis' in Africa. Watts notes that 'As a particular form of crisis, famines can be usefully situated with respect to current debates over crisis theory (Offe, 1984)'. Given the scale of the problem, surely famine deserves the title of 'catastrophe' rather than a mere crisis?

Zoonotic Disease

Famines are often the foundation for an outbreak of infectious disease. Contemporary approaches to the vulnerability to zoonotic disease in Africa also adopt an historical political economy approach to the 'structural violence' that lies behind the social inequalities that increase the risk of disease', such as trypa-nosomiasis in Zimbabwe, Ebola and Lassa fever in Sierra Leone and Rift Valley fever in Kenya (Dzingirai et al. 2017). I return therefore to the issue of zoonotic disease – or disease transmitted from animals to humans – which is a growing challenge on a global scale. The challenge is to understand the nexus between society, ecology, environment, and disease. While it is a long-standing challenge, the threat has increased as the environment has been corrupted by industrialization, population growth and urbanization. The COVID-19 pandemic dramatically and palpably illustrates the global impact of disease on society. While COVID-19 has clearly changed the way we live and work, life-threatening diseases are not a new global experience. We can refer, for example, to the spread of malaria that now kills half a million people annually. It has evolved in ways that make it difficult to control and there is no effective vaccine. Getting an exact picture of the effects of climate and social change on the spread and control of malaria is affected by changing weather conditions.

Zoonotic disease, or disease transmitted from animals to humans, is a major cause of human suffering and death. The problem has increased with the domestication of livestock, but also from pets, including rats as pets. Jared M. Diamond (1999) in *Guns, Germs and Steel* claimed that recent diseases – such as smallpox, malaria, measles, and cholera – are infectious diseases that have evolved from animals. There are many other examples of zoonotic diseases that have spread rapidly because of globalization, especially labour migration. We can take the recent examples of monkey disease or monkeypox. It is caused by a virus, that is a member of the *Orthopoxviral* genus in the family of *Poxviridae*. Various animal species have been identified as susceptible to the monkeypox virus, such as squirrels, rats, dormice, and various primates. Many such viruses circulate in animal populations and are therefore difficult to detect and control. Monkeypox is a viral zoonosis with a range of symptoms that are similar to but less severe than those found in smallpox patients. Smallpox was eradicated in 1980 and monkeypox has become the most important example of *orthopoxviral.* Although it is relatively common in the tropical rainforest of North and West Africa, it came to public attention in 2022 when a small number of cases were identified in the United States, Canada, and various European societies. Monkeypox is transmitted to humans because of close contact with an infected person or animal, or with material that has been contaminated with the virus.

Catastrophe and Civil Unrest

Misfortune falls hard on the shoulders of the unfortunate, but perhaps the whole of political life is the subject of fortune. Martin Wight, the great political theorist of international relations, believed that 'The word "fortune" describes the most ancient and fundamental experience in politics' (Chiaruzzi, 2016: 79). The politics of civil unrest after a catastrophe is certainly part of this politics of fortune. The literature of the extent of civil conflict following a disaster was extensively reviewed by Philip Nel and Marjolein Righarts (2008). They considered the effects of disasters especially on developing societies with a youthful population whose life chances had been undermined. One aspect of civil unrest included the presence of the 'youth bulge' in the age range 15–24 years who were most affected by the destruction caused by earthquakes. These findings can be generalized to include men in that age range in developed societies whose life chances have been undermined by social change in general. This concatenation of misfortunes is unfortunately well illustrated by the recent history of Lebanon. Cholera has been spreading from Syria through many adjacent societies. Lebanon shares a long border with Syria. Cholera was detected in Lebanon on 6 October 2022, which is the first outbreak since 1993. By November there were 803 suspected cases. Medical provision is woefully in short supply, following the political and economic crisis in the country where three-quarters of the population are living in poverty with basic amenities such as clean water in short supply. The causes of these misfortunes are basically political (Traboulsi, 2002). With independence from France in 1943, there was a power-sharing agreement involving 18 religious sects. While Lebanon has enjoyed periods of prosperity, it is caught in a conflict between various states involving Iran and Israel. The presence of cholera unfortunately well illustrates the sequence between war, civil unrest and disease.

The growth of European-wide co-operation in response to the Russian invasion of the Ukraine may be interpreted as one positive political development, but it is not clear whether the consensus will survive in the long run. President Erdogan of Turkey raised problems for the coherence of NATO in his attitude towards extending membership to Finland and Sweden. To take one of the issues facing the democratic countries of the West, COVID-19 has illustrated the problems that democratic governments have in imposing basic measures such as universal vaccination, social distancing, lockdowns, and masking. Government interventions have occasioned violent responses in otherwise stable cities such as Melbourne and Sydney in Australia. There has been in 2020–2022 little sustained evidence of the emergence of a community of risk in Ulrich Beck's terms. Prosperous societies in the West have been slow to share vaccines with other countries. If there are any communities of risk, they are small and local rather than global. Civil protests in many democratic societies were as much about wider issues to do with employment, wages, and housing as with the pandemic, but the protests illustrate a wider malaise in liberal democracies. The most dramatic example was the attack on the US Capitol Building by Donald Trump's supporters that was fuelled by a range of disaffected groups in U.S. society. The United States has been among the least effective countries to come to terms with COVID-19, especially following the Trump administration's failures to respond effectively and to accept scientific evidence from the ubiquitous Dr. Anthony Fauci. While there is much talk about a post-COVID environment, Omicron sub-variants such as BA.5 spread rapidly in the United States from August 2022.

The COVID-19 crisis is clearly not a one-issue threat to the global order, and it is likely not the last of the zoonotic infections. We are confronted by four interconnected catastrophic threats – political instability, natural disasters, climate change, and zoonotic disease. The political crises are all too obvious: Chinese expansion in the Pacific; President Putin's quest to rebuild the Soviet Union prior to the fall of the Berlin Wall; the political paralysis in the United States between Democrats and Republicans; political tensions in Europe after Brexit; political instability in Westminster after 'Partygate' and the rise of authoritarianism especially in Eastern Europe. Recent natural disasters are equally daunting. Major bush fires in California and Western Australia have burnt out of control, destroying ancient forests. Other parts of the world suffer from devastating droughts. COVID-19 has caused countless fatalities and threatened to undermine small communities with limited resources. Will the 21st century be the age of catastrophes? In these multiple catastrophes, there is little sustained evidence of a community of risk and scant indication of collective hope.

Conclusion: What is COVID-19?

Is COVID-19 a plague? To call it so would be regarded as emotive, ignorant, and possibly dangerous. To call it a catastrophe might equally be dismissed as only seeking public attention. Medical dictionaries generally reject the label 'plague' as applied to outbreaks such as COVID-19. We might say that, unlike our medieval ancestors, we have the benefit of modern science and have sophisticated strategies to contain the pandemic and possibly to prevent its future development. Scientific associations have developed organizations to anticipate future pandemics such as the *Coalition for Epidemic Preparedness and Innovation* (CEPI). One arrangement for the effective control of future pandemics would involve sufficient early production of manufacturing facilities to produce a large number of vaccines to be distributed globally. In defence of the superiority of medical science, one might point out that poliomyelitis, as a devastating disease among children under the age of 5 years, has been contained through a national programme of vaccination and careful monitoring. However, one critical response is that the scientific advice about COVID-19 was not always conclusive or coherent and that governments were faced with a difficult set of choices, including protecting the population or defending the economy to support households and their breadwinners. The origins of the pandemic became a topic where conspiracy theories could prosper and multiply. As I have indicated, the scientific interpretations of the causes of the Black Plague and subsequent plagues have not arrived at a consensus about its causality. Finally, we should not underestimate the rationality of early responses to the plague that included isolation, quarantine, and masks. The plagues of the past, like the pandemics of modernity, have exposed the obvious social outcome that the primary burdens fall on the poor, the elderly, and the outcast.

Chapter 5
Colonial Catastrophes and Genocide

Introduction: Genocide and Slavery

The history of colonialism from the early 17th century to the end of the 20th century, and the attendant episodes that accompanied those colonies, cannot be described under any bland notion of a history of disasters. The persistence, scale and consequences of this history can only be described as a series of catastrophes, the effects of which have persisted long after the abolition of slavery and contemporary processes of de-colonization. While this history was tragic for the many aboriginal communities who were the unfortunate victims of colonization and occupation, we are left with an uncomfortable question: for whom were these colonies catastrophic? For the colonial powers and the empires that participated in these colonial ventures, colonies had many positive economic and political consequences. Church missions greatly increased the influence of Christianity even when that influence contradicted the moral system that is embedded in Christian doctrine. The Church avoided, as it were, this contradiction by not recognizing indigenous people as truly human, but the contradiction remained in the case of those natives who were converted to Christianity and yet remained in subjugation or slavery. Colonialism also brought into question social and political values, such as 'liberty', that inspired both the American and French Revolutions. The 'rights of man and of the citizen' were contradicted by the regimes of torture and violence that characterized French colonialism all the way to the occupation of Algiers in 1830 to the war of independence in 1962. The colonial legacy continues to trouble French politics today (Lazrig, 2007). The death of Queen Elizabeth II had the unintended consequence of raising once more the role of colonialism in building the present-day Commonwealth.

Alongside the dispossession of native communities and the effects of war and disease, there is also the history of slavery in the Americas (Blackburn, 2011). Christopher Columbus, who was sponsored by the Monarchs of Spain, landed on what is now known as the Bahamas in 1492. It was occupied by the Lucayan people. While the Vikings had arrived in North America in the late 10th century, the modern era of colonization starts with Ferdinand and Isabella of Spain who gave authority for the transport of African slaves to the Americas. The first slaves arrived in 1502. The Roman Catholic Church through its missionary work by the Franciscans and the Jesuits was heavily involved in these early colonies. Over time, the Jesuits came to own thousands of slaves in Peru, who were used to support missions and the

https://doi.org/10.1515/9783110772364-005

establishment of colleges. By the time the Society of Jesus was expelled from Spanish America, the colleges were among the largest slave owners.

The role of the Church in the colonization and settlement of the Americas was confirmed by the Papal Bull *Inter Caetera* by Pope Alexander VI in 1493 that claimed that land not occupied by Christians could be occupied and exploited. This papal Bull became the basis of the Doctrine of Discovery that gave Spain a monopoly over the New World. Indians had de facto occupancy, but those entitlements could be expunged at will. The Roman Catholic Church through its missions became part of the institutional structure that controlled slave labour throughout the Americas. However, there was also division within the Church whereby, for example the Dominicans and Franciscans sent eight memorials of protest to the Council of the Indies in 1533 complaining that, when white settlers claimed that 'Indians' were not human, this assumption was merely an excuse to make slavery less objectionable (Banchoff and Casanova, 2016). The Dominicans of Salamanca – the so-called 'school of Salamanca' – condemned the strategies of Spanish conquest that involved warfare, violence, appropriation of property and forced conversion of natives. These movements to end slavery by the Capuchins and Propaganda Fide were eventually silenced by the ecclesiastical hierarchy.

The conclusion is that the history of the Roman Catholic Church in the Americas has many varied and contradictory elements. In coming to a conclusion much will depend on which country, what association within the Church and in what period of history we conduct an inquiry. For example, Pamela Voekel (2002) conducted an imaginative study of the origins of modernity in Mexico by a study of cemeteries, burial rituals, graveyards and graveside architecture. One aspect of her research methodology involved a study of 2,100 wills from Mexico City. She divides the history of Catholicism in Mexico into two periods: the baroque and the modern. In the baroque period burial practices were elaborate and reflected the social structure of the society whereby the elite had elaborate funerals and graves. The graves of the elite were often built in city centres to display their wealth and piety to the vulgar masses.

In the period 1767 to 1827 an enlightened Catholicism rejected the sensuality, exuberance and elitism of the Baroque and instead offered an 'internal, individual and direct spirituality that exalted moderation, reason and discipline' (Voekel, 2002: 44). The enlightened Catholics condemned religious cults and were critical of the proliferation of saints. Cemeteries were to be built in the suburbs where they could be hygienically maintained and not town centres where they would spread disease. In short, their reforms were a parallel to the reforms undertaken by Protestants. While modernity in Mexico involved an internal reformation of the Church, Voekel's larger claim is that Catholicism in the Americas was not a rigid monolithic institution intractably hostile to liberal change.

Various developments brought an end to slavery in the Americas. The first was the gradual abolition of slavery in Europe by the beginning of the 19th century, which made the continuity of slavery in America problematic. The Abolition Bill was passed through the English Parliament in 1807. The second was another contradiction. Many Christian churches held the view that a Christian could not be a slave and therefore the various missions in converting slaves and indigenous people to the Christian faith exposed the contradiction of Christian teaching in relation to converted slaves. The British campaign to end slavery was driven by the so-called Clapham Sect of evangelical Anglicans between the 1780s and 1840s, by various Protestant groups and, by the Quakers who developed a global advocacy movement (Stamatov, 2013).

The other forces bringing slavery to an end were resistance and rebellion. These were probably more important forces than a change in moral attitudes on the part of western reformers. The other development was the slow erosion in the economic logic of slavery. Various critics in the first half of the 19th century argued that slavery degraded labour and made white workers less willing to engage in plantation work. It was also claimed that white settlers had become lazy through enforced idleness. Skilled labourers in search of employment were going to the northern states rather than to the South. Slave, unlike free, labour, had no capacity for consumption which imposed another constraint on economic prosperity. Furthermore, slavery involved a large outlay of capital to bring slaves to the Americas leaving little available capital for investment in machinery. While the northern states began to enjoy economic growth and industrialization, the southern states stagnated. This pattern of economic backwardness was eventually described in terms of the 'development of underdevelopment' especially by Marxist critics (Foster-Carter, 1973; Frank, 1967).

It may be perverse to ask, who benefitted from slavery? Obviously, the slaves, who were forcefully extracted from their traditional communities in Africa and forced to labour both on the plantations and in domestic service, did not benefit. Many died on the way to North America. It is possible to argue that slavery had, in the long run, serious consequences for the United States. The American Civil War, which I consider in chapter 6, was not exactly fought over slavery in 1861–1865, but the issue of a divided nation between north and south was clearly a central issue. Despite the abolition of slavery, the experience of slave labour continues to divide American society between black citizens, who, struggle with many disadvantages, and white Americans, who by comparison, are privileged.

The Great Land Rush and the Malthusian Catastrophe

This phrase 'the great land rush' is the title of a publication by John C. Weaver (2003) on 'the making of the modern world 1630 – 1900', which describes the discovery, colonization and development of North America, Canada, South Africa, Australia, and New Zealand. His research documents the colonization and genocide of native peoples across the expanding imperial system. Colonization raised an important issue, because, while the 'land rush' was catastrophic for the inhabitants of these regions, it brought great economic and political benefits to the European powers. One benefit was cultural as the English language became the basic means of communication for trade across the globe, contributing greatly to Britain's 'soft power'. Weaver explains how British understanding of land, cultivation and property rights implanted a framework on these colonies, associated with their economic and political success. The experience of slavery and colonialism was brutally different for the colonists on the one hand and the colonized on the other.

While slavery is normally discussed by reference to its historical contradiction in terms of America's claims to stand at the beginning of the evolution of liberalism and democracy, we need to consider it from a different perspective. Slavery was a cruel answer to the scarcity of available labour in North America. In this chapter, I return briefly to Thomas Malthus and the debates about population in relation to the available land in Britain. I turn to Malthus, because the early formulation of demographic theory, was closely connected with the growth of British colonies and what was to become the British Empire. The early American colonies and the development of Australia as a convict settlement were the early stages of what was to become the beginning of over two centuries of British colonial expansion. Colonialism, and its genocidal consequences, bring to the foreground the problem of values, history, and ethical judgement. From the perspective of the European powers, colonialism brought obvious benefits in terms of trade, enhanced food supply, precious minerals, and land for settlement. The long-term consequences also include the social and political problems that confront liberal democracies as they continue to struggle with the consequences of slavery in terms of racial divisions and racial conflict.

In April 1770, James Cook of the Royal Navy planted the First Union Flag at Botany Bay and in August the same flag was placed on Possession Island, proclaiming the whole eastern border of Australia as a British territory. The start of the settlement of Australia in 1788 was a solution to overcrowded prisons and provided a labour force to do the early work of establishing a settlement. From the colonial point of view, Australia was in terms of the 'doctrine of discovery' *terra nullius* or 'nobody's land' or an 'empty land'. From the legal and political view, aboriginal tribes did not constitute a state. Therefore, it was not possible for the British colonial authorities to sign treaties with aboriginal leaders. Aboriginal customs, ritual practices and laws were unwritten, and thus there were no legal grounds for any political settlement. As late as 1971, Justice Richard Blackburn in the Northern Territory Court case of *Milirrpum v Nabalco Pty Ltd* ruled that Australia, at the time of settlement, had been considered a land that was 'desert and uncultivated' and in which the inhabitants were uncivilized.

From the perspective of the inhabitants, colonialism was a catastrophe. While there were many violent conflicts between the settlers and the inhabitants that are now known as 'The Australian Wars', aboriginals suffered more from the introduction of diseases against which they had no natural immunity. Smallpox was discovered among the aboriginals at Sydney Bay in 1789 and infections had devastating consequences with 70 % of the population dying from the disease. Aboriginals were also to suffer from measles, tuberculosis, influenza, and sexually transmitted disease. In general, disaster studies do not include colonialism and genocide in research on disaster. From the perspective of the communities that suffered from, and in many cases, disappeared as a consequence of colonialism, we can only call this period of modern history from the late 16th to the 19th century a global catastrophe.

Thomas Malthus is an important figure in the history of colonialism for several reasons. Although typically described disparagingly as 'parson Malthus', he was in fact a professor of political economy in the East India Company College. This position put him in direct touch with an expanding imperial world, and for many years he taught candidates for service in the Company as clerks destined for India (Tribe, 1995). The Company had been given a legal identity by Queen Elizabeth I in 1600 when it was mainly focused on trade in tea and spices with South-East Asia. Over time it became heavily involved in trade with India. In its Chinese trade, it was bringing tea to Britain and exporting opium to China. By the 1750s it had become a military power and took over Bengal in 1757. In its trade with the outside world, it played a predatory role. In the Bengal famine of 1769 – 1770, thirty million people were affected, but the Company offered little relief and in fact exploited the situation by creating grain monopolies. The Company was also involved in the slave trade from Africa to the Americas. These early trading companies were inevitably, if implicitly, operating as agencies of the state (Bowen, 2006). The East India Company survived until 1858 when it handed Bengal to the British State.

Malthus was very much in touch with this expanding colonial world (Bashford and Chaplin, 2016; Macfarlane, 2018). He had argued in his *An Essay on Population* in 1798 that, given the limitations of food production on the available arable land, if population growth was not restrained, then the inevitable results were famine followed in the long run by civil unrest and revolution. Poverty, he claimed, was the inevitable lot of most of the population. As population increased when harvests were good, so the poorest sections of the population would perish when times were bad. Disease and famine served as natural checks to over-population. In demography, there is the notion of a 'Malthusian Catastrophe', or the 'Malthusian trap' when population growth greatly outstrips agricultural production, resulting in poverty and famine. Malthus concluded, 'I see no way by which man can escape from the weight of this law which pervades all animated nature. No fancied equality, no agrarian revolutions in their utmost extent, could remove the pressure of it even for a century' (Malthus, 2004: 14).

One way out of this dilemma was colonialism and the transportation of those unwanted and idle sectors of society such as the convicts who were a burden on the domestic economy (Winch, 1963). Colonies were an obvious solution to domestic population growth, but the effects on the colonies were quite the opposite in terms of a demographic collapse rather like the disastrous population collapse in the 14th century in Europe that was associated with a combination of warfare and disease.

While colonies were an answer to limited arable land and an expanding population in Britain, Malthus's view of population and poverty had little obvious relevance to colonial America with an immense land mass and a small colonial population (Hodgson, 2009). Thomas Jefferson (1743–1826), however, was seriously interested in Malthus's ideas while recognizing the obvious differences between the cramped spaces of Europe and the open prairies of North America. The ample availability of uncultivated and fertile land gave opportunities to a settler population willing to work, to marry young and raise a large family. He assumed that America would become a society of land-owning farmers. Jefferson was also a slave owner, and, in his notebooks, he justified his continuing ownership on the basis that freeing them would cause civil unrest among the settlers. In the period leading up to the Civil War, Malthusianism was used in support of both pro-slavery and anti-slavery advocates (Hoff, 2012). It was claimed that in a slave system the slave owner had an obvious interest in the well-being of his slaves as the basis of labour power and income. In addition, a slave owner would control population growth on his estate by controlling the sex ratio of his work force – for example, by having a predominance of male slaves. However, as the extensive landmass supported an ever-increasing population and the West was eventually closed, at that stage America would become a land of over-crowded cities and, with defeat in the Civil War, the aristocratic vision of an orderly and hierarchical South would be destroyed.

The Sociology of American Slavery

In addition to convict settlement, the exploration, settlement, and exploitation of colonial holdings in America and the Caribbean involved a vast network of institutions overseeing slavery, transportation, and exploitation of slaves primarily from Africa for the extraction of natural resources. While the British played a key role in this extractive process, other European countries such as the French in Algeria and Asia, the Germans and Dutch in Africa, and the Italians in North Africa were involved in colonial conquests and exploitation. Eventually colonies, evolving from military conquests and exploitative trade relationships, covered much of the planet from islands in the south Atlantic to the Kingdom of Hawaii (Kirch and Sahlins, 1992).

Although plantations were the basis of the slave economy, slavery reached every level of American society. While cotton picking on colonial plantations was back-breaking laborious work, the relationship between slave, especially the domestic slave, and slave owner has often been portrayed as warm and sympathetic. Slaves as domestic servants often appeared in the family portraits of the wealthy elites, for example, in Frans Hals' *Portrait of a Dutch Family* (1648) or they appear alongside aristocratic figures in Anthony van Dyck's *Henrietta of Lorraine* (1634). The early universities, many of which, such as Harvard, became the dominant universities of the 20th century, were based on the wealth generated by slavery. Colleges basically expanded on the eastern seaboard with the growing wealth of merchants, who sent their sons to the newly established colleges. Once the local native tribes had been contained or subdued, the number of colleges went from three to nine between 1746 and 1769. These included the foundations of what were to become Princeton in 1746, Pennsylvania in 1749, Rhode Island in 1764 and Rutgers in 1766. The economic growth of the east coast was stimulated by slavery which also had the consequence of transforming the economies of the West African coastline from agriculture and fishing to slavery. The principal investigation into this forgotten history of America's famous universities was undertaken by Craig Steven Wilder (2013) in *Ebony and Ivy. Race, Slavery, and the Troubled History of America's Universities*.

A key figure in transforming white understanding of the problems facing blacks in the development of slavery was Booker T. Washington (1856–1915), who had been born a slave on a Virginian plantation. He gained an education and came to promote the idea of industrial training for black men as the alternative to resistance and protest. At the Atlanta World Exposition, he gave his famous Atlanta lecture that became known as 'the Atlanta Compromise' in which he argued that the black man got almost as much out of slavery as the white slave owner. His response to slavery at Atlanta must be seen against the background of growing social unrest with lynching in the South coming to a peak in 1895. He was embraced by the white establishment who promoted his career. In 1881, Washington was appointed as the principal of Tuskegee Normal Institute for Industrial Education where he could promote his philosophy. Max Weber visited the Tuskegee Institute in 1904 and was impressed by the effort to develop a moral order for black society. Weber recognized that the 'colour-line' was the 'paramount problem' of the present time and of the future everywhere in the world (Radkau, 2009: 229). Washington's ideas were also welcomed by the emerging school of Chicago sociology which accepted his Darwinian account of black inferiority and the importance of education if Blacks were ever to become fully civilized. Washington believed that the social and economic progress of Black Americans would depend on education, but their advance would not come quickly.

The legacy of Washington was challenged by W. E. Du Bois (1868–1963) who was a representative of northern free Blacks, acquired a degree from Harvard and did further study in Germany at the University of Berlin with Gustav von Schmoller (Morris, 2015). In Berlin before the rise of fascism, Du Bois felt he had escaped the racism of America. He came to widespread public attention for his *The Souls of Black Folk* (Du Bois, 2007). As a challenge to Washington, he helped create the Niagra Movement in 1905 and was instrumental in the development of the *National Association for the Advancement of Colored People* (NAACP). He died one year before the passing of the *Civil Rights Act* in 1964. The acceptance of Du Bois into mainstream American sociology was slow and hesitant. However, through the Laboratory in Sociology at the University of Atlanta, Du Bois laid the foundations for a sociology of race that was both empirical and theoretically sophisticated. He developed the idea of a 'double consciousness' to describe the experience of being marginalized and experiencing the self through the eyes of others.

Despite movements to improve the standing of Blacks, significant inequalities remain. Health statics are ultimately our best measure of well-being. A survey of mortality rates from all causes from 2016 to 2018 from thirty of the most populous cities in America found that Black mortality was 24% higher than for White Americans (Benjamins, 2021). However, mortality data for all young persons in the age range 15–24 years are causes for serious concern. A report from the Population Reference Bureau in 2022 found that the main causes of death are poverty, race, gender, education of parents and region. Six of the ten states with obvious health and mortality problems were in the South. In comparative global terms, America has the highest number of drug-relative deaths and increasingly from the synthetic opiate fentanyl.

The obvious conclusion is that slavery casts a long shadow. This stain or shadow was explored in another famous sociological publication, namely in Gunner Myrdal's *The American Dilemma* (1944) in two volumes. At the core of the study is a recognition that the racial inequality in America contradicts its founding principles as a liberal and democratic society. The dilemma is that racial inequality is a contradiction involving a perpetual moral struggle. Having dismissed the idea of racial inferiority, the main problem facing the United States was a failure of its institutions. He concluded that the so-called 'Negro Problem' is in fact a white man's problem, but he remained optimistic about future developments regarding racial integration and affirmative actions. Given the nature of the issues, *The American Dilemma* received mixed reviews. However, Du Bois enthusiastically reviewed the publication, because it completely covered the field. The work was monumental and did not hide the brute facts of inequality. However, Myrdal's analysis of the United States was eventually overshadowed by the growing political organization of Black Americans to transform their economic, legal, and political status in the United States. The 1960s were an important turning point with legislation that began to at least change the voting rights of Black Americans – Civil Rights Act 1964, Voting Rights Act 1968 and the Fair Housing Act 1968. The movement for social change was often driven by such charismatic and controversial figures as Martin Luther King (1929 – 1968) (Taylor, 1998) on the one hand and Malcolm X (1925 – 1965) (Marable, 2011) on the other. King was assassinated in 1968. Malcolm X was assassinated in 1965.

Revolution and Resistance

Just as the racial inequality between white and black citizens contradicts the founding principles of American society from the perspective of the revolution of 1799, slavery in the Americas contradicts the French Revolution of 1789 which embraced three principles: liberty, equality, and fraternity. The Declaration embraced the rights of man and of the citizens. How could slavery be accepted in lands which were under French sovereignty? This contradiction between the revolution and slavery was critically exposed by the uprising of slaves in Saint-Domingue in 1794. As free men, the former slaves struggled against invading British forces. Under the leadership of Toussaint-Louverture, a black army defeated the British forces, which set in train a process that resulted in the suspension of the slave trade in 1807 (Buck-Morss, 2000). Another example of protest and uprising comes from Cuba. In 1825 a violent conflict occurred between armed white settlers and soldiers in the Guacamaro Valley and the port city of Matanza in western Cuba near the coffee plantation. The insurgents were dealt with by extreme measures including torture, execution, and decapitation. In fact, Cuba had a history of conflict underpinned by anxieties about the demography of white settlers and African slaves (Allahar, 1988). In 1815 the Spanish government introduced a scheme to redress the demographic imbalance by introducing a programme to make Cuba a society of white Roman Catholic settlers.

The American Holocaust

Although Malthus's theories have been the topic of extensive criticism, some historians of North America have accepted the idea of a Malthusian demographic catastrophe in the destruction of aboriginal communities between the end of the 15th century and the massacre at Wounded Knee in 1890. Here again Catholic missions were involved, directly or indirectly, in the settlement of North America from the east coast to California (Jackson and Castillo, 1995). David E. Stannard's history of the conquest of North America refers to this aspect of American history as the 'American holocaust' (Stannard, 1992). He estimates that a total of 100 million people were killed through a combination of disease, starvation, dispossession, and military activity. Russell Thornton (1990) also referred to 'The American Indian Holocaust'. Jefferson regarded the Indians as a noble race, but he had little sympathy with those tribes that joined forces with the British forces and threatened the revolution. When the Cherokee attacked white settlements, he promised to 'never cease pursuing them while one of them remained on this side of the Mississippi' (Meacham, 2012: 111). A similar decimation of native peoples took place in Canada. James Daschuk (2013) in *Clearing the Plains* records the history of how diseases such as smallpox and policies of starvation subdued and then destroyed native communities in Canada.

The alternative history of the settlement of North America is contained in the 'Turner Thesis' of Frederick Jackson Turner (1920) which is also known as 'The Frontier Thesis'. His thesis was first announced in a lecture in 1893 and published in 1920 as *The Frontier in American History.* Turner's theory was that the experience of the frontier had laid the basis for individualism, independence, and democracy. These virtues owed a great deal to the entrepreneurship behind the early fur trade and the life on the frontier settlement. The experience of the frontier explains how America avoided autocratic government. In short, the frontier created American democracy. There has, however, been considerable historical debate about exactly what was 'the Turner Thesis' (Klein, 1997). There was no discussion of genocide in this early history and the background assumption was a simple division: civilization or savagery. This version of the settlement and colonization of North America was not questioned until anthropologists began to offer an alternative account of the suffering and survival of Native Americans.

There are various legal and philosophical issues surrounding the concept of 'genocide' from the Greek *genos* (tribe or race) and *cide* (killing). It is commonplace to distinguish between the physical destruction of a people or the destruction of their culture and way of life. The early work on the idea of genocide was undertaken by Raphael Lemkin (1944) in a short pamphlet on *Axis Rule in Occupied Europe* on physical and cultural destruction. For Lemkin, these two forms were of equal importance. The destruction of a culture robs a community of its collective memory, its language, and the practices that cement a community together. These ideas are important in the study of aboriginal cultures since, in many cases, they were not physically destroyed completely. They may have lost their lands but often many elements of their cultures have been preserved. The destruction of aboriginal cultures often took place in missionary schools for aboriginal children. In the literature, there is broad agreement that genocide constitutes a catastrophe, but there is ongoing controversy as to what constitutes a genocide or a pogrom. My interest in these definitions and these examples is, however, neither an exercise in etymology nor in historical research. It is rather to develop a more precise sociological approach to the different, but related, crises that currently confront us.

One can argue that the beginning of the end for indigenous peoples of America was the purchase of Louisiana by the Jefferson Administration from Napoleon Bonaparte in 1803. The purchase immediately doubled the size of colonial America. The new territory was home to many tribes including the Sioux, Cheyenne, Arapaho, Crow, and Comanche. Oklahoma was soon designated as Indian Territory (Dunbar-Ortiz, 2014). A controversial figure in this historical transformation of America was Andrew Jackson (1767–1845), the 7th President. He had a distinguished military career forming the Tennessee Militia and becoming eventually the General of the US Army. He is much revered as an American president and as founder of the Democratic Party. In fact, Alexis de Tocqueville referred to the American party system as 'Jacksonian Democracy'. It is believed that he kept the nation together during various crises and he is seen to be a defender of the 'common man'. However, he rejected the abolition of slavery and has been accused of genocide during his various campaigns against Native Americans, such as the Creek Wars, 1813–1814.

With the 1830 Indian Removal Act many tribes from the Southwest were moved to what became known as 'Indian Territory'. In the 'Trail of Tears' some 60,000 native inhabitants were removed to Indian Territory between 1830–1850. This development was in line with Jefferson's view that, if it proved impossible to civilize the Indians, it would be necessary to remove them (Mennell, 2007). The main concern of the Bureau of Indian Affairs just before or after the turn of the century was the rapid assimilation of Indians into white society. Assimilation meant that the Indians had to be de-tribalized so that they would no longer think of themselves as belonging to a viable community or tribe, but rather see themselves as individuals in the process of merging into white society. This process was accelerated by the

Dawes Act of 1887 which provided for the elimination of tribal lands in favour of individual allotments. Any remaining 'surplus land' was opened to white settlement. The result was that reservation land shrank from 138 million acres in 1887 to 48 million by 1934. Other changes included the Court of Indian Offenses to undermine traditional forms of dispute resolution. This disappearing world was famously and poetically captured in the photographs of Edward S. Curtis (Gidley, 1998).

Perhaps it is commonplace to focus on the impact of American settlement and colonialism on the nomadic lifestyle of male warriors. Beth H. Piatote (2013) in *Domestic Subjects* has drawn attention to the impact of colonialism on women and family life as reflected in the publications of Native American writers. Through several fictional works Piatote (2013: 9) explores how white colonialism was an attack on family life, but nevertheless 'the domestic is also the locus through which Indian families and nations have expressed resistance'. The title of her book is taken from an opinion of the U.S. Attorney General in 1856 to the effect that 'Indians are not citizens of the United States, but domestic subjects'.

There are many accounts of heroic survival of Native American communities, such as *Holding Our World Together: Ojibwe Women and the Survival of Community* (Child, 2012) and *We Are Still Here!* (Wittstock and Bancroft, 2013), but their land had been confiscated, their means of survival destroyed with the disappearance of the buffalo herds, and their way of life undermined. Many tribes may still be present on reserves today, but their culture and way of life were destroyed by colonialism. At the height of their power, the Lakota controlled the Great Plains as far as the Mexican border (Hamalainen, 2019), but by the 1880s their nomadic life no longer existed. The Cheyenne after the passing of the Indian Reorganization Act of 1934 were treated essentially as prisoners under the daily control of the army. They did not become citizens until 1924 and the Bill of Rights was not extended to them until 1968. The remains of the Cheyenne killed at the Battle of Summit Springs were repatriated from the Smithsonian in 1993 to be laid to rest in a traditional ceremony (Moore, 1996). Oglala Lakota Indians, who appeared in circus performances with Buffalo Bill (William Cody) did not continue their traditional culture; they participated in a farce (Bridger, 2002).

While I have described these historical events as catastrophes, aboriginal communities survived colonialism and genocide. Is it survival? Aboriginal populations in modern-day North America and Australia continue to experience problems associated with drug dependency, degenerative diseases, and high rates of incarceration. Alcoholism has long been recognized as a major health issue among aboriginal communities under colonialism (Saggers and Gray, 1998). Opioid addiction has also become a major problem among aboriginal people in recent years. Mortality rates for Native Americans are almost 50 % higher than that of their white counterparts (Bauer and Plescia, 2014). Additionally, Native Americans have an infant mortality rate that is 1.5 times the rate of whites. While research shows that white Americans experienced a significant decline in all-cause mortality rates from 1990 to 2009, Native Americans did not (Espey et al., 2014).

I do not underestimate their struggle for respect and recognition. Protests against this colonial history and present conditions emerged in the 1960s with the American Indian Movement (AIM) in 1968 and the National Indian Youth Council. Bradley G. Shreve (2011) argues that the origins of native activism can in fact be dated from the 1950s. As these associations gained in influence, there was a move to declare a separate native Republic of Lakota in 2007. There have been many notable activist native women such as Joy Harjo, a Cree Indian and the first Indian to become the poet laureate. There have been cultural protests against the commercial exploitation of Indian culture. George Tinker complained about 'New Age aficionados who have mistakenly seen Indian spirituality as a new trade commodity' (Tinker, 2003: 517). The fundamental questions about the survival of First Nations people remain: where and whether they can find hope in the face of total devastation? These questions were debated by Jonathan Lear (2020) in his *Radical Hope.* The book is an account of Many Coups, the last Chief of the Crow Nation during the period when his people were forced onto a reservation. Many Coups summarized the devastation when observing, 'When the buffalo went away, the hearts of our people fell to the ground'. Many Coups, response was not, however, one of nostalgia, but an attempt to forge new conditions of existence for the Crow, eventually in a world beyond the reservation.

Conclusion: Hope versus Underdevelopment

This chapter once more raises questions about the possibilities of any optimism regarding the colonial experience of the Americas. Perhaps in these colonial histories, there is only space for narratives of suffering (Wilkinson, 2005). The general conclusion has been that the legacy of colonialism has been one of economic under-performance. In this chapter I have only touched upon the Marxist economics of underdevelopment, especially as it was applied to Latin America. It is argued that the long-term consequences of colonial power have been a history of failed economic progress. Perhaps the main criticism of this analysis came from the economist Albert O. Hirschman (1915 – 2012), who spent much of his career working on development problems primarily in Latin America (Adelman, 2013). Hirschman argued that the Marxist analysis failed to recognize the many achievements of ordinary people in creating sustainable economic activity (Hirschman, 1968). He was in fact critical in more general terms of economics as a discipline that was focused on the single, self-interested, and isolated individual. For Hirschman, it is impossible to understand economic change without considering the political context of all economic activity. He based his own empirical studies of economic change on Latin America, believing that there was always scope for optimism in the face of depressing economic and political conditions. He developed the idea of 'possibilism' to describe his optimistic view that change is always possible. He was critical consequently of the underdevelopment thesis for its defeatism. Much of his work on development fought against what he called 'fracasomania', namely the persistent view that all attempts at improvement in the developing world end in yet another failure. Many of his ideas were unorthodox from the perspective of conventional economic theories on how to achieve development. One example is his views of the black market. In the context of authoritarian governments, it is through the black market that people can secure what they need to survive. The black market opened opportunities for ordinary people to be creative. In response to the pessimism of Marxist economics, he argued in favour of hope (Hirschman, 1971).

In a book on catastrophes, it is important to look for avenues of survival and change that can offer hope for the future. As a defence of his optimism and commitment to the possibility of progressive change, Hirschman examined the history of the 'rhetoric of reaction' under three headings (Hirschman, 1991). The first is the perversity thesis, according to which any purposive action to improve the life of the people can only serve to exacerbate the circumstances which are necessary to remedy or alleviate the situation. The second thesis is the futility thesis, which suggests that any attempt at change will be futile in the face of entrenched interests or rigid social structures. Finally, the jeopardy thesis argues that the costs of change are always high and in fact can compromise many existing improvements to the common life. Hirschman had of course confronted all three forms of reaction during his engagement with Latin American politics but retained his commitment to possibilism. Any study of the accumulation of catastrophes in modern times needs to entertain the possibility of hope, which is explored in my final chapter – perhaps on the assumption that hope is modest and appears at the end and not at the beginning.

Chapter 6
War: The Cascade of Catastrophes

Introduction: Centuries of War

All wars can be unquestionably catastrophic, especially for the immediate victims, but modern wars have become more devastating and horrific with the technological development of military weaponry. Unarmed civilians have become the principal victims of modern warfare. More precisely, the principal casualties of modern warfare are not the soldiers as the combatants, but women and children. As in the invasion of Ukraine, women are raped in large numbers, often as an act of cultural genocide to wipe out the biological inheritance of an ethnic community. Systematic rape of women and the killing of their husbands in Ukraine are the means to demoralize a community and undermine the will to resist. Rape camps and mass rapes in Bosnia and East Timor were a deliberate strategy of social and cultural destruction. In modern warfare 'rape is a war economy' because it is cheaper and more effective than dropping bombs on a community (Münkler, 2005: 82). These common strategies constitute rape as genocide. In this chapter I describe the common features of modern warfare that have catastrophic consequences for civilians, who have become the principal casualties of wars in this century. Although in this chapter I am concerned primarily with modern or industrial warfare, we cannot underestimate how wars from the past have shaped the modern world. The use of gunpowder has been used by humans in conflict for some five hundred years. The Thirty Years War, 1618–1648, which I consider in this chapter, had highly destructive consequences for European societies and is often regarded by historians as the first modern war. Of continuing interest to a modern audience is *The Peloponnesian War* (431–404 bc) between Athens and Sparta that was recorded in great detail by Thucydides (460–400 bc). Its continuing interest lies in the fact that, in the fifth century, Athens was a democracy whereas Sparta was an authoritarian state.

Wars have become more destructive with the technological improvement of weapons. This development is basically equivalent to the industrialization of warfare alongside the general modernization of society. We can argue that the first examples of this industrial development were the Crimean War (1854–1856) and the American Civil War (1861–1865). In the American case, there were 750,000 casualties. However, WWI involved an extensive development of military technology in mechanized trench warfare and gas attacks. With the development of machine guns, chemical weapons and land mines, there were approximately 6.5 Million

https://doi.org/10.1515/9783110772364-006

military and 8.5 million civilian casualties. George F. Kennan, the famous American diplomat, in his *The Decline of Bismarck's European Order*, described WWI as 'the great seminal catastrophe' of the century.

In WWII there were 15 million military casualties, 25 million wounded and 45 million civilian casualties. All statistics regarding war casualties are always only approximations, given the fact that the bodies of the victims are often never found. The nuclear bomb dropped in Hiroshima killed 66,000 and injured 69,000, while the bomb at Nagasaki killed 39,000 and injured 25,000. These figures, albeit appalling, always hide the true number of deaths and injuries, including civilians who died subsequently of hunger, starvation, disease, and despair. They take no account of those who died later from drug dependency, psychological trauma, and suicide. Wars continued through the 20th century in Korea (1950–1953) with 2.5 million casualties and numerous atrocities against civilians. The Second Indochina War that involved Vietnam, Laos and Cambodia lasted from 1955–1975. It involved 58,220 American military casualties and 254,256 South Vietnamese casualties. Agent Orange disfigured many children who were born in later decades.

Thirty Years War, 1618–1648

The Thirty Years War is often regarded as the first modern war and the most destructive before WWI (Wilson, 2011). It involved European-wide struggles over power, territory, and religion. The war (in fact a number of separate wars) started when Ferdinand II, King of Bohemia, attempted in 1618 to impose Roman Catholic absolutism over his lands. The Protestant nobles of Bohemia and Austria revolted against Ferdinand and the conflict created opportunities to grab territory in Europe. In 1625 King Christian of Denmark attempted to gain territories in Germany. The invasion was not successful, and his defeat was confirmed by the Peace of Lübeck in 1629. Gustav II Adolph, King of Sweden, with the support of many nobles for his anti-Catholic campaign, invaded Germany and took over many German territories. The conflicts brought in mercenaries from across Europe. Irish and Scottish troops were recruited to serve alongside the Swedish contingents of Gustavus in support of the Protestant cause. While many areas of Germany remained unaffected by the wars, other regions lost up to 60–70% of their population. After the cities were captured and plundered, the lords could not prevent the surviving peasantry from quitting the land. Displaced farm labourers could only move to the cities where there was no work for them. Land cultivation declined and livestock could not be fed. As the cities declined, urban culture was also impoverished. The War was cruel and protracted and the large number of mercenaries who had been recruited to fight were often not paid for their services. These unpaid soldiers turned to harassment and plundered the villages and the countryside. None of the many battles fought in the Thirty Years War resulted in a clear military outcome. As the wars progressed and clear victories did not eventuate, an alternative strategy emerged, which was to achieve the economic exhaustion of the enemy (Münkler, 2005: 42). The historical result was thereby to establish what became a regular feature of warfare, namely the connection between war, mercenaries, and black markets. This response has become a common pattern of war. Russian troops have been looting homes in villages captured during the war in Ukraine and then selling the loot in Belarus.

The peasants often responded by forming small, militarized units or mobile guerrilla forces to protect their farms and villages. In response, military units of the contending states punished the peasantry with cruel revenge. Epidemics became common. In 1636 – 1640 the plague returned, devastating an already weakened population, especially in western and southern Germany. The demographic result was the severe reduction of the German population from 15 – 16 million in 1620 to 10 million in 1650 (Vierhaus, 1988: 3). Famines became widespread across Europe as planting and harvesting were severely disrupted. This cascade of catastrophes – war, rape, famine, demographic decline, and disease – had multiple long-term consequences that transformed societies, cultures, and environments.

In many respects the Thirty Years War was the military aftermath of the Reformation in which the Peace of Augsburg in 1555 had recognized Europe as a patchwork of Catholic and Protestant towns, or more precisely between Catholic and Lutheran towns and countries. The Peace of Augsburg was signed by Charles V, the Holy Roman Emperor and the Protestant Schmalkaldic League – an association to promote Protestantism – to end the religious wars between Catholics and Protestants. The key component of the treaty was the doctrine of *cuius regio, eius religio*, namely that each ruler would decide what the faith of his people would be (Von Friedeburg, 2011). If anyone rejected the ruler's religion, they had to emigrate. While the treaty achieved a temporary peace, it ultimately failed, because the agreement applied to Lutherans, thereby excluding the Calvinists, who at the time were a small Protestant group. However, Calvinism expanded rapidly through the German states and disrupted the simple solution offered by the Augsburg peace.

The long conflict in Europe was finally settled by the Peace of Westphalia in 1648 that was signed at Osnabruck and Münster. It brought an end to the Eighty Years War (1568 – 1648) and the Thirty Years War (1618 – 1648) in which eight million people died. The effect was the final recognition of the claims of the Holy Roman Empire over Europe. The provisions of the Treaty allowed the rulers of the imperial states to choose what religion would be permitted in their lands. Catholics and Protestants were to be recognized as equal by law. The Dutch Republic was granted independence in which its commitment to religious tolerance included the Jewish community. Political historians argue that the Treaty established the principle of national sovereignty, whereby independent nations were legally guaranteed immunity from external interference. The so-called doctrine of Westphalian sovereignty, creating sovereignty of inviolable borders and non-interference in domestic affairs, survived until the late 20th century when the growth of human rights began to establish universal norms to protect domestic populations from 'crimes against humanity'.

Guerrilla Warfare: The Peninsula War

Guerrilla warfare. as a strategy to defeat large, disciplined, and well-equipped occupying forces. was invented in response to Napoleon's invasion of Portugal in the Peninsula or Iberian War of 1807–1812. Napoleon intended to create a naval force to invade Britain and began his campaign by attacking the British in Portugal in 1807. He then invaded Spain which had been his ally and appointed his brother Joseph Napoleon as king of Spain. The result was a series of wars of liberation. The wars against Napoleon were fought by a new strategy whereby small groups of men would attack the supply lines and outposts to wear down the enemy. The Peninsula War involved the rape and plunder of the civilian population. These horrors of war were depicted by Francisco Goya (1746–1828) in 82 prints that were created between 1810 and 1820. They were given the title *The Disasters of War* and have been used ever since to depict the suffering that typically accompanies war. Goya called them *Fatal Consequences of Spain's Bloody War with Bonaparte, and Other Caprices.* Because of their political message, the prints were not made public until after Goya's death. The prints have forever served to remind us that there is nothing glorious about war, especially when the principal victims are unarmed civilians. While Napoleon had appeared invincible before the campaign in Spain, his ability to sustain his military adventures was limited by the high casualty rates inflicted on his forces. As a result, of the 148,000 men in the *Armée de L'Allemagne*, 47,000 were underage conscripts (Kennedy, 1990: 134).

The Industrialization of War

Writing on the general problem of violence in the wars of the 20th century, Hannah Arendt starts her reflections with the observation, 'The technical development of the implements of violence has now reached the point where no political goal could conceivably correspond to their destructive potential or justify their actual use in armed conflict' (Arendt, 1970: 3). The increasing mechanization of war from the 19th century onwards has greatly increased the number of fatalities and casualties of both civilians and military personnel. The American Civil War (1861–1865) is seen as the most destructive confrontation in the period between the Napoleonic wars in 1815 and WWI in 1914. It was fought to preserve America as a united society rather than as a collection of separate sovereign states (Brogan, 1985). It was fought after Abraham Lincoln pledged to end slavery and, in response, the seven slave states formed the Confederate of the States of America. The high casualty rates were possibly a consequence of Lincoln's decision long before 1865 that it would have to be a hard war because he insisted on the unconditional surrender of the Confederate forces before there could be any serious talk about peace (Wilentz, 2009: 207).

The first confrontation of the two sides occurred at Fort Sumter in 1861. While these are the basic facts, there is little agreement among historians as to the causes of the conflict (Keegan, 2010). Was it a struggle to end slavery or an economic conflict between two different economic systems, or a cultural conflict between two contrasted elites, or was it a struggle over democratic values? What is not open to dispute is the scale of the conflict with estimates of fatalities ranging between 625,000 and 752,000 men. It is referred to as an 'industrial war' because it involved the use of railroads to carry troops and weapons, telegraphs for messages, steamships to conduct blockades, and mass-manufactured weapons. The American Civil War was the opening scene of modern military mechanized carnage.

WWI is often referred to as 'The Revolution in Military Affairs'. The pace of technological change in weaponry was staggering with the invention of advanced artillery, machine guns, mortars, hand grenades, rifles, poisonous gas, flame throwers, and submarines. Another critical development was the use of aircraft to bomb enemy positions thereby taking the war to the skies. The British developed strategic bombing which was also directed towards undermining the morale of the home front (Travers, 1987). Although WWI has been described as 'total warfare', there were differences between the various forces. For example, the French strategy of bombing showed far greater restraint than the British strategy (Barros, 2009). In many ways the most revolutionary change came in 1917 towards the end of the 'Great War' when the British developed the tank that was able to go over German trenches and wire fortifications. The Germans were slow to develop tanks and by the end of the war they were fighting from a defensive position. It was not until 1939 that the German cavalry was mechanized with the development of modern tanks and troop carriers (Poehlmann, 2016). The result of the deployment of mass armies and technological improvements in weaponry resulted in massive loss of life. Some 8 million men lost their lives in WWI. These figures do not fully incorporate the fatalities from the outbreak of Spanish influenza and typhus that became widespread after the War. France lost 1 in 10 of its active male population, but these figures do not take into account the lives that were destroyed by the effects of devastating injuries and gas attacks.

After the War, there was some recognition of the needs of the 'destroyed men' and 'wounded patriarchs' who were no longer capable of reintegration back into civilian life. Suicides were common and many drank themselves into oblivion, leaving behind many 'fatherless communities'. The social and cultural consequences were equally significant. Many institutions, especially state and religious institutions, lost credibility, and authority. Family life was transformed with high divorce rates, often leaving young people without guidelines or models. In response to declining populations, many states wanted women to leave work, return home and have babies. There were attempts to limit contraception. For example, the German Reichstag banned contraception after the publication of the pamphlet *Geburtenrueckgang* (*Birth Decline*) in 1927. Catholic teaching against contraception and abortion grew more stringent with Pope Pious X1's 1930 encyclical on the sanctity of marriage, and in Britain the 1929 Infant (life preservation) Act made abortion a statutory offence with life imprisonment. However, there was no rapid upturn in birth rates despite official attempts to limit abortion and promote motherhood. This was the 'Dark Continent' of Europe's 20th century as described by Mark Mazower (1999). These terrible social and cultural consequences in Europe were brought about primarily by technical developments in the machinery of 'modern warfare' (Joas, 2003).

If the Great War had been a catastrophe for the European continent, the peace settlement was equally tragic in laying the foundations for the next war. In France the pacifists did not want another repeat of the Somme and Verdun, and they were equally troubled by the apparent irrationality of defending the settlement of Versailles in which nobody believed. In addition, Hitler, Mussolini, and their French supporters were able to portray the War as futile and the peace settlement as a gross international injustice (Judt, 1992: 220). If wars appear to start because of a concatenation of accidents, the resulting peace can be equally tenuous and fragile. After 1918 the age of parliamentary democracy was short-lived. With the Russian Revolution of 1917, there was political polarization in Europe and in response 'Ruling elites in many countries soon showed themselves to be anti-communists first, democrats second' (Mazower, 1999: 2).

Old Wars versus New Wars

The idea of 'new wars', 'hybrid wars', 'privatized wars' or indeed 'post-modern wars' has been much discussed in the last quarter of a century. In benefitting from this debate, I concentrate on the work of Mary Kaldor and Herfried Münkler. Kaldor (1999) published her *New and Old Wars, Organized Violence in a Global Age*. For Kaldor, the Balkan Wars were the definitive start of new wars. The war over Yugoslavia was at a deeper level a turning point in the West in terms of a struggle against an alien 'Other' (Hansen, 2006). It raised profound questions: are the Balkans part of the West or is their history too deeply influenced by and embedded in the Orient? Understanding the war was obscured by a history of 'balkanization' that constructed the region in terms of its 'otherness' (Todorova, 1997).

Münkler published *Die Neuen Kriege* in 1988 which was translated in 2005 with the same title – *The New Wars*. There is considerable overlap between their approaches, but I include a later publication by Kaldor in which she defends the idea of new wars. I start with definitions of new wars before exploring the value of the concept as the route to understanding modern warfare as a *civilian* catastrophe. Münkler's principal thesis in *The New Wars* is simply that there has been some degree of 'de-statization' of military conflict with the privatization and commercialization of the military. Thus, the new wars simply reflect the fact that the state has lost its monopoly on military force (Münkler, 2005: 16). In recent years, two groups have been controversial examples of so-called PMCs (Private Military Companies). Blackwater was created in 1997 by Al Cark and Erik Prince (Siddhartha and Joshi, 2009). From being a small-scale security group, it evolved into a major company with global operations. The invasion and occupation of Iraq formed the occasion for the expansion of many PMCs as the United States struggled to stablish its control over Iraq. Eventually the number of private soldiers and security people grew into many thousands. Blackwater came to public attention in 2007 when, in the Mansour district of Baghdad, Blackwater employees opened fire in a traffic jam, killing at least twenty unarmed civilians. No criminal charges were brought against the group, because of technical legal issues surrounding their status in the country (Scahill, 2008). The other security company that has been involved in controversial operations in the Central African Republic, Mali and Ukraine is the Wagner Group, which is privately funded by the oligarch Yevgeny Prigozhin, but has close connections with the Kremlin. It was created by Dmitry Utkin, a former Russian soldier. The group is named after Richard Wagner, because of the composer's subsequent association with German fascism. The Wagner Group is accused of multiple human rights abuses by Human Rights Watch. It is alleged that the group was responsible for executing 300 people in Mali. Given the founder's attachment to fascism, it is ironic that President Putin supports the Wagner Group in his drive to 'de-Nazify' Ukraine.

New wars are often driven by identity politics and hence ethnic cleansing is often a strategy, as it was in Serbia. New wars are typically genocidal wars. While old wars were fought by soldiers attached to states, new wars often include security contractors, mercenaries, drug lords and jihardists. New wars often recruit teenagers from refugee camps and urban slums to fight local conflicts over identity issues. Old wars were often fought over territory and involved a decisive battle to bring them to an end. New wars involve the erasure of populations, their displacement, and may continue without obvious 'victors'. With new wars there is an increase in the destructiveness of new technologies making symmetrical wars between similarly armed opponents increasingly destructive and difficult to win.

Other authors argue that 'war' is not appropriate as a description of the conflicts carried out by thugs or criminals who organise violence for political or commercial ends. The drug wars and gang warfare in major Mexican cities would be another illustration. Münkler (2005) argues that conventional wars were fought between sovereign states, whereas new wars are fought by a plurality of groups for status and material benefits, but the combatants have little or no interest in a lasting peace. On the contrary, the continuation of these conflicts is the basis of their ongoing income and status. Wars in sub-Saharan Africa, wars associated with the collapse of Yugoslavia, armed conflicts in the Caucasus and the wars in Afghanistan since the 1980s shared these characteristics, with warlords forming the local leadership. These wars 'all bear much greater resemblances to the Thirty Years War than to the interstate wars of the eighteenth to twentieth centuries' (Münkler, 2005: 3).

Another perspective on the rise of new wars is to think of them as 'Post-Heroic Wars' (Luttwak, 1995). Whereas most British citizens and soldiers believed they were fighting German fascism to avoid occupation and the radical transformation of their society and culture by Hitler's planned invasion, later conflicts in Korea and Vietnam or colonial conflicts in Asia did not exhibit such a clear ideological definition. Furthermore, western societies, and especially the United States, were reluctant to accept the high casualties that followed from putting 'boots on the ground'. Soldiers returning in black bags sent a clear but negative and damaging message to the public. The war in Vietnam gave rise to considerable public opposition in the United States, whereas in Vietnam it was the 'people's war'. General Vo Nguyen Giap was successful in manipulating American public opinion. While his forces often had significant casualties, he realized that the American public would not accept high casualties. Giap could also rely on conscription, which contemporary democracies are often reluctant to impose. Much of his strategic success had been developed in his war against the French (1946–1954), culminating in his victory at *Dien Bien Phu* which the French and American generals had regarded as an 'invulnerable' military camp. Giap would have been more successful, but the intervention of the Politburo in the exercise of the war produced unwanted errors (Vetter, 1997). Because the western public will not tolerate high casualties in wars fought in distant lands, command of the skies has become the key issue in allowing the use of aerial bombardment of enemies. Such strategies no longer have a heroic aura and involve enormous civilian casualties.

Martin Shaw (2003: 5) in *War and Genocide* adopts a similar approach in what he calls 'degenerate war'. This form of warfare can be seen in 'the armed conquests and aerial bombing of great powers and in guerrilla and counter-insurgency wars'. He goes on to argue that 'genocide utilizes the logic of war and can be seen as an extension of degenerate war'. However, because genocide is a form of war situated within the context of wider military confrontation, it can only be terminated through the use of considerable military force.

The violence raised questions about what was 'new' about the New Wars given the history of mercenaries, slaughter of civilians, and futile destruction of towns that has characterized wars on European soil for centuries. Kaldor looked forward to a period when the politics of inclusion would replace the criminality of the warlords (Kaldor, 1992). She argued that the failures of peace keeping activity after the Cold War, but especially in the Balkans, were the result of misunderstanding the nature of new wars and by continuing to think in terms of traditional Clausewitzean military confrontations. It was necessary to cultivate a global civil society against nationalism in the history of warfare (Kaldor, 2003). The changing phenomena of new wars include the destruction of historic monuments and other cultural objects, displacement of civilian populations, wide-spread social disruption, and the erosion of the distinction between organized crime and warfare. In response to these new circumstances, she proposed the development of humanitarian politics. Apart from developing international agencies, this approach would require that all United Nations operations be open to public scrutiny and evaluation. In addition, it is necessary to address the problem of masculinity behind all forms of conflict (Chinkin and Kaldor, 2013). Kaldor's interventions also point to the prominence of warlords in new wars. In recent years, they have enjoyed a growing importance from West Africa to Central Asia. The notorious warlord Charles Taylor (b. 1948) came to dominate much of Liberia and Sierra Leone. In 2012, a court found him guilty of terror, murder, and rape, and sentenced him to 50 years in prison. The recent history of Afghanistan has also been primarily under the control of warlords.

Chechnya

It is important to understand the wars against Chechnya if we are to understand Vladimir Putin's strategy in the Crimea and Ukraine in his response to the breakup of the Soviet Union (Kipp, 2001). Chechnya is a state in the Caucasus that is composed of three ethno-cultural groups: Chechens, Russians, and Ingush. Chechnya became a Muslim society in the 14th century. Chechnian Islam has been influenced by Wahhabism which had its 18th century origins in the Arabian Peninsula in a reformist movement begun by Mohamed ibn Abd al Wahhab (1703–1791). His aim was to restore the early purity of Islam to return Islam to a strict interpretation of the *Qur'an*. In the 1820s another religious movement swept through the region under the leadership of Mullah Muhammad Yaraghi, who introduced the Sufi Naqshbandi movement. He also called for the suppression of customary law and the enforcement of the *Shari'a*. In 1829, Qazi Mullah, one of his followers, called for a *Jihad* against the Russians. Various conflicts between Russian forces and Chechen fighters did not end until 1864 with a Russian victory. When war broke out between Russia and Turkey in 1877, Chechens organized an uprising against Russian control over their lands. Their Islamic identity has thus played an important role in their conflicts with Russia dating back to the middle of the 19th century. Chechens are overwhelmingly Muslim and tensions with Russia were exacerbated by Soviet secularism after 1917 and by the general process of Sovietization.

I dwell on the Chechen crisis, because many ways it is the precursor of the Russian military strategy in Ukraine. Conflict between Chechnya and the Russian state has a long history. Attempts to establish an Islamic state were undertaken by the Chechen leader, Imam Shamil, and his fighters in 1858. Islam provided the ideology and platform to rid the country of outsiders and their political over-lords. The attack on religious freedom was a basis of the world view of the Soviet Union with its commitment to secular atheism (Khalid, 2007). Islam survived by being practised in the home in secret as children were taught by their parents. Muslims continued to practise under Soviet rule, but always at the risk of losing their jobs. In response to Boris Yeltsin's policy of encouraging self-rule within the Soviet Republics, in November 1990 Chechnya split into two regions – the Republic of Ingushetia and the Chechen Republic. Eventually the growth of crime and terrorism in Chechnya was seen as a threat to Russia.

The First Chechen War, 1994–1996, followed a Russian invasion into Ichkeria, where the Russians sought to overturn the Ichkerin government. In 1994 the Russian forces claimed the Chechen independence movement to be an illegal uprising and launched a military attack to destroy it. The Russian government officially declared war in 1994, declaring it to be a military action for restoration of legality, law, and order in the territory of the Chechen Republic. The Russian Army came to Chechnya from three directions: Dagestan, Ingushetia, and North Ossetia. From December onward the Russian Army bombed Grozny for three months until they destroyed the capital city completely. Russian forces attempted to gain control over the mountainous regions but were confronted by resistance from Chechnyan guerrillas. Despite the disparity in resources, the Chechen insurgents, employing guerrilla tactics, were able to expel the Russians, despite the superior military equipment of the Russian forces.

The Chechnian forces sought to continue the resistance through guerrilla warfare or try to move the war from Chechnya to Russia, turning to the use of terrorist acts. In June, Basayev opted for terrorism and headed with his fighters into Russia where he took over a hospital in Budyonnovsk. Shamil Basayev, who would later become the most important Chechen terrorist leader and mastermind behind the most infamous terror acts, including the Beslan school hostage incident in which children, fleeing the scene, were shot in the back by the terrorists, was at this time not yet fully under the Wahhabist influence. Returning from this phase of the war, he was hailed as a great hero. He was greatly respected by Chechens of all ages, but particularly by young boys and men who admired how the great Russian Army had been repelled through his leadership during the war.

Basayev claimed that he was able to cross Chechnya and get as far into Budyonnovsk by bribing corrupt Russian forces at checkpoints. One hundred and thirty hostages were killed in this attack, whereas at this point in time more than 50,000 civilians in Chechnya had been killed and about 150,000 wounded. In July of 1995, after eight months of war with more than 50,000 casualties on the Russian side, a negotiated peace settlement was proposed but not fully realized. At this time Yeltsin declared that there was international terrorism in Chechnya and therefore the Russian Army could not win the war. Consequently, Yeltsin was forced to accept a cease fire, withdrawing Russian forces in August 1996. Afterwards there was an armistice over a five-year period during which time law and order continued to deteriorate.

The official Russian figure for military fatalities was 5,732, but other estimates put the number as high as 7,500. Although there are no reliable figures for the number of Chechens killed, estimates put the figure as high as 17,000 dead or missing. Various figures estimate the number civilian deaths at between 30,000 and 100,000 killed and possibly over 200,000 injured, while more than 500,000 people were displaced through the conflict. The bombing campaigns reduced many cities and villages to ruins, that were no longer fit for human habitation. The conflict led to a significant decrease in the non-Chechen population due to violence and discrimination.

The second Chechen War was in Chechnya and the border areas of the north Caucasus from August 1999 to April 2009. In August 1999, Islamic fighters from Chechnya entered Dagestan, declaring it an independent state, and calling for a jihad. In September 1999 in response to Chechen incursions into Dagestan and under the new Prime Minister Vladimir Putin, the Russians embarked on a systematic pacification of Chechnya. During the initial campaign, Russian military and pro-Russian Chechen paramilitary forces faced Chechen separatists in open combat and seized the Chechen capital Grozny after a winter conflict that lasted from December 1999 until February 2000. Russia established direct rule over Chechnya in May 2000. However, Chechen resistance in the North Caucasus region continued to inflict heavy casualties on the Russian forces and challenged Russian political control over Chechnya for several years. Both sides carried out attacks against civilians. These attacks on civilians were widely condemned.

Vladimir Putin staked his own rise to power on a successful military outcome which involved the destruction of Grozny. In mid-2000, the Russian government transferred various military responsibilities to pro-Russian Chechen forces. The military phase of operations was terminated in April 2002, and the coordination of the field operations was given eventually to the Ministry of Internal Affairs in 2003. By 2009, Russia had severely disabled the Chechen separatist movement and large-scale fighting ceased. Russian Army and Interior Ministry troops ceased patrolling Grozny, which underwent reconstruction efforts and much of the city and surrounding areas were rebuilt quickly. However, sporadic violence continued throughout the North Caucasus; occasional bombings and ambushes targeting federal troops and forces of the regional governments in the area continued. In April 2009, the government operation in Chechnya officially ended.

As with other new wars, in the Chechen wars it was often difficult to distinguish between military violence and routine criminal behaviour. Soldiers and officers in the Russian forces were easily corrupted by access to black markets, often resulting in tacit agreements over loot between Russian and Chechens in the mid-1990s (Goytisolo, 2000). In the Second Chechen War, there is evidence of kidnapping and a trade in corpses as a means of rewards for both Russian officers and men (Nivat, 2001). Both sides were involved in the illegal trade in booty, bodies, oil, and captives to fund their involvement in war (Politkovskaya, 2008).

Ukraine: A Modern Civilian Catastrophe

The 1917 Revolution was a drastic attempt to impose secularization and to eradicate all manifestations of religion. The Orthodox Church was a problem, because it was, on the one hand, deeply embedded in the religious and cultural practices of the peasantry and, on the other, it was closely connected to Tsardom. However, the strategy of general secularization failed, to some extent as a result of peasant and worker resistance. During WWII, the communist state sought a political peace with the Church in its conflict with Germany and concluded that Orthodoxy, especially at the parish level, could be politically useful. With the collapse of the Soviet Union in 1991, the Orthodox Church began to recover. The traditional doctrine of the relationship between state and church had been understood as an institutional harmony or *symphonia*. This traditional political theory has been restored and the Orthodox hierarchy supports the state in both domestic and foreign affairs. In particular, the Orthodox hierarchy, and especially Patriarch Kirill, have supported the war against Ukraine, defining the struggle with the West as a war against Satanic Forces, which are illustrated by homosexuality, political liberalism, consumerism, and secularity. The Church and the state have thus returned to *symphonia* restoring the historic relationship between Church and state that had been forged by the Tsar and Patriarch.

The independence of the Ukraine Church had become a problem for Moscow and the Russian Orthodox Church. In response to this religious and political division, Putin has rejected the idea of Ukraine as an independent sovereign state and instead regards Ukraine as a member of the Slavic community of nations. The Orthodox Church views its canonical authority as including all the lands that were part of the former Soviet Union. In all other former Soviet lands, including Ukraine, the Church claims canonical jurisdiction, no matter how Ukrainians see their own identity. Putin now employs a religious justification for reuniting the Ukrainian and Russian peoples again, so the Caesaropapist relationship of the Tsars and the Church, which the communists had interrupted, has returned.

The modern-day Russian Orthodox Church has been restored to its original position as closely connected to the state apparatus (Bourdeaux and Popescu, 2008; Bremer, 2013). The various churches have enjoyed considerable freedom to develop their parishes and recruit new priests. While the overwhelming majority of Russians identify as Orthodox, church-going has declined. What is remarkable is the convergence of attitudes between the Kremlin and the Orthodox hierarchy. This convergence includes their negative view of the West and their support for restoring the territory of the Soviet Union, if necessary, by force, before its collapse. While the state has been able to work with the church hierarchy, it can be said that 'the Soviet authorities would ideally like a church with a hierarchy but no believers' (Walters, 1986: 144).

Ukraine has a complicated relationship to Russia regarding borders and sovereignty. In November 1990 the Ukraine-Russian treaty recognized Ukraine's borders. The Russian executive argued that the break-up and disintegration of the Soviet Union made the treaty no longer valid. By contrast, the United Nations and western governments disagreed, wanting to support the treaty and opposed territorial claims made by the Russian parliament between 1991–1996. The history of this relationship is complicated by the fact that Russia had never been in the pre-Soviet era a state. However, Russians have been reluctant to accept a fixed Russian-Ukraine border. With the May 1997 treaty, Russia supported the view that the Sea of Azov would be held in common. However, Russian authorities continued to dispute the ownership of the Donbas and Crimea (Kuzio, 1998).

The war against Ukraine has in many respects been a repeat of Russian military strategies that were used in Syria and Chechnya. Rather than expose Soviet troops to local fighters who are familiar with the urban terrain, the strategy has been to destroy the towns and cities by aerial and artillery bombardment. Where there has been a need for 'boots on the ground', President Asad and his Russian supporters have often relied on mercenaries such as the Wagner Group. In Ukraine, Russia has also relied on starvation and lack of clean water in the attempt to force Ukraine's leadership into submission and a peace treaty guaranteeing some basic aspects of President Putin's original ambition, short of Ukraine independence and sovereignty. By July 2022, almost 20% of Ukraine territory was under Russian control. The occupation is resulting in numerous health issues. What assessments we do have suggest that with the hot summer weather, human contact with insects such as ticks will result in the spread of infectious disease. This repeats a typical pattern of warfare that it creates further health crises, such as infection and famine. The duration of the war may be decided, not on the battlefield, but by forthcoming elections in the West.

As in other new wars, rape and the black market have played a role in subduing and demoralizing the civilian population The casualties on both sides have been tragic. Russian conscripts were not well prepared for either the weather or the war. Fatalities and injuries of war are difficult to calculate and may not be known for years after the fighting has stopped. There are many missing persons whose fate may never be determined. As with other wars, truth has been one of the first casualties. The domestic control of information regarding the war in Russia has returned to techniques that were developed by Stalin (Adler, 2022). The consensus is that we have returned to the circumstances and consequences of the Cold War. The Russian invasion has been justified in terms of the attempt to de-Nazify Ukraine, to prevent further persecution of ethnic Russian minorities. Russia's attack on Georgia and the annexation of the Crimea, the Trump Presidency, tensions over Taiwan and Chinese expansion into the Pacific, Brexit and the war in Ukraine and its justifications, have demonstrated the collapse of the liberal international order (Mulligan, 2022).

Russia's Coming Demographic Catastrophe

The future of Russia will depend to some degree on its demographic future and the possible role of Islam in that development. The Islamic *umma* was divided in 1992 as a result of internal Muslim politics in response to the changed circumstances that had arisen from the Russian Law on Freedom of Confessions in 1990. By 2006, these internal divisions had been reconciled, providing the institutional conditions for an Islamic revival. New mosques have been built and educational institutes or *madrasah* to train Muslim leaders or *muftis* were re-established. Islamic leaders have also seen an opportunity to emphasize their historic presence in the Russian 'motherland'. Islam has in the past and equally today played an important role in the geo-politics of southern Russia where mosques were in frequent contact with Muslim centres in the Middle East (Matsuzato, 2007).

One key figure in the revival is the Mufti Talgat Tadzhuddin. He claims to have Tartar ancestors and hence to be heir to the legacy of Islam as a basic element of Russian history. He joined forces with Orthodox Church leaders in their condemnation of the corrupt morality of the West. For example, in 2006, he joined with Orthodox priests in Moscow in a protest against a gay march. As the chairman of the Central Spiritual Board of Muslims in Russia, he has considerable influence. Speaking in 2022 in Ufa, the capital of the Republic of Bashkiria, he offered his support for the military invasion of Ukraine. In the celebrations for Eid al-Adha, he prayed for the Muslim and non-Muslim soldiers in Ukraine. Tadzhuddin has also issued a *fatwa* establishing a religious obligation to fight in the Ukraine, and stated those men who die there will be recognized as religious martyrs. These events have been occasions to reiterate the official Orthodox view of the West as a Satanic Force. This criticism of the West is a view widely held by state-sponsored Muftis in their condemnation of Gay Rights and other expressions of western liberalism. While Putin is willing to accept the endorsement of the Muslim hierarchy, we can assume that in private he does not see Muslims as members of the historic homeland of Finnish, Ukrainian, and Russian Slavs.

The Russian community is confronted by a serious demographic future with a steeply declining fertility rate. This demographic crisis may be one reason why Putin must be open to the idea of Muslim membership of the motherland (Eberstadt, 2004). The Russian population is in decline, because of a low fertility rate, a rising mortality rate, and an increase in Russians leaving to establish themselves overseas. Population replacement requires a total fertility rate (the number of hypothetical births per woman if she completes her reproductive cycle around 49 years) of 2.1. The TFR fell in the 1990s to 1.247 and then climbed to 1.823 in 2021. However, we do not know how many Russians have died during the COVID-19 pandemic. One other issue for Russia is that three-quarters of its population lives in European Russia. However, this demographic scene can only become more acute if the war in Ukraine continues with significant Russian fatalities. With a continuing demographic decline, it is estimated that by 2030, Muslims will constitute the majority ethnic population in Russia. The Muslim fertility rate is around 2.3 and thus well above the Russian average. Their reproduction rate is related to their religious beliefs in that observant Muslims refrain from alcoholism whereas one cause of high mortality rates among non-Muslim Russians is drug abuse, especially alcoholism (Plant, 2017). When faced with these domestic problems, Putin's willingness to embrace the Muslim hierarchy becomes understandable.

The Russian Orthodox Church under Patriarch Kirill has become a key player in the official political and cultural project in opposition to the secular West and its Satanic influence. The Orthodox Church adds a moral critique of western decadence which complements Putin's belief that the collapse of the USSR was both a moral and a political failure. The idea of an independent Ukraine outside the Russian homeland, in this perspective, is a political fiction which has been embraced and propagated for political reasons by the decadent West. Putin has in public claimed that there exists an historical unity between Russians, Ukrainians and Belarusians that can be traced back to Ancient Rus. This claim that Ukraine was in fact never a sovereign nation state was frequently rehearsed prior to the invasion of Ukraine (Mulligan, 2022). Putin's understanding of the continuity of Russian history is captured in the traditional anthem of the Russian Federation – *So it was, so it is, and it will always be so* (Adler, 2022).

Conclusion: The Banality of Evil

While Putin has spiritual endorsement for the catastrophe unfolding in Ukraine, we might ask ourselves, when faced with accounts of mass killing, rape, torture, and amputations in journalist accounts of the war in Ukraine, 'why does evil exist'? Furthermore, why is evil banal? (Arendt, 1951). These questions of course have been around since humans emerged to ponder the nature of their own vulnerability. The Abrahamic religions – Judaism, Christianity, and Islam – have developed theodicies to account for these uncomfortable exigencies of our mere survival. In a modern secular society, it may be that few people encounter and accept these religious traditions. We might say that we experience evil because our peculiarly human vulnerability exposes us to forces that can easily prey on our frailty both physical and mental (Turner, 2009b: 246–251). Secular individuals are unlikely to find religious accounts of good and evil convincing. If they do encounter Abrahamic notions of evil, it may come in a disguised form such as the film version of J.R.R. Tolkien's *The Lord of the Rings*, in which a village of innocent hobbits are drawn into a battle with an evil force that threatens hobbits, humans, and elves. They might not realize that the four *ringwraiths* in the early stages of the story who attempt to track down the hobbits are drawn from the four horsemen in *Revelation* who represent conquest, death, war, and famine. The struggle between Gandalf and Sauron represents the eternal conflict between good and evil, in which Sauron is a fallen angel. Other figures in the story, such as Gollum, represent the corruption and decay of goodness (Treloar, 1988: 58). The orcs are also corrupted elves, while the *ringwraiths* are corrupted men. These examples are confirmations of an observation by Elrond that 'nothing is evil in the beginning. Even Sauron was not so' (*Lord of the Rings* vol. 2:2: 267). The final destruction of the ring at the end of the story as Gollum falls into the flames is the eucatastrophe of the drama. The debate was partly ignited by Tom Shippey's *Tolkien – Author of the Century* (2001) in which he argued that the story has two conflicting views of evil. One is Augustinian in which evil is simply the absence of good and can be resolved, because ultimately evil has no substance. The alternative reading is that Tolkien's understanding of evil is a reflection on the horrors of the trench warfare of WWI. Other commentaries on Tolkien's fairy stories have argued that the question of evil runs through all his fictional works (Bergen, 2017). While Tolkien draws on the Christian themes, he was also influenced by the dark pessimism of Norse and German sagas.

But why refer to Tolkien's fiction in a study of catastrophes? One answer is that Tolkien invites his readers (or cinema-goers) to contemplate horror and evil through his epic account of the struggle to protect the future of the world of the hobbit. However, his story of the hobbits invites us to think about war, destruction and more deeply about the meaning of evil. While based on his reading of medieval literature such as *Beowulf*, the story also reflects the influence of Roman Catholicism on his fiction and his world view. His epic always asks us to think about evil in our times through a fictional world. In this respect, it has chilling relevance to our present concerns, including the war in Ukraine, because the Ukrainian fighters in the war are now referring to Russian troops as 'orcs' based on the degenerate and evil characters in *The Lord of the Rings*.

Chapter 7
The Economics of Catastrophe

Introduction

In this chapter I discuss two issues. Firstly, the connections between the business cycle in terms of economic growth and depression and the dire consequences for the generations that suffer from the resulting economic and social hardship. The first theme of this chapter is the unstable history of capitalism from boom to bust. Speculative crises are a common aspect of capitalism. Instability in modern financial markets with the introduction of the crypto into the currency market is one example, but we could go back to Holland in the 17th century to the Dutch Tulip Bulb Market Bubble (Vries, 1976). There have been many attempts to explain the business cycles in the history of capitalism. Kenneth Arrow, writing on the financial crisis, commented that, 'The history of capitalism has been marked by repeated collapses of the financial system, situations in which the markets for loans disappear for extensive periods of time' especially after 1819 (Arrow, 2013). The instability of capitalism in terms of the long waves of growth and depression has been an established theme of critical analysis such as by Ernest Mandel (1978: 109–110) in *Late Capitalism*, who wrote about 'capital accumulation, decelerated capital accumulation, and under-investment'. Thomas Piketty's (2014) *Capital in the Twenty-first Century* rehabilitated Marx's economics.

Behind these waves are the workers and their families coping with unemployment and hardship. I examine one important attempt to develop a socialist city plan that is known as 'Red Vienna' as an alternative to the 'free market' principle of unfettered capitalism. In the conclusion I examine the problems of waste, demography, human ageing, and consider how mainstream economics has not systematically addressed the question of inter-generational justice.

The second theme of this chapter concerns the damage done to the environment by economic growth and the endless demand for natural resources. It also includes the creation of waste in economic progress. I turn to the 'bio-economics' or 'ecological economics' of the Romanian economist Nicholas Georgescu-Roegen (1906–1994) who argued that all economic activity is confronted by the degradation and decline of the natural environment, namely by the law of entropy (Mayumi, 2001). He criticized economic science for failing to take into account the limitations of natural resources and the failures of economics to confront the problem of waste. The question of waste impinges on the issue of inter-generational justice. The aim should be that the life chances of our children are no

https://doi.org/10.1515/9783110772364-007. The original version of this chapter was revised. Passages on pages 107–109 have been corrected. An erratum is available at https://doi.org/10.1515/9783110772364-011.

worse than our own. Consequently, he complained, with some degree of humour, that economics was an opportunistic science, so that, 'An inflation, a catastrophic drought, or a stock-exchange crash leaves absolutely no mark on the economy' (Georgescu-Roegen, 1975: 348). In this chapter I will explore his work with special reference to climate change, the degradation of our natural environment and the production of waste.

This chapter contrasts capitalism and communism, both of which have promised and failed to deliver on substantial and sustainable prosperity. The socialist attempt to revise and reform capitalism such as that undertaken by 'Red Vienna' also failed, but the final failure of their socialist experiment arose from political causes outside Vienna, such as the rise of fascism. Vienna after the catastrophe of WWI went through a period of remarkable intellectual growth and excitement that included significant developments in sociology and economics from both socialists and conservatives. It also witnessed extraordinary developments in architectural theory and urban development. These progressive movements were eventually cut short by the arrival of another political catastrophe, namely the emergence of German fascism. Through Adolf Hitler's *Anschluss* (annexation), Austria was eventually united with Germany in 1938, thereby bringing to an end the creative period of Red Vienna and establishing the next catastrophic European war.

In the standard account of economic growth, both classical economic theory and Marxian political economy can be criticized for the neglect of the natural world and its degradation by unregulated economic development. Neither economics nor sociology has taken sufficient interest in the environment as a potential constraint on socio-economic progress. The underlying question of this chapter, for which Nicholas Georgescu-Roegen gave a decisive negative response, is whether the degradation of the environment can be significantly remedied or indeed reversed, for example, by improvements in technology and by an exit from fossil-based energy. Perhaps the broader question that confronts us in this century is whether we can imagine a time and a set of causes that might render the human species extinct. These pressing concerns have given rise to a range of scientific responses that have sought to give answers to this most fundamental of questions.

Georgescu-Roegen's approach to economics is of particular interest for any analysis of the relationships between economic growth and environmental degradation (Carvalho and Suprinyak, 2022). His work assumed, amongst other things, that natural resources are finite, in fact, subject to degradation through entropy. His analysis therefore raises an important issue about whether degradation of the natural world could be moderated or indeed reversed. Is there any space for hope when faced by environmental catastrophe? To understand Georgescu-Roegen's economics, it is important to consider him in the context of the economists of his generation, who worked on related issues in the context of the European recovery after WWI. The post-war context saw various experiments to provide socialist alternatives to capitalist development. These figures included Karl Polanyi, Otto Neurath, Ballod-Atlanticus, and Josef Popper-Lynkeus.

I concentrate on this generation of economists because they struggled with the idea that socialism could be an answer to economic insecurity and economic underdevelopment, but without its negative consequences for the environment. Their work also involved a thorough revision of classical economics and questioned its foundations in methodological individualism, utility theory, rational choice theory and the belief in the merits of an unregulated free market. In this critical confrontation, they also engaged with the legacy of Karl Marx and Marxism. Thomas Malthus also enters this debate, because his analysis of population pressures also assumed a world of finite or at least limited resources. In this context, Malthus and Marx can be described as 'catastrophe theorists'. Malthus predicted demographic catastrophes with growing populations on limited arable land, while Marx developed economic theories that anticipated the collapse of capitalism through the inevitable class conflict between workers and capitalists or their mutual destruction. The other figure in this debate was David Ricardo whose idea of the three classes – workers, capitalists, and landlords – and his analysis of the tendency of the rate of profit to fall were the background to Marxist sociology and political economy. In summarizing this introduction, it can be said to present a single question of significance to both conservative and socialist audiences: is capitalism a catastrophic mode of production?

Marx, Class, and Capitalism

Karl Marx's analysis of the periods of historical transformation from feudalism, capitalism, and communism found, perhaps unlikely, inspiration in Georg Hegel's philosophy of history as the unfolding of the spirit of freedom through a series of historical transformations (Hook, 1962). For Hegel, the Battle of Jena in 1806, when the French revolutionary army defeated the Prussian military, was a significant turning point in European, indeed, world history. Hegel saw Napoleon prior to the Battle of Jena and described him as 'the world soul'. From this perspective, the European societies had a dynamic and often revolutionary history, whereas the Orient was, in Marx's view, a stationary realm. In fact, the Orient had no history. Marx adopted much of this historical scheme, including the idea that the Orient had no history, from Hegel's philosophy of history. The idea of Oriental stationariness was developed in the famous Asiatic Mode of Production (AMP) in which the state dominated society through the management of large utilities such as water systems. The AMP was also employed to study the imperial history of pharaonic Egypt and Inca Peru (Krader, 1980). Paradoxically, it was British imperialism in India that laid the foundation for historical change by introducing private property, a railway system, and newspapers (Turner, 1979).

Marx's class theory regarding the ultimate transformation of capitalism can be said to have given Hegel's view of history a materialist foundation. Marx's development of the theory of capitalist crisis also simplified Ricardo's class theory. Richard Wiltgen (1998: 451–460) provides a useful critique of Marx's dependence on Ricardo. With the development of capitalism, the petty bourgeois class was absorbed into the capitalist class or downgraded into the working class. Consequently, the principal conflict was between capitalists and workers. The peasant class remained a problem in Marx's account of social change. For Marx, the peasantry was always a conservative force. The role of the peasantry in revolutionary conflict was also explored in 1850 by Friedrich Engels (1950) in *The Peasant War in Germany*, where he saw the conflicts of 1525 as the forerunners of the 1848 revolutions. Thinking mainly of the French peasantry, according to Marx, the peasants do not form an integrated class. Their lifestyle and place in agriculture promote their social isolation or indeed their social atomism. He once described peasant society as a bag of potatoes to express its size, uniformity, and lack of leadership. Hence, the revolution had to be fought by the industrial working class who would lead and represent the peasants. Marx's view of the peasantry shaped the strategy of Lenin and the communists towards the peasantry, who constituted most of the Russian population. The Russian peasant might hate the local landlord, but they worshipped the Tsar. Only through proletarian leadership would the peasants become independent from the landlords through the ultimate destruction of feudalism.

After the 1917 Revolution, the political solution involved the collectivization of peasant holdings and the destruction of the influence of the Russian Orthodox Church – in fact the destruction of the influence of all religions over the world view of the peasantry. The peasant would disappear from the movement of world history. From Marx's class theory, we can conclude that he rejected evolutionary notions of social change that were popular in the 19th century. For Marx, significant social change came through class struggle. The transformation of modes of production was the outcome of a revolutionary conflict between dominant and subordinate classes, resulting in either their mutual destruction or the emergence of a new mode of production.

Marx's theory of capitalist collapse through class conflict suffered from at least three, potentially fatal, problems. The first was that the collapse of capitalism did not occur and hence it was not followed by socialism in Europe. Secondly, a communist revolution was undertaken in a backward society, namely Russia, in 1917 with a weak bourgeoisie and a numerically dominant peasant class. Thirdly, capitalism was to some extent modified and reformed, not by revolutionary struggle, but by the early development of welfare states through parliamentary legislation. Capitalism, rather than suffering a catastrophic collapse, entered a period of reformism (Turner, 1986). In Britain, post-war social and economic reform in the 1940s, based on Keynesian economic policies to sustain full employment, involved an expansion of citizenship rights (Marshall and Bottomore, 1992) through legislation over health and education. In the conclusion to *The General Theory*, Maynard Keynes (1957: 372) summarized the failures of capitalism, 'The outstanding faults of the economic society, in which we live are its failure to provide for full employment and its arbitrary and inequitable distribution of wealth and incomes.'

In fact, Chancellor Otto von Bismarck had introduced legislation to create social insurance programmes in the late 1880s to protect the German workers after work-related accidents. His legislation was not entirely altruistic. It was designed to reduce the electoral appeal of the Social Democrats, but the legislation brought about an important improvement in the lives of the working class.

For many contemporary economists, modern capitalism has been transformed not by revolution, but by neo-liberal economic reforms that are associated with Ronald Reagan (1911–2004) and Margaret Thatcher (1925–2013) in the second half of the 20th century. Reagan was President of the United States from 1981 to 1989. Thatcher was Prime Minister of the United Kingdom from 1979 to 1990. Reagan inherited a deep recession which he tackled by reducing government spending, cutting taxes, and reducing regulation. These had the effect of stimulating growth and reducing unemployment. Thatcher had similar strategies, but she also sought to control and limit the effect of militant trade unionism. Whether her policies were successful in the long run is disputed. Certainly, the long-term consequences had serious negative outcomes in terms of civility and communal solidarity. Her control over the Conservative Party probably depended more on a successful war in the South Atlantic than it did on the success or failure of her economic policies.

The changes that Reagan and Thatcher introduced to the management of the economy involved a process of financialization in which fortunes were made through speculation rather than by industrial production. With financialization, industrial profits were not reinvested in capital, technology, and wages, where the risks are high and the return on investment is often slow and uncertain. The source of profits was now associated with the return on dividends, interest on international bank loans, retirement, and investment funds (Marazzi, 2007). This form of capitalism can be said to involve profits without any accompanying production. Thatcher's economic policies saw London emerge as the global centre of finance capitalism and witnessed the decline of northern England and Wales with the erosion of coal mining. Although financial speculation is as old as capitalism itself, the strategy for the financial re-organization of capitalism gained traction in the 1960s. Policies such as deregulation and privatization are often associated with the growth of neo-liberalism, especially in the United States and Britain. The process produced a new culture occasionally described as 'neo-conservatism' or 'Thatcherism' or 'Reaganomics' to capture similar changes in both Britain and America. These changes, in capitalism, lay behind the global crisis of 2008–2011. While some economists, who favour liberalization, have argued that de-regulation of the economy produces substantial benefits, others have argued that it is detrimental to economic productivity or that the financial sector is too large and that there is a problematic gap between the 'real economy' and the 'artificial economy' (Sawyer, 2013: 14).

In recent history, the collapse of Lehman Brothers Holdings Inc. in 2008, following the failure of two hedge funds in Bear Stearns in 2007, caused a profound shock to the American economy that had global consequences. The crisis was seen as the consequence of deregulated markets with the adoption of neo-liberal economic strategies. The banks were criticized for issuing sub-prime mortgages to customers who could not effectively afford them (Malloy, 2014). The crisis in the housing market and the rise in mortgage defaults were immediate causes of the failure of Lehman Brothers (Dosdall and Rom-Jensen, 2017). The economic and political consequences of the bankruptcy were profound as governments struggled with the consequences of what was also recognized as the rise of finance capital. 26,000 employees lost their jobs because of the Lehman collapse. Whatever view one takes of neo-liberalism, the result has been to produce greater social inequality and economic instability. For those societies, such as Greece and Spain, that faced major economic and political difficulties as the financial crisis became a global problem, the outcomes were catastrophic. While the US government adopted measures to stimulate the economy, the European Union imposed austerity packages that had serious economic consequences for Greece, Italy, and Spain (Semmler, 2013). The unintended political consequence was to promote the growth of populist movements, such as Podemos in Spain (Booth and Baert, 2020). The crisis was especially problematic in Greece where the economic policies imposed on Greece by the EU and the IMF were seen to be humiliating and draconian. Syrizia, a populist party of the Left, came to power in January 2015 and rejected the austerity packages (Palaiologos and Pelagidis, 2017). Alexis Tsipras, the political leader of Syrizia, proclaimed that Greece was leaving the policies of destructive austerity, fear and authoritarianism. However, despite the criticisms of its creditors, the populist government was forced to accept a third bailout and continued to struggle towards solvency.

The History of Economic Depressions

Marx's analysis of the crisis tendency of capitalism was, despite its limitations, shared by many mainstream economists. The cycle of economic growth and depression has been a regular aspect of capitalism since the 19th century. Joseph Schumpeter (1942) invented the phrase 'creative destruction' to describe how capitalism creates superior goods and services and, as a result, destroys existing technologies and goods. In the process, it also undermines the occupations that are connected to specific technologies with little hope of new occupations emerging with technological change. This pessimistic view of economic development has been labelled 'the Luddite Fallacy' after the workers who destroyed the weaving machines that were replacing human labour in Hucknall Nottinghamshire, on Lord Byron's estate. It was thought to be a fallacy because it is claimed that technological change also creates new forms of employment – at least in the long run.

The fact of growth and depression is now recognized in terms of the major trade cycle (six to eight years), the Kuznets building cycle (fifteen to twenty years) and the Kondratieff cycle (fifty to sixty years). This destructive-creative process is the 'business cycle' of the capitalist world (Schumpeter, 1939). Depression and recovery are seen to be basic and inevitable components of economic development. For example, in an early work, Arrighi and Silver (1999) referred to the chaotic character of capitalist development. In a subsequent work, Arrighi (2010), in *The Long Twentieth Century,* documented the history of 'the systemic cycle of accumulation' which starts with the depression of 1873–1896.

The Great Depression from 1929 to 1939 was a catastrophic event that shaped the lives of a generation (Elder, 1974). Triggered by the Wall Street crash in October 1929, the Great Depression was a challenge to existing economic assumptions that, for example, unused industrial plant and widespread unemployment could not last over any span of time, because workers would accept lower wages and thereby stimulate a return to full employment and robust economic activity (Galbraith, 1994). Sooner or later, competition would drive prices down and production would rise in response to sales. This process was seen to confirm Say's Law that the sale of any item would be matched by the capacity to buy it. Say's Law also claimed that a general glut of supply over demand could not last for long. As a result, the economy was a self-correcting system.

The Great Depression delivered a different message which was that the economy had settled at an equilibrium, but at a much lower level of activity. Workers without incomes did not stimulate sales and a run on the banks only added to the depth of the Depression. The Depression also resulted in a crisis in the agricultural sector. The conservative response to the Depression was to say that swings in economic activity were normal and that the Depression would be short-lived. The result, however, was almost 13 million unemployed and a depression stretching over a decade. However, the conservative response was to argue that any government interference in the economy would undermine business confidence and deepen the depression. One leading view of capitalist instability was presented by Friedrich Hayek in 1933 in his *Monetary Theory of the Trade Cycle* (Hayek, 2012). As the title suggests, the business cycle was determined ultimately by the activity of the banks whereby investment produced excessive business activity.

President Roosevelt's legislation to bring an end to the Depression – such as a major investment in the TVA (Tennessee Valley Authority) programme in 1933 to harness the water of the Tennessee valley and bring employment to a depressed area of the United States – departed from the conventional economic wisdom. To get his programme accepted, Roosevelt had to struggle with the Supreme Court that ruled against many of his projects. In retrospect, opinion is divided as to whether Roosevelt's interventions brought an end to the Depression or whether they prolonged it. In the long term, FDR's economic programme continues to be rejected by many Republicans who see it as socialism by a different name. What is clear is that WWII brought an end to the Depression and unemployment. It took a wartime catastrophe to end an economic and social catastrophe.

Are socialism or communism the ultimate answers to the dynamic instability of capitalism? Both capitalism and communism promised a life of plenty for the masses. Were they utopian dreams and have they faltered and failed? Susan Buck-Morss (2002) in *Dreamworld and Catastrophe* describes both capitalism and communism as utopian dreamworlds that failed to deliver on the promise of peace, plenty, and prosperity for the majority of citizens. The main contrast was that communism was a utopia of production, while capitalism was a utopia of consumption. However, they shared a common dream of a mass society without any material scarcity. The dream was to be achieved by massive industrialization that would completely transform both the natural and social world. Buck-Morss claims that both dreamworlds now lie in ruins. She refers, for example, to the ruined factories that were left in Detroit which was technically bankrupt. The rust belts of America are repeated in the blighted landscapes of Poland and Russia. Because the modern consumer world rests on the endlessly new, it also sits on the discarded and outmoded products of past production and consumption.

She notes that this world of dreams was captured by Walter Benjamin in his study of the Paris arcades (*Passagen*) (Buck-Morss, 1989). In his *The Arcades Project*, Benjamin (1999) studied the emerging world of modern consumerism and the social and cultural changes that were evolving as a result. The arcades began to develop after 1822 when their emergence was associated with the boom in the textile trade. The arcades also depended on important technical developments in the use of iron and glass. The arcades launched a new world of consumerism that was celebrated by World Exhibitions that had in fact already begun in 1798. City planning became a new art with the principal aim of crowd control. For example. streets were to be wide to make the construction of barricades no longer possible. Rising inner-city rents also pushed the working class into the suburbs.

Austrian Economics and Socialism

Benjamin's critique of the consequences of modern capitalism provides a convenient backdrop to a study of the cohort of Austrian economists who struggled with the problems associated with creating a socialist economy. To understand the work of this group of economists, we need to see their work in the context of 'Red Vienna' in the period 1918–1934 (Alier, 1987; 1992). The city itself was run by the Social Democratic Workers Party of Austria (SDHP). They introduced a raft of policies to improve housing, education, health care and sanitation. Their policies are often associated with the work of Karl Polanyi (1886–1945) who was a major critic of the laissez-faire policies that were advocated by Friedrich Hayek (2012). Polanyi was born in Hungary and became active in the generation that worked to modernize and develop Hungarian society. At a later stage, he and his wife were involved in Red Vienna. Although Polanyi was a prolific writer, he is primarily known by his *The Great Transformation* (Polanyi, 1944). His topic was not capitalism as such, but the market and the marketization of society, and the damage it had inflicted on society and the natural world. The background to the confrontation between Polanyi and Hayek concerned the debate over 'socialist accountancy' in terms of the feasibility of creating a socialist economy without having to depend on market-determined prices. Polanyi rejected the idea of 'free markets', arguing that they always depended on state intervention. In fact, laissez-faire was planned to protect the property values and the wealth of the bourgeoisie. The gold standard played a crucial role in protecting the assets of the elite who managed the City of London. At the same time, the 'free' labour markets were designed to force workers to accept the employment conditions on offer to avoid the harsh conditions of the poor housing and rental markets.

Polanyi's work has continued to inspire contemporary criticisms of the social costs of neo-liberal theories of the market in the idea of 'market fundamentalism' (Block and Somers, 1984; 2014). Polanyi's idea is of a 'double movement' of conservatives who mobilized behind the movement to impose market rationality on society and those forces that opposed it. The market regime of early 20th century's global economy was the condition driving the growth of populist, nationalist, and authoritarian social movements in the 1920s and 1930s. The same driving force explains the contemporary rise of radical populist politics. Wolfgang Streeck

(2013) has also worked with the legacy of Polanyi. In several recent contributions Streeck has developed a critique of the consequences of capitalist globalization. He makes a distinction between the *Staatsvolk* (the citizens of a democratic national community) and the *Marktvolk* (the global elites who run finance capital). These financial elites exercise considerable influence over governments either directly or by funding political parties that favour free markets and globalization. Thereby they can also escape taxation and avoid control from democratic institutions. In this regard his arguments support Polanyi, who was not blind to the political force of market-driven policies. Furthermore, it was not the case that such strategies were amoral. On the contrary, economic strategies were awash with moral sentiments. Any movement seeking to over-turn the economic order of capitalism must understand the appeal of its moral underpinning (Somers, 2022).

The ideas of the economists behind the experiments in Red Vienna were often rejected as being unrealistic – in fact utopian – in their assumptions behind their plans to create a socialist society. The work of these socialist economists is important for my research on catastrophes, because in my final chapter I consider whether socialist utopianism is dead. Otto Neurath (1882–1945) and his generation were accused of naïve utopianism (Nemeth and Stadler, 1996). While I am here concerned to look at the utopian theme in socialist plans for an alternative to capitalism, we should keep in mind such fictional works as H.G. Wells's (2005) *A Modern Utopia* in 1905, which envisioned a world state as enjoying control of the earth as the sole landowner. Humans would be free from physical labour as technological progress would develop machinery to replace labour. The critics of socialist utopias included Karl Popper (1902–1994) and F. A. von Hayek (1899–1992), who rejected the Austrian strategy of social reform as creating the conditions for totalitarian socialist engineering. Socialist economists and centralized planning were attacked by Hayek in *The Road to Serfdom* and by Popper in *The Open Society and its Enemies* (Popper, 1945) and by Mannheim in *Freedom, Power, and Democratic Planning* (Mannheim 1951). Popper's *The Poverty of Historicism* (1957) was probably directed at the ideas of Neurath. Both Hayek and Popper saw the work of the ecological economists as naïve and a danger to individual freedom. However, Hayek's criticisms did not consider resource depletion, pollution, and waste. In addition, the critics did not take into account questions about inter-generational justice.

It must be borne in mind that the socialist experiment in Vienna inherited a difficult economic context. From the end of the War until the destruction of Social Democracy by the Austro-Fascists in 1934, Red Vienna was confronted by economic difficulties in terms of slow growth rates, a lack of capital, and high unemployment. Eventually redistribution was achieved by tax reforms, the new housing programme, improvements to public transport, and the welfare and health systems.

Karl Popper is often seen as one of the most famous critics of closed societies, especially communist societies. His fame as a critic of utopias and as a philosopher of scientific method has perhaps overshadowed the influence of his ethics of cosmopolitanism and the cosmopolitan legacy of the community of assimilated Jews in the culture of Vienna in the 1930s. The cultural diversity of Vienna was condemned by Hitler in *Mein Kampf* who complained that Vienna was a city of diverse races and especially of Jews.

Karl Popper's parents had converted to Lutheranism, becoming members of the high bourgeois culture of Vienna. This cosmopolitan culture remained an essential part of Popper's life and philosophy. It was the basis of his early recognition of the emerging danger of German fascism and his concern that the Viennese socialists were slow in responding to the threat posed by fascism and the specific dangers to European Judaism. There was also the suspicion that the Viennese socialists were naïve in their understanding of the authoritarian strand in Russian communism. Popper's fears and foreboding regarding the development of racism and nationalism were tragically confirmed by Hitler's entry into Vienna in 1938. For Popper fascism was a return to tribal society.

Otto Neurath (1882–1945) was the secretary to the Austrian Association for Settlements and Small Gardens, but he spent much of his adult life fleeing from the consequences of the German occupation of Austria seeking refuge in the Netherlands in 1934 and in England in 1940. He and his wife Marie Neurath were famous, not so much for his economic and social ideals, but for the development of the Isotype, a visual language employing infographics.

His radical views on wealth and value sought to refocus economic theories on the satisfaction of needs rather than on the standard measures of prices and wages (Vianna Franco, 2020). By offering ecological arguments to show the different elements of the economy were not commensurate, he proposed *Naturrechnung* rather than money as the unit of wealth. His version of ecological utopianism claimed that the economy cannot be adequately understood simply by reference to the traditional priorities of economic planning. His work brought into sharp focus a set of issues that are typically neglected in mainstream economics, namely the question of the inter-generational allocation of resources that are of necessity limited because they are exhaustible. In response to the deprivations of the urban working class, he developed a socialist housing strategy. The aim was to create a socialist style of housing that was sensitive to a proletarian 'form of life' (Blau, 2006).

Josef Popper-Lynkeus (1838–1921) was another member of the 'Other Austrian Economics', a contemporary of Otto Neurath and a relative of Karl Popper. He was a strident critic of economic science which had failed to promote social reform. However, unlike Neurath he was not particularly interested in the methodological issues behind explanations of economic development.

Popper-Lynkeus worked as an engineer for much of his adult life, engaging in research in a variety of fields of the natural sciences such as thermodynamics, mechanics, electricity, and aerodynamics. He developed various schemes for harnessing the power of waves and waterfalls to create electrical energy. After his retirement, he turned his attention to questions of social reform and philosophy.

He argued that every society has a duty to provide its citizens with basic goods plus a public system of health care and education. In return, every citizen was obliged to participate in labour not requiring a special education for the creation of the material basis of the national economy such as farming and mining. His main publication in 1912 was *The General Obligation to Nourish as a Solution to the Social Question* which is regarded as his most important contribution to social science. More controversial was the *Right to Live and the Duty to Die* (1903). Citizens would not have a duty to die for the state.

The basic requirements of social justice were security and a criminal justice system to provide protection to offenders rather than punishment. He also proposed a universal conscription to a nationwide service to produce basic goods such as food, clothing, shelter, education, and health care. These important and valuable services would unfortunately require access to non-renewable resources. He was aware of the ecological costs of such a scheme but recognised there was no available alternative (for the last four paragraphs, cf. Vianna Franco, 2020).

Within this generation of economists and social reformers, we should also consider the contributions of Karl Ballod-Atlanticus (1864–1931). Born in Latvia into a poor uneducated family, he was largely self-educated. He became a Latvian priest serving in both Russia and Latvia. He was dissatisfied that his Christian ministry did nothing to alleviate the suffering of his flock of parishioners. To gain a better understanding of the difficulties facing his parishioners, he began to collect demographic data especially on mortality rates. With a colleague, he published a Russian volume on *The Mortality of the Russian Population of Russian-Orthodox Faith 1851–1895*. It won the Tolstoy Prize from the Academy of Science in St. Petersburg. For much of his adult life he was a professor at the University of Berlin. He is remembered for his German publication *A View of the Future State, Economic Ideal and Economic Reality* in 1898. In his Preface, Karl Kautsky praised the book as the first attempt to confront the economic problems of a post capitalist society. He eventually returned to Latvia to apply his economic theory to improving agricultural productivity.

Atlanticus was critical of Marxism, because it was basically a theory of the breakdown of the capitalist system. Marx had failed to explain a how a post-capitalist socialist economy would actually work, and how it would improve the conditions of existence of the workers. Atlanticus had attempted to fill this theoretical gap by calculating how, with modern technology, constant labour productivity, and a shorter working day, it would be possible for a socialist economy to increase output and become more productive than free-market capitalism (Balabkins, 1973). As with other members of the Red Vienna generation, Atlanticus's ideas were also frequently dismissed as utopian.

To conclude, these socialist economists developed a critique of classical economics on a variety of issues. The classics took for granted existing state borders and failed to consider the role of cheap colonial imports. Conventional economics failed to calculate externalities and could not put a value on future, uncertain and unknown effects. Methodological individualism, which is a basic assumption of economics when addressed to the maximizing individual, has failed to include future generations into its analysis of the economy. A competitive economy transfers waste and diminished resources to the next generation. Many physical and biological processes are irreversible and cannot be understood in terms of the circular flows of capitalism favoured by many economists. In general terms, these Austrian economists rejected the optimistic view of mainstream explanations of 'sustainable development'. Their innovative approach to economics was cut short by the catastrophe of fascism that plunged Europe into another destructive war (Mayumi, 2001).

These criticisms of conventional economic theories have also served to underline the fact that sociology had an 'aversion to the environment' (Buttel, 1986). This criticism has also been applied to classical sociology, for example, in the work of Émile Durkheim. A similar criticism of sociology has been to claim it adopted as 'human exemptionalist paradigm' whereby humans were exempt from natural-environmental influences (Catton and Dunlap, 1978). Alongside Durkheim, there is a considerable dispute as to whether Max Weber did or did not consider ecology and environment in his sociology (Foster and Holleman, 2012). There is in fact ample, if scattered, evidence that Weber took the environment and technology seriously (Weber, 2005). There is the remarkable chapter in *General Economic History* on 'Industrial Technique' where he comments on the destructive consequences of economic development with the deforestation of England. 'Everywhere the destruction of the forests brought the industrial development to a standstill at a certain point' (Weber, 1981: 304). Industry then with new technologies would be able to switch to coal. He was also aware, however, of the limits of coal in *The Protestant Ethic and the Spirit of Capitalism*. Observing how 'the technical and economic conditions of machine production' determines the everyday life of the worker, he speculated 'Perhaps it will so determine them until the last ton of fossilized coal is burnt' (Weber, 1956: 181). The point of this comment on Weber's economic sociology is to illustrate awareness among social scientists of the destructive capacity of capitalist development, but also how the environment threatened to place a finite limit on that development. The prospects of future economic growth through technological progress were much debated in German sociology in early meetings of the sociological association (Weber, 2005).

Georgescu-Roegen on Entropy

Nicholas Georgescu-Roegen was well known for his work on development economics based on his research of development issues in Latin America, especially Brazil, but also Africa. His principal contribution to development economics rests with his work on peasant societies rather than his publications on inflation and inequality in Brazil (Carvalho and Suprinyak, 2022; Gowdy and Mesner, 1998, Maneschi, 2006). Coming from Romania, he believed that he was well equipped to understand the problems of economic backwardness and underdevelopment. In Romania, Russia and in various parts of eastern Europe, the main question for economic modernization was what to do with the peasantry. Georgescu-Roegen was influenced by Alexander Chayanov, the Russian Narodnik movement, and the neo-populists who sought to explain why the economic behaviour of peasants could not be understood based on traditional economic models. The science of economics is city economics, and it is blind to different types of society, including peasant society. The peasant agrarian economy had one basic issue, namely an over-supply of population. The problems of a peasant economy could not be explained by the classical notion of the marginal utility of labour, because Georgescu-Roegen argued that in a peasant economy the marginal utility of labour would be zero. In that situation, profit maximization would result in more unemployment and less wealth. In the period 1965 to 1971, he developed his analysis of the limitations to economic growth in his bio-economic approach in *The Entropy Law and the Economic Process* (1971) and 'Energy and Economic Myths' (1975).

The background to his bio-economics involved a Malthusian argument regarding the pressure of a growing population over limited and possibly declining natural resources pushing a less-developed society into the classic Malthusian trap. The main problem with classical economics was that it assumed its theories would fit every type of society. He was critical not only of classical economics in general, but also attacked the remoteness of highly abstract economic models from economic reality. While his 'ecological utopianism' was criticized, in fact it helps one to grasp the limitations of economic planning and its claims about the rationality of the market. While he drew inspiration from Marx's political economy, he was also critical of Marx's neglect of the natural environment within which economic activity took place. Georgescu-Roegen's main argument was that natural resources are finite and cannot be replaced once they are destroyed or consumed. Since the economy is entropic, there is an inevitable exhaustion of resources which is accompanied by the production of waste. Marxists and socialists optimistically envisioned a future of plenty and abundance. Against Marxist sociology, he recognized that the social and political conflicts of modern societies are not the consequence of the division of society into classes, but a product of the struggle over low-entropy resources.

Economic theory all the way back to Adam Smith and the Scottish Enlightenment imagined the growth of a world of plenty. Once again Malthus is relevant to this debate on the limits of growth (Wrigley, 1989). The idea of an endless world of luxury has been challenged by Nicholas Xenos (1989) in *Scarcity and Modernity*. Following Rousseau's critique of luxury in a world of inequality, Xenos showed how the growth of consumerism in societies with considerable inequality, results in a general experience of scarcity, not affluence. Georgescu-Roegen's economic theory also predicts scarcity but based on the entropy law that shows how all resources are limited. He argued that the economy is entropic and hence there is both the exhaustion of finite resources and the inevitable production of waste (-Georgescu-Roegen, 1986). 'Ecological utopianism' argues that decisions on the economy cannot be taken by appealing to the priorities set by economic planning or by appeals to the rationality of the free market (Mayumi, 2001). Many physical and biological processes are irreversible and cannot be understood in terms of the circular flows of production and consumption favoured by most economists. We need to recognize the obvious fact that outputs consist of both commodities and waste.

He complained that the waste from large cities is not used for fertilization. Human waste from large cities such as Berlin had to be removed at great expense, but with no obvious economic benefit. He opposed the modern dependence on motor cars which were often merely status symbols and argued for public transport in response to population growth and the finite volume of natural resources. As with other Red Vienna socialist intellectuals, he was critical of economists who believed in ever-present 'sustainable development'. Much of the modern thinking about the 'stable state' has been influenced by two publications by Herman Daly (1991; 1996).

The Utopian Technology of Survival

The blunt message of Georgescu-Roegen's bio-economics was that what has been lost cannot be restored. His critics might reasonably ask: Can resources not be replaced? Can waste be successfully recycled? There is ample evidence of state support for technology to maintain extensive programmes for the recycling of domestic and commercial waste. There is also growing public awareness of the dangers of plastics especially in terms of plastic waste that contaminates the oceans. There are various effective alternatives to many plastic items which the public has in the past taken for granted. These might include simple measures such as the use of paper bags to replace plastic bags at supermarkets. It is also possible, that with further development of cloning, to store and protect endangered species. In response to contemporary shortages in the food supply, there is now a discussion of how basic food such as meat could be artificially produced in laboratories on a commercial basis. None of these developments of course can return us to the world of past generations who often grew much of their own fruit and vegetables on small patches of land such as allotments. However, the counter-argument would be that technological developments can produce new procedures to create what we might call 'laboratory food'. With desalination plants it may be possible to increase the supply of drinking water. Many of these technological developments are already in place, but it does mean that the natural world is being replaced by an artificial world that one assumes will lack the diversity and richness of the world we have lost. In fact, I may need to use quotation marks for 'the natural world' to register the question: what and where was that?

While one might be optimistic about human creativity to resolve problems of sheer existence, the scale of the difficulties is daunting. Many species are extinct. It would be difficult to remove the plastics floating in the sea. By 2050, worldwide municipal solid waste generation will have increased by 70 % to 3.4 billion metric tons because of population growth, urbanization, and consumer habits. It is unlikely that the factors behind this global growth of waste can be readily corrected. There is widespread public recognition of the dangers confronting humans from climate change. In 2022, it is difficult not to be aware of the heat wave in southern Europe or the drought in Italy, or the forest fires in California, or the flooding that has occurred regularly in the eastern states of Australia in 2021 and 2022. However, many democratic governments are also under pressure from companies and electorates that depend on the mining of fossil fuels such as Queensland in Australia or Virginia in the United States to limit restrictions on traditional forms of energy.

Conclusion: Scarcity, Long Life, and Inter-generational Justice

Demography is a crucial discipline if we are to understand the global challenges to our well-being and survival as a species. But demography often fails to be included in sociological and economic approaches to the basic issues of human survival. There is of course general awareness of the steady increase in the world population. The United Nations Population Division issues its *World Population Prospects*. Recent reports indicate that the world population is 7.97 billion in 2022. However, the rate of growth has declined from 2.2 % per annum to 1.05 % currently. The improvement in child health has been a result of vaccination programmes, improvements in the quality of the water supply, food, and general improvements in child-care. However, we need also to consider the child mortality rates in the developing world. Many communities in the developing world do not have basic sanitation which is an important cause of diarrheal disease, resulting in more than 11 million children under five years old who died from the condition worldwide. The fatalities in Africa are particularly high. Over 330,000 children under five died in Africa in 2005 (Bryce et al., 2005).

World population growth is also a result of increasing life expectancy, at least in the developed world. In many north European societies, life expectancy for women is 83 years. Life expectancy for women in Italy is 85.8 years. In fact, the growth of privatized medicine, 'rejuvenative medicine' and cryonics offer the rich the prospect of 'living forever' (Turner, 2009a; Turner and Dumas, 2016).

The availability of these techniques does of course clearly illustrate the unequal promise of longevity. The ageing of the populations of the developed world is also combined with fertility rates that are well below the 2.1 Total Fertility Rate (TFR) that is required to ensure population replacement. This combination of an ageing and declining population presents significant problems for developed societies: the rising cost of medicine, the decline in the population that is available for work, and the rising burden of the elderly and the sick on hospitals, retirement homes and hospice care.

Some societies can be said to be already confronted by a population catastrophe. For example, at 1.082 in 2022, South Korea has one of the lowest TFRs in the world. This development is the result of successful modernization including the national emphasis on work, the rising cost of living and house prices. It also comes with gender equality and the pressure on women to work full-time. It is estimated that the population may shrink from 9.6 million in 2020 to 7.2 million by 2050.

Contemporary biomedical gerontologists have claimed that ageing is an effect of a limited number of conditions for which there are various promising solutions in medical and technological progress. Aubrey De Grey is the Chief Science Officer of SENS and co-author of *Ending Aging* (De Grey and Rae, 2008). His ambition is to demonstrate that people in their mid-life in this century will not need to die from such conditions. It is more likely that they will die from accidents such as being run over in a car accident or falling off a ladder in the prime of life, as in Leo Tolstoy's famous story of the unexpected death of Ivan Illyich from falling off a ladder (Tolstoy, 2001). But are there strong ethical arguments in support, not of living forever, but in favour of limiting life expectancy?

I focus here on the implications of ageing in response to Popper-Lynkeus's (1903) *Das Recht zu leben und Die Pflicht zu sterben – Sozialphilosophische Betrachtungen* (*The Right to Live and the Duty to Die*). His idea of a duty to die anticipated many of the issues we confront today. Let us remind ourselves of two important assumptions that guided his argument. The first is that we are confronted by scarce and declining resources that cannot support population growth indefinitely. In other words, it involved a Malthusian set of assumptions. The second is that the ethical principle of inter-generational equality is worthy of our assent and respect. Bioethicists have claimed that we cannot avoid rationing resources and that a life of 75 years can be regarded as 'having lived the good life'. Bioethicist Ezekiel Emanuel, who is a member of the Center for American Progress, was born in 1957 and has argued in *The End of Human Life* (Emanuel, 2014) that, with the decline in the quality of life after 75 years, the quest for unlimited life cannot be justified on ethical and social grounds. He includes himself in arguing that he has no desire to continue his own life after 75 years, because he thinks inevitable mental and physical decline robs life of its value. Life after 75 years is not worth saving because it is, so to speak, a poor investment. A shorter life might have the benefit of permitting a greater transfer of wealth to the next generation.

Although his views are seen to be controversial – indeed for many they are unethical – his argument is persuasive. In a context of scarce resources, whose life has more value and what is the cut-off point to conclude successful ageing? Much of the literature on old age is written from the perspective of the ageing individual rather than the ageing society. Popper-Lynkeus asked a slightly different question, namely does the citizen have an obligation to die? My response is that there should not be a fixed age such as 75 years beyond which life is seen to be selfish, pointless, and unethical. It is rather that there should be no social stigma attached to euthanasia, and it should be couched in the argument that, to avoid an environmental and resource catastrophe, the citizen should embrace the view that there is no virtue in living forever. The notion of a duty to die was proposed by a generation of economists who were intent on building a socialist society. His argument might not win widespread support in a modern society built on individualism and consumerism. However, to reject the argument also implies that we have no strong commitment to inter-generational equality. In rejecting the arguments of Popper-Lynkeus, we would adopt the position that the problems of the next generation are not our concern.

Chapter 8
Catastrophe and Utopian Hope

'As utopian oases dry up, a desert of banality, and bewilderment spreads'
Jürgen Habermas (1986: 68) 'The New Obscurity'

Introduction: The End of Utopia?

The year 2023 marks the century – old publication of the two-volume set of Oswald Spengler's *The Decline of the West* in 1923. Is the West in terminal decline? The theme of the maturation and final decay of civilizations continues to fascinate the West today as we face multiple problems that appear to have no convenient or convincing solutions. As the final touch to the year 2022, Queen Elizabeth II died in September, bringing to a close 70 years on the throne and concluding an era of British history as a society that combined relative political stability with slow economic decline. The end of her reign has established a context for radical changes to the Constitution, the role of the Church of England, the political future of Britain as a United Kingdom, the future of the Commonwealth, and the constitutional future of Northern Ireland after the problems created by Brexit. With her departure, we might wish to quote Oliver Goldsmith (1730 – 1774) from *The Deserted Village*, 'ill fares the land, to hastening ills a prey, Where wealth accumulates, and men decay' (Goldsmith, 1996). Goldsmith's publication was a reflection on the great changes occurring in England and Ireland with the decline of traditional agriculture and village life, the enclosures, and the depopulation of the countryside under the impact of early industrialization. He believed that kingdoms and empires, such as Rome, were undone by the accumulation of vice and wealth. Britain in 2023 is not England in the 1770s, but there is a similar sense of untidy endings, that are social, cultural, and political.

In reference to my opening chapter, I commented that one of the few ideas that philosophers may agree on is that the aim of all human activity is to enhance our happiness. Of course, the concept is difficult to define and there are different frameworks or 'regimes' that have defined happiness, but it typically includes good health, friendship, security, prosperity and longevity (Contreras-Vejar, Jen and Turner, 2019). Although the utilitarian political theorists have been much criticized, for example, by J. S. Mill (Stillinger, 1971: 86 – 89) as he turned against the legacy of his father and Jeremy Bentham (1748 – 1832) for the simplicity of their idea of 'happiness', the majority of liberal democratic societies abide by some version of the principle of creating the greatest happiness for the greatest number. As an elemen-

https://doi.org/10.1515/9783110772364-008

tary policy objective, this commitment involves security, employment and welfare. My analysis of catastrophe accepts the centrality of the components of the modern view of happiness as health, friendship, security and longevity and asks how these can be secured in the face of the catastrophes of modern times. If these objectives are slipping away for the current generation, can they be secured for future generations by taking action now? If our mismanagement of the environment, for example, threatens and compromises the happiness of the next generation, then a significant injustice has clearly been committed.

The many modern catastrophes – real and potential – facing the world are daunting. Is it possible to respond with utopian hope? Catastrophes bring things to an end rather than creating new hopeful beginnings. As in a Greek tragic drama, the *cata-strophe* is the end of a sequence. The origin of the idea of catastrophe as the denouement of a drama is often attributed to Aristotle's *Poetics* (2013). The roots of the word are from the Greek *kata* (down) and *strophien* (turn) whereby we might think of catastrophe as an over-throwing of an established order of things. Shakespeare in *King Lear* had the stability of the kingdom overturned at the beginning and not the conclusion of the play. By bringing the overturning to the beginning of the drama, Shakespeare makes the play into a long and unfolding political catastrophe. The Greek tragedy is also important in bringing our attention to the connections between Greek tragedies and Greek politics (Carter, 2010). The epic struggles over ethics and politics laid the foundations for a theory of catastrophe.

I have also proposed that catastrophes tend to come in multiples, whereby, for example, wars create famines and in turn famines create conditions for the spread of disease. The result is a demographic collapse. Such multiple events can often end in civil unrest and in some cases in revolution. Wars are catastrophic, but so are colonialism, genocide, economic collapse, famines and plagues. Such events tend not to have 'good' outcomes. After a revolutionary overthrow of government, there may be a new order or no order. One other issue to emerge from this inquiry is that there is no sharp division between natural and socio-political catastrophes. The global effects of climate change that were experienced dramatically, for example, in Europe during the summer of 2022 can be found in environmental changes, but the causes and effects have many features: demography, environmental damage, urbanization, political ineptitude, and so forth. In chapter 4, I examined the research on famines in Nigeria which were a consequence of colonialism, capitalism, and the failures of development plans as much as climate change.

As I conclude this book, new questions have emerged about the legacy of colonialism and slavery. The anti-colonial and anti-racist agenda in politics has intensified in the West. Slavery and racism created conditions that were catastrophic for the victims, but was slavery good for the colonizers? Some scholars have argued that without colonialism Britain, and the West more generally, would not have enjoyed rapid industrialization and growing prosperity. However, a history of slavery has left the United States with a racial divide between white and black communities that has not been resolved. As the Commonwealth begins to unravel, a similar legacy of slavery and exploitation has become politically more pressing. New generations in the Commonwealth demand apologies and reparations for the past and for the legacy of failed economic development. These catastrophes – slavery, racism, genocide, famine, and war – do not feature regularly, if at all in disaster studies, but we need to build them into a comprehensive theory of catastrophes.

Having started this book with a focus on COVID-19, I have to include now the invasion of Ukraine and the possibility of nuclear catastrophe, the spread of Omicron variants and monkeypox, food shortages in Africa, a drought across much of Europe, a potential Chinese invasion of Taiwan, North Korean missile attacks, rising authoritarianism in eastern Europe, democratic instability in many European societies, especially Britain, the home of modern democracy, the threat of civil unrest in the United States, the other home of democracy, the potential collapse of the legal and economic framework of the EU, and a possible return to 'The Troubles' in Northern Ireland. This potential 'cascade of catastrophes' cannot be easily ignored. However, if we believe we are 'all doomed' (to quote a signature line from the TV Series *Dad's Army*), why would one write a book about it? Does writing a book about catastrophes in fact imply optimism that we can survive this catastrophic period in modern history? Are there any credible utopian dreams that can paint an optimistic future? Is the prospect of human happiness ruled out by the scale of contemporary problems?

There is a *Journal of Utopian Studies* that first appeared in 1987, which suggests that there is significant academic interest in utopian ideas to support such a publication, but many contemporary philosophers and social scientists have claimed that the age of utopian thought is over. These pessimistic conclusions often mean in fact that the dream of a socialist alternative to capitalism is dead. This is the conclusion reached by Jürgen Habermas.

The specific problem for my conclusion to this study of the age of catastrophe is, however, to answer a related but different question: if my analysis or any analysis of modernity results in bleak pessimism and supine resignation, would it be dishonest to write a book about it? In response to this challenge, I examine various attempts to defend hope and optimism in the face of contemporary catastrophes, and thereby to uncover the possibilities for utopian dreams against the view of many observers that utopian times are over (Habermas, 1989; Jameson, 2005; Levitas, 1982). I consider the potential of inter-generational justice with respect to climate change as one way forward to avoid unremitting pessimism.

What steps might we take to protect or to improve the prospects of future generations?

A systematic analysis of the traditions of utopian and dystopian literature has been undertaken by Krishnan Kumar (1987) in *Utopia and Anti-Utopia in Modern Times*, in *Utopianism* (Kumar, 1991) and in his many related publications on the sociology of utopia (Kumar, 2010). Much of his research has, however, focused on literary accounts of utopia, where he concludes that this genre of work is indeed more or less exhausted. If a utopian tradition continues at all, it is in the genre of science fiction. He also notes that many feminist authors have opted for dystopian rather than utopian fiction such as Margaret Atwood's *The Handmaid's Tale* (1985). Another example would be the more complex *Parable of the Sower* by Octavia Butler (1995). Her novel depicts 21st-century California in a state of collapse and where the streets are militarized. The rich inhabitants live behind walls in urban enclaves. Despite the dystopian view, her apocalyptic vision is intended as a call to communal action. However, her bleak portrayal of social decay offers 'survivalism' rather than a real alternative to the coming catastrophe (Phillips, 2002).

The key issue for much contemporary thinking about utopia has been the failures of socialism and the survival of capitalism in various forms. Thus Fredric Jameson (2005) in *The Desire Called Utopia and Other Science Fiction* struggled to identify any genuine tradition of utopian writing that could address this political failure outside the world of science fiction. Many authors including Zygmunt Bauman (1976) in *Socialism: The Active Utopia* have confronted the problem of failed socialist revolutions (Postpone and Brick, 1982).

In response to this literature on utopian traditions, there are only two possible foundations for utopian hope. One is the secular tradition of Marxism-socialism, aspects of which I explored in chapter 7 on economics, where I considered various socialist experiments in 'Red Vienna' in the 1930s (Cunha, 2013; 2015). In the second tradition, I refer to the messianic theologies of the Abrahamic religions, namely Judaism, Christianity, and Islam. These three monotheistic religions share various traditions relating to prophecy, the Messiah, and the world to come. In the Islamic world, Shi'ism represents the critical messianic tradition in the figure of the Mahdi, but in this conclusion, I will focus on Judaism and Christianity. More specifically, I consider the contemporary interest in the theology of St Paul and the idea that we are already living in the messianic age. The issue becomes, in a predominantly secular age, whether the religious message of hope continues to have any currency. Despite their distinctive qualities, these two traditions overlap at various points in their view of the character of history. Walter Benjamin, whose view of history has influenced my approach at various stages in writing this account of catastrophe, combined Marxism and Jewish messianism (Ware, 2004). Given the overlap both historically and intellectually between socialism and messianic religion, perhaps there is only one, and not two, foundation for contemporary utopian thought.

Melancholy

If the great age of utopian thought has come to an end, are we left with pessimism as the only option? If our times are pessimistic in the face of an assembly of modern catastrophes, are we only left with melancholy? If we need to discuss melancholy, we also need to include nostalgia. Robert Burton's *The Anatomy of Melancholy* was published in 1621 and went through many reprints. He rejected what he called unlawful remedies and relied ultimately on 'our prayer and physic both together' (Burton, 1927: 296). It purports to be a medical treatise, but it is more frequently regarded as a literary masterpiece. The volume contains various ironic reflections as when he admitted that he wrote the study to avoid boredom and melancholy. The issue of boredom is part of the story indicating that human beings are prone to melancholy. The debate about melancholy was a basic aspect of Elizabethan psychology and Timothe Bright (1550 – 1615) published his famous *A Treatise of Melancholie* in 1586. It provided the basis for Shakespeare's *Hamlet* (O'Sullivan, 1926). Hamlet's inability to take decisive action was treated as a key indicator of melancholy. These historical details are important in bringing to light how disease categories tell us a lot about social and political conditions, and why different manifestations of melancholy, for example, indicate important features of social change. In the history of medical thought, melancholy was seen to be the companion of intellectuals and monks, who suffered from isolation, contemplation, inactivity, and the complaint of 'acedia'. A special problem was associated with monks who suffered from boredom and spiritual lethargy (Raposa, 1999). In summary, the nostalgic paradigm has four dimensions: a sense of historical loss and decline; a feeling of the loss of personal wholeness; a sense of the loss of simplicity, and finally an awareness of the erosion of authenticity and spontaneity (Turner, 1987).

The nostalgic critique of culture tends to be elitist, conservative, and backward-looking (Davis, 1974; Elliot, 1948). Conservative critiques of modernity are powerful, but nostalgia may not be conducive to restoring or inventing utopian alternatives to catastrophic thought. Modern – day intellectuals may also suffer from what Antonio Gramsci called 'Pessimism of the intellect, optimism of the will'. The expression was taken from Romain Rolland and developed by Antonio Gramsci in his 'Address to Anarchists' and recorded in his prison notebooks (Gramsci, 2007). Gramsci was reflecting on the paradox of pessimism in the face of growing political authoritarianism in the 1930s and the optimistic opportunities for political action. Despite imprisonment, his politics and stoicism were a struggle against nostalgic resignation (Carling, 1993).

In many respects, the contemporary analysis of catastrophe and utopian hope continues to return to the legacy of Thomas More (1478–1535) whose *Utopia*, published by Erasmus in Leuven in 1516, has enjoyed a remarkable longevity (Elias, 2009). His vision of society is often thought to be a socialist response, before socialism, to the difficulties of the age in which he lived. I have in a previous chapter noted that Karl Kautsky (1927) among others in his *Thomas More and his Utopia* saw More as a socialist responding to the crises of his age. It is easy to overlook the fact that More was a devout Catholic statesman who was beatified by Pope Leo XIII in 1886. More opposed King Henry's attempts to change Catholic teaching on divorce and marriage to solve the problems of the continuity of the House of Tudor (1485–1603). More rejected the King's decision to become the head of the Church of England. As a devout Catholic, More supported the removal of Lutheranism from English life and accepted the necessity of the burning of heretics. While socialists such as Kautsky saw More as a socialist, we might equally say that *Utopia* reflected the place of monasticism in the Catholic tradition. *Utopia* followed the basic rules and simple lifestyle of the Catholic monastic tradition, while anticipating the arrival of socialism some three hundred years later. These divergent interpretations of More as a socialist and a devout Catholic point to the ironic convergence between socialism and Christianity.

Weltschmerz

While these early texts are a valuable part of the tradition, my aim in this conclusion is to focus on Germany in the 20th century. It is interesting that Germany has a well-established vocabulary for unhappiness and melancholy such as *Weltschmerz* or 'world weariness' or 'world pain'. The idea of *Weltschmerz* can be traced back to Jean Paul Richter (1763–1825) in his novel *Selina* or *the Immortality of the Soul*, which was published posthumously in 1827. The idea that the world, as it is, cannot satisfy the needs of the mind, became part of the regular currency of Romanticism and the *Bildungsroman*. My focus here, however, is not the tradition of Romanticism, but rather to consider the consequences in 20th-century Germany of two world wars. Many aspects of my attempt to study catastrophes have inevitably been influenced by German authors. In fact, we can trace this theme of a negative critique of modernity starting with Friedrich Nietzsche (1844–1900). The idea of nihilism begins to appear in Nietzsche's notes in the late 1880s, when he comments that 'Nihilism stands at the door: whence comes to us this uncanniest of all guests?' in *The Will to Power* (Nietzsche, 1968). It did not get his full attention until *On the*

Genealogy of Morals (1887) where he concentrated on the connections between nihilism, art, and science. At that point, he declared his attention to write the 'History of "European Nihilism"'. For Nietzsche, pessimism was a preliminary form of nihilism, while 'radical nihilism' emerged out of the 'death of God'. At the pathological stage of nihilism, the world appears to be meaningless.

Nietzsche had a profound impact on European thought after his death. For example, Sigmund Freud (1917) was influenced by Nietzsche. In his 'Mourning and Melancholia', melancholy involved a range of dispositions including heightened self-criticism. Freud's psychoanalytical theory evolved from the early study of frustrated sexuality to the later sociological problem of authority. Freud, as with other intellectuals of his time, suffered from the cultural rather than economic collapse of the civilized world. For Freud, human evil is unavoidable and ubiquitous, because it is rooted in the basic instincts of our nature. Freud's *Civilization and its Discontents* (2002) is the most – cited work of his many publications (Kaye, 2019). The fact that Freud described the book as an 'inquiry into happiness' perhaps provides a misleading description. His psychoanalytic therapy aimed to help patients cope with the normal unhappiness of their lives rather than to make them happy. Freud had originally called the book *Das Unglück in der Kultur (Unhappiness in Culture)*, but then replaced *Unglück* (unhappiness) with *Unbehagen* (discontent or discomfort). Freud wrote the book during a period when he was in constant pain from operations for his cancer of the mouth, but he obviously rose above the pain, and avoided self-pity, thereby exhibiting heroic steadfastness.

Human suffering from war is more than merely cultural, but it can be displayed culturally. The traumatic effect of WWI on young German military recruits can be seen in the artwork of Otto Dix (1891–1969), who served in the war, participating in the Battle of the Somme and on the Eastern Front. He was awarded the Iron Cross. He emerged as a scathing critic of the war and many of his artworks were later destroyed by the Nazis, because of their anti-war themes. His post-war art is famous for the grotesque representation of post-war Germany in brothels, bars and theatres in the collection known simply as *Der Krieg* (Fischer, 1981). He also depicted crippled and disabled war veterans. Dix was a founding member of the *Neue Sachlichkeit* (the New Objectivity) which was critical of what was seen at the time as the romanticism of the expressionist tradition. He was also influenced by Nietzsche's notions of power and nihilism. After the war he settled in Dresden where he worked with socialists, expressionists, and the Dada movement. After WWI and the unsatisfactory peace under the conditions of the Versailles Treaty, the generational angst from WWII can once more be seen in the artwork of German Neo-Expressionism. In Freudian terms, this artistic tradition was driven by mourning for the calamity of WWII or by melancholic attachment to a mythically heroic Germany in the past (Kuspit, 1991).

My discussion of melancholy and nostalgia in this conclusion is, however, less concerned with artistic representations of war and its aftermath. My aim is to explore the possibility of a sociology of melancholy with special reference to the culture of Germany in the last century. The most valuable starting point is with Wolf Lepenies (1992) in *Melancholy and Society*, which was first published in Germany in 1969. Lepenies, in a chapter on 'Bourgeois Melancholy', traces the origins of *Weltschmerz* to the peculiar status of the bourgeois class in the German power structure in their relationship to the land-owning aristocracy. In particular, the petit bourgeois stratum was excluded from the expanding economy and from participating in real political power. Their resignation was the first step towards melancholy. Lepenies (1992: 61) argues that this melancholy of social status eventually assumed a 'general and cosmological' manifestation. The main therapy for the bourgeois class was hard work and economic success. In many respects, the most interesting section of his research concerns the legacy of Arnold Gehlen, who had identified the origin of the idea of the melancholy in the bourgeoisie. Three conditions gave rise to this melancholic condition: the beginning of German industrialization, the science of psychology, and sentimental-psychological literature such as the publication of Johann Goethe's *The Sorrows of the Young Werther* in 1774. This legacy promoted resignation not engagement. Lepenies studied Gehlen's views on melancholy, the end of history or *post-histoire*, and the end of the Enlightenment tradition. *Post-histoire* means that there is no future, and we enter Now-Time or *Jetzt-Zeit*. Lepenies (1992: 183) concluded that Gehlen's views that we have moved into a pattern of world events that do not fit into history at all only 'served to water down the similarity between his ideas and theories' and those of Oswald Spengler. Judith Shklar, in her introduction to *Melancholy and Society*, is critical of both the aristocracy and intellectuals who feel melancholic about modern times, but do not have to suffer the real melancholy of ordinary citizens suffering unemployment, poverty, and despair. However, much of the driving force in Germany after both world wars was the sense of suffering and loss from warfare with no tangible or beneficial outcome. We need to see this problem in generational terms rather than in status terms.

Max Weber is strangely missing from Lepenies's text, but he must play an important role in any account of post-war pessimism. In 1898 Weber suffered from severe neurasthenia due to years of overwork. He spent the winter semester at the Konstanzer Hof sanatorium for nervous disorders on Lake Constance. The condition forced Weber to withdraw from teaching in 1900. In the depth of his depression, he read Jacob Burckhardt's *History of Greek Culture* (2002) from which he adopted the historian's 'distinctively Greek pessimism'. Weber saw happiness, following Nietzsche, as a superficial emotion of the masses and celebrated the struggle for life as a manly vocation. He died in 1920 with pneumonia having contracted the Spanish flu. In the two years between the end of the War and the tragic provisions of the Treaty of Versailles he had time to write some of his most provocative reflections on the fate that had befallen Germany. The two most influential lectures are 'Politics as a Vocation' and 'Science as a Vocation'. However, Weber's sense of the rise and fall of civilizations had occupied him through much of his career. In his biography of Weber, Joachim Radkau (2009: 71) describes how the young Weber read Homer with enthusiasm and describes how 'Inhabiting antiquity in his inner life, Weber found alien the modern belief in progress – or at best could detect progress only up to the "Renaissance", the revival of antiquity.'

In these two lectures, given in Munich and published in 1919, Weber explored the conflicts between what he called, reflecting on Tolstoy's philosophy, an 'ethic of ultimate ends' and an 'ethic of responsible action'. The bitterness of these public lectures and his late essays reflected the horror of industrial warfare in the Great War, the post-war German crisis and Weber's disillusionment with the peace and professional politicians. Once more Weber rejected happiness or *eudaimonia* as the ultimate end of human action, in pursuit of a disciplined calling in politics – 'Politics is a strong and slow boring of hard boards. It takes both passion and perspective... steadfastness of heart' (Weber, 2009a: 128). The underlying mood of 'Politics as a Vocation' and of Weber's sociology more generally is one of pessimism. The contents and direction of these lectures were aimed a particular audience, namely to students who wanted a constructive message of hope. We might interpret his harsh remarks about Germany's future as pointing specifically to the students' own future if the peace agreement did not offer Germany any prospect of change and renewal. In rejecting happiness as a goal of public policy, his personal ethic might be described in terms of endurance. Men who are neither heroes nor leaders must 'arm themselves with that steadfastness of heart which can brave even the crumbling of all hopes' (Weber, 2009a: 128). In 'Science as a Vocation', Weber (2009b: 143) once more found inspiration in Nietzsche's critique of superficial ideas about happiness: 'After Nietzsche's devastating criticism of those "last men" who "invented happiness", I may leave aside altogether the naïve optimism in which science – that is, the technique of mastering life which rests upon science – has been celebrated as the way to happiness.' In short, Weber, like Nietzsche, rejected the idea of happiness as being connected to pleasure.

Another key figure in this period of intellectual and moral uncertainty was Charles Darwin (1809–1882). Raymond Aron (1971: 92) noted with reference to Weber's Freiburg lecture that we must see in Weber's *Weltanschauung*, 'a Darwinian component (the struggle for life), a Nietzschean component (not the happiness of mankind, but the greatness of man)'. Weber was certainly attracted to charismatic 'personalities' such as the circle around Stefan Georg (1868–1933) and their attempts at artistic creativity. At one stage Nietzsche saw artistic creativity as the essential escape route out of the morass of Darwinian positivism and evolutionary theory. Hence his early infatuation with Richard Wagner and the total work of art is easily understood. However, as we know, Nietzsche eventually became disillusioned by the bourgeois character of Bayreuth and came to believe that Wagnerian culture was just another substitute for the Christian religion whose days were numbered.

The fundamental question for Nietzsche was: How can humans rise above their primitive ape-like origins to become higher moral beings and hence achieve authentic happiness – or joy – that is not simply equated with pleasure? Weber, like Nietzsche, saw the heroic life as based on endless struggle. Darwinism offered its own version of struggle, but this time blind struggle to reproduce in an environment of scarcity and uncertainty. In this confrontation with Darwinism, Nietzsche (and Weber) believed that modern man could not be genuinely happy. In Nietzsche's criticisms of modernity, the mass of humanity constitutes a herd that is incapable of lifting itself above the iron law of animal evolution. With the death of God and the crisis of Christian values, it requires a superhuman effort to live a satisfying and creative life. The task facing the *Übermensch* is indeed daunting. It is only through perpetual struggle and the will to power that the *Übermensch* can lift themselves out of the animal foundations of Darwinian nature.

The End of Utopian Dreams

Jürgen Habermas (1989) has addressed the problem of the exhaustion of utopian thought in a lecture he gave in 1984 and reprinted in *The New Conservatism*. He identified two forms of thought that appear to be opposed, namely historical thought which is saturated with the evidence of actual experience versus utopian thought which imaginatively opens new alternatives for action. Habermas starts his essay with More's *Utopia* which was overtly a fictional account of a future state which Habermas contrasted with historical thought. Interestingly Habermas also noted that Marx and Engels were critical of 'utopian sociologists'. Habermas recognized that it was Karl Mannheim in 1936 in *Ideology and Utopia* who clearly distinguished 'utopia' from 'utopianism'. The German edition of 1929 consisted of two separate essays. He argued that utopia is constructed by the will for change and hence utopian thought is a force for social and political change. There is, however, little substantive evidence that the Marxist-socialist alternative to capitalism has enjoyed substantial and lasting success. In the essay on 'The Utopian Mentality', he considered the chiliasm of the Anabaptists, the liberal-humanitarian idea, conservatism, and the socialist-communist tradition. These traditions are now more or less exhausted and Mannheim concluded his discussion by observing that after a long 'heroic development, just at the highest stage of awareness, when history is ceasing to be blind fate, and is becoming more and more man's own creation, with the relinquishment of utopias, man would lose his will to shape history and therewith his ability to understand it' (Mannheim, 1997: 236).

The mood of resignation is also evident in the work of Giorgio Agamben. He has been an influential philosopher whose work raises new questions about catastrophe, primarily in political theory. He first came to widespread attention with the publication of *Homo Sacer* (Agamben, 1995) in which he discussed the consequences of sovereignty on human rights and the role of 'biopolitics'. He concluded with three theses. The first concerns the 'exception', namely the power to over-ride the law in the declaration of an emergency. This notion rejects the idea that the state is based on a contract and the assumption of citizens 'belonging' to state. This exceptional power creates 'thresholds' outside the state. The second is that the fundamental activity of the state is to create 'bare life' as a threshold between nature and culture. Under 'bare life' Agamben incudes concentration camps, medical experiments conducted on the inmates of such camps, people declared 'brain dead', refugees, and the entire population of the Third World. Finally, today it is the camp and not the city that is the fundamental political paradigm of the West (Ek, 2006). He is important in this conclusion, because he argues that sovereignty is not, as it were, accidentally connected to lawlessness and disorder or that these conditions can be averted. On the contrary, catastrophe occurs, because of sovereign violence. In developing his admittedly complex political theory, Agamben had in mind the extreme examples of Auschwitz and Guantanamo Bay. It is Guantanamo Bay that perhaps best illustrates Agamben's notion of the 'camp'. It was opened in 2002 when 800 Muslim prisoners were admitted following the issue of the *Authority for the Use of Military Force* by President Bush in 2001. This 'authority' opened the door to extra-judicial transfer and various measures – waterboarding and 'rectal feeding' or rape. What became the *Torture Report* has never been de-classified and only twenty-two prisoners have been charged with terrorist activity. Thirty-five people are still detained at Guantanamo.

While Agamben has been influential, his work has also received systematic criticism. James Finlayson (2010: 124), who describes Agamben's work as 'not just refreshingly radical, but self-consciously eschatological', demonstrated that Agamben's understanding of the distinction between *bios* and *zoe* with overline on each in Aristotle is fundamentally mistaken, thereby rendering much of his argument invalid. Another criticism, perhaps more relevant to this conclusion, is by Jessica Whyte (2013) in her *Catastrophe and Redemption*. The Redemptive moment is the context for hope that comes into sight over the ashes of sovereignty and the wreckage of democratic politics. Whyte argues that Agamben fails to recognize the importance of political struggle against the retreat into hopelessness. She notes that

Auschwitz was not a condemnation of the West, and, without the military role of the Allies, the horrors of fascism would have been even more terrible. Agamben recognized that he is often accused of relentless pessimism and in his defence often refers to the idea of 'the hope of the hopeless'. He also referred in an interview to 'the courage of hopelessness' (Skinner, 2014). In another interview, Agamben responded by saying 'I am sure that you are more pessimistic than I am' (Smith, 2004).

Although through much of the last century, sociologists concluded that modernity involved a fundamental secularization of society, religion has shown a remarkable resilience, including in the public sphere. In this volume on catastrophe, religion enters any discussion of optimism or otherwise about the future. Various modern authors have been drawn to ideas about messianism and to the legacy of the notion of 'weak messianism' in the work of Walter Benjamin. Jacques Derrida (1994) has addressed these issues in his reflections on religion where he draws a distinction between 'messianicity' as a universal experience that provides an openness to the future and the actual historical manifestation of messianism. These concepts bring him to consider whether all actual historical messianisms are failures to actualize the 'to come' (Ware, 2006).

An equally important 'turn to religion' occurred in the work of Alain Badiou (2003) who turned to St Paul to consider the temporality of the 'truth-event' and the prospects of universality. These truth-events involve major disruptions to our lives, from which we emerge as different beings. A conversion is an obvious example, and it is for this reason that Badiou turned to Paul whose universal gospel had world-changing consequences (Wellborn, 2009). Badiou concluded his study of Paul with a discussion of hope. Thus 'Hope, for its part, pertains to endurance, to perseverance, to patience; it is the subjectivity proper to the continuation of the subjective process' (Badiou, 2003: 93).

The interest in St Paul has to be seen within a larger intellectual interest in apocalyptic thought within the broader focus on 'the return of religion'. To some extent, the crisis of Marxism that followed the collapse of the Soviet Union in 1989 created a space for thinking about politics and theology within a new framework that is 'messianic thought outside theology' (Glasgova and North, 2014). A major contribution to understanding New Testament apocalyptic thought in the context of modernity came from Jacob Taubes (2004) in *The Political Theology of Paul* (Taubes, 2004) and *Occidental Eschatology* (Taubes, 2009). For Taubes, we cannot consider Paul outside the context of the Jews in European history. In his analysis of such texts as Romans 11.25, the blindness of the Jews makes them the enemies of God. This New Testament exegesis relates to the idea in Carl Schmitt that all distinctions in politics relate to the opposition between friend and enemy.

The implication of this commentary on recent philosophical debates about what I may call the 'messianic imagination' is that there is only one western utopian tradition which is an amalgam of the Judaeo-Christian and secular-socialist imagination. This conclusion confirms a familiar interpretation that Karl Marx's vision of the collapse of capitalism was dependent on or at least influenced by the Judaeo-Christian understanding of the end of times and the coming of the Messiah and the creation of a new Kingdom (Kurian, 1974). Both traditions have seen the coming of a new order as the overthrowing of the powerful rulers of the earth and the uprising of the poor, the needy and the oppressed. The crucifixion of Christ is interpreted by Paul in the New Testament as the overthrow of the military and political might of the Roman Empire. For Marx, the class struggle would overthrow the power and privilege of the capitalist class and usher in an age of equality and justice. Are these utopian traditions exhausted?

Conclusion: Inter-generational Justice

A critic of my development of the theory of catastrophes might argue that, while we may continue to struggle to ban nuclear weapons, there are areas where social change is possible. These improvements do not have to be on a large scale. We may be able to manage further global pandemics by improvements in vaccines and advanced planning. The future spread of new zoonotic disease can also be addressed. We need to learn from the lessons of COVID-19 and build a global system for research and development (Lurie, Keusch and Zou, 2021). With the decline in the sperm count in the western male, we need to invest more capacity for sperm storage. There are modest changes that might limit the effects of climate change. The decline in petrol-driven engines will no doubt limit the impact of pollution from private modes of transport. On health grounds, we might persuade more people to use bicycles to get to the office. At the same time, western societies have survived world wars in the past and perhaps the Russian invasion of Ukraine can be contained. UN efforts to increase the supply of grain to the rest of the world are promising. The decline in life expectancy in the United States may be reversed in coming years. The question arises as to whether multiple catastrophes can be, if not reversed, as least contained. These are reasonable pragmatic responses, but they fail to address the compelling ethical issue that confronts those who have survived the catastrophes of recent history, namely the issue of inter-generational justice. It is here that the question of climate change gains in urgency. Acting on climate change now can have no benefit for me, because the consequences of taking action may have no positive effect until after I am dead. So why take action? One line of argument is developed by Amartya Sen (2009: 205–207) in *The Idea of Jus-*

tice. He refers to the teaching of the Buddha that we have a responsibility towards animals precisely because of the asymmetry of power. The Buddha went on to illustrate his argument by referring to the relationship between mother and child. The mother can do things to influence the child's life, that the child cannot do for itself. The mother receives no tangible reward, but she can, in an asymmetrical relationship, undertake actions that can make a significant difference to the child's well-being and future happiness. In short, the idea of mutual benefit is not the only reason for taking action to help others. Acting now on climate change can be reasonably expected to enhance the benefits of future generations to come, then it is reasonable to do so. Such actions can be seen to be 'justice enhancing' in Sen's terms.

The idea of inter-generational justice does encounter philosophical difficulties but mainly if we approach it from the perspective of John Rawls's account of justice in which fairness is seen from the perspective of a contract that is mutually beneficial. Rawls (1999) cannot ultimately explain why I should be concerned with future generations any more than I would be concerned with past generations (Mathis, 2009). If we approach this issue from the perspective of human rights, one might equally ask why – from the standpoint of liberal individualism – should I care for the next generation? Why should I care about the treatment of Muslim Rohingya in Myanmar within a human rights framework? To escape from the dominant model of justice in John Rawls, we must think of alternatives to egoistical calculation. These issues emerged in chapter 7 when I discussed Georgescu-Reogen's idea of entropy. The decline of natural resources and the accumulation of waste are problems that affect everybody regardless of their wealth and status. What is required, however, is a deeper and more compelling notion of what it is to be human. I have argued elsewhere that the idea of the 'dignity of the human being' that underpins human rights is not adequate because of its cultural baggage (Turner, 2006; 2022). An alternative is to consider the vulnerability of all human beings. Climate change perfectly illustrates the shared vulnerability of all human beings and the need for common action to secure a future for our children.

This line of argument can be consistent with consequentialism. Briefly consequentialists argue that, if the outcome of an action is beneficial, then it can be regarded as valuable and laudable. There is a reasonable presupposition that we are morally obliged to make the world a better place to live in when there are opportunities to do so. If there are no objections that reveal a need or opportunity beyond consequences, then these consequences alone determine what is morally right or wrong. This conclusion might be treated as too modest and too simple to address the catastrophes that have been considered here, but it has the merit of avoiding despair and melancholy. In the absence of compelling political or religious visions of a world to come, the merit of small acts to protect the planet for future generations is self-evident.

References

Acemoglu, Daron, and Robinson, James A. (2012) *Why Nations Fail. The Origins of Power, Prosperity, and Poverty.* New York: Crown Business.

Adelman, Jeremy (2013) *The Worldly Philosopher. The Odyssey of Albert O. Hirschman.* Princeton and Oxford: Princeton University Press.

Adler, Judith (2022) 'Russian Regress: Reading Victor Zaslavsky in a Time of War' *Society* 59: 268–273.

Adorno, Theodor W. (2005) *Minima Moralia, Reflections from a Damaged Life.* London: New Left Books.

Adorno, Theodor W. (1973) *Negative Dialectics.* London: Routledge.

Adorno, Theodor W. (1964) *Jargon of Authenticity.* London: Routledge.

Adorno, Theodor W., Frankel-Brunswick, Else, Levinson, Daniel J., and Sanford, Nevitt (1950) *The Authoritarian Personality.* New York: Harper.

Adorno, Theodor W., and Horkheimer, Max (1973) Dialectic *of Enlightenment.* London: Allen Lane Penguin Press.

Agamben, Giorgio (2005) *State of Exception.* Chicago: University of Chicago Press.

Agamben, Giorgio (1998) *Homo Sacer: Sovereign Power and Bare Life.* Stanford: Stanford University Press.

Alalykin-Izvekov, Vlad (2020) 'Pestilence and Other Calamities in Civilizational Theory: Sorokin, McNeil, Diamond and Beyond' *Comparative Civilizations Review* 83(Fall): 1–43.

Alier, Juan Martinez (1987) *Ecological Economics. Energy, Environment and Society.* Oxford: Basil Blackwell.

Alier, Juan Martinez (1992) 'Ecological Economics and Concrete Utopias' *Utopian Studies* 3(1): 39–52.

Allahar, Anton L. (1988) 'Slave Merchants and Slave Owners in 19th Century Cuba' *Caribbean Studies* 21(1/2): 158–191.

Anderson, Perry (1976) *Considerations on Western Marxism.* London: NLB.

Arendt, Hannah (2003) *Responsibility and Judgment.* New York: Schocken Books.

Arendt, Hannah (1994) *Eichmann in Jerusalem. A Report on the Banality of Evil.* New York: Penguin Books.

Arendt, Hannah (1970) *On Violence.* London: Allen Lane. Penguin Press.

Arendt, Hannah (1951) *The Origins of Totalitarianism.* New York: Henry Holt.

Arendt, Hannah (1945) 'Nightmare and Flight' *Partisan Review* 12/2(Spring): 259–260.

Aristotle (2013) *Poetics.* Oxford: Oxford World Classics

Arjomand, Said A. (2020) *Messianism, and Sociopolitical Revolution in Medieval Islam.* Oakland: University of California Press.

Aron, Raymond (1971) 'Max Weber and power-politics' in Otto Stammer (ed), *Max Weber and Sociology Today.* New York: Harper & Row.

Arrighi, Giovanni (2010) *The Long Twentieth Century. Money, Power and the Origins of Our Times.* London: Verso.

Arrighi, Giovanni, and Silver, Beverly J. (eds) (1999) *Chaos and Government in the Modern World System.* Minneapolis: University of Minnesota press.

Arrow, Kenneth Joseph (2013) 'Economic Theory and the Financial Crisis' *Procedia: Social and Behavioural Sciences* 77: 5–9.

https://doi.org/10.1515/9783110772364-009. The original version of this chapter was revised. A reference has been corrected. An erratum is available at https://doi.org/10.1515/9783110772364-011.

Atwood, Margaret (1985) *The Handmaid's Tale.* Houghton Mifflin Harcourt.
Badiou, Alain (2003) *Saint Paul: The Foundation of Universalism.* Stanford: Stanford University Press.
Baker, Keith Michael (2004) 'On Condorcet's "Sketch"' *Daedalus* 133(3): 56–64. doi: https://doi.org/10.1162/0011526041504506
Balabkins, Nicholas (1973) 'Carl Ballod: his *Zukunftsstaat* and his place in Independent Latvia' *Journal of Baltic Studies* 4(2): 113–126.
Banchoff, Thomas, and Casanova, José (eds) (2016) *The Jesuits and Globalization. Historical Legacies and Contemporary Challenges.* Georgetown University Press.
Bancoff, Greg (2003) 'Cultures of Coping: Adaptation to Hazard and Living with Disaster in the Philippines' *Philippine Sociological Review* 51: 1–16.
Barnes, Jonathan (1984) *The Complete Works of Aristotle.* Princeton: Princeton University Press, vol. 2.
Barros Andrew (2009) 'Strategic Bombing and Restraint in "Total War" 1915–1918' *The Historical Journal* 25(2): 413–431.
Bashford, Alison, and Chaplin, Joyce E. (2016) *The New Worlds of Thomas Robert Malthus* Princeton: Princeton University Press.
Battiskelli, Fabrizio, and Galantino, Mira Grazia (2019) 'Dangers, Risks and Threats: an alternative conceptualization' *Current Sociology* 67(1): 64–78.
Bauer, Ursula, and Plescia, Marcus (2014) 'Addressing Disparities in the Health of American Indian and Alaskan Native People: the importance of improved public health data' *American Journal of Public Health* 104 Suppl.3(S3).
Bauman, Zygmunt (2017) *Retrotopia.* Cambridge: Polity Press.
Bauman, Zygmunt (2016) *Strangers at Our Door.* Cambridge: Polity Press.
Bauman, Zygmunt (2011a) *Collateral Damage. Social Inequalities in a Global Age.* Cambridge: Polity Press.
Bauman, Zygmunt (2011b) *Socialism. The Active Utopia.* London: Routledge.
Bauman, Zygmunt (2004) *Wasted Lives. Modernity and its Outcasts.* Cambridge: Polity Press.
Bauman, Zygmunt (2000) *Liquid Modernity.* Cambridge: Polity Press.
Bauman, Zygmunt (1998) *Work, Consumption, and the New Poor.* Philadelphia: Open University Press.
Bauman, Zygmunt (1995) *Life in Fragments: Essays In Postmodern Morality.* Oxford: Blackwell.
Bauman, Zygmunt (1991) *Modernity and Ambivalence.* Ithaca N.Y.: Cornell University Press.
Bauman, Zygmunt (1989) *Modernity and the Holocaust.* Cambridge: Polity Press.
Bauman, Zygmunt (1976) *Socialism: the Active Utopia.* London: Allen & Unwin.
Beck, Ulrich (2015) 'Emancipatory Catastrophism: What does it mean to Climate Change and Risk Society? *Current Sociology* 63(1): 75–88.
Beck, Ulrich (2014) 'How might climate change save the world?' *Development and Society* 43(2): 169–183.
Beck, Ulrich (2011) 'Cosmopolitanism as Imagined Communities of Global Risk' *American Behavioral Scientist* 55(10): 1346–1361.
Beck, Ulrich (2009) *World at Risk.* Cambridge: Polity Press.
Beck, Ulrich (2000) *What is Globalization?* Cambridge: Polity Press.
Beck, Ulrich (1996) 'Word Risk Society as Cosmopolitan Society? Ecological Questions in a framework of Manufactured Uncertainties' *Theory, Culture & Society* 13(4): 1–32.
Beck, Ulrich (1992) *Risk Society. Towards a new modernity.* London: Sage.
Beck, Ulrich, and Beck-Gernsheim, Elizabeth (2014) *Distant Love: Personal. Life in the Global Age.* Cambridge: Polity Press.

Beck, Ulrich, and Beck-Gernsheim, Elizabeth (1995) *The Normal Chaos of Love.* Cambridge: Polity Press.

Beckett, Samuel (1956) *Waiting for Godot.* London: Faber.

Beilharz, Peter (2016) 'All that is Solid... Maelstrom and Modernity in Zygmunt Bauman, Marshall Berman (and others in between: Marx, Troeltsch, Faust and Spengler' *Revue Internaionale de Philosophie* 277(3): 291 – 304.

Bellah, Robert N., and Joas, Hans (eds) (2012) *The Axial Age and its Consequences.* Cambridge, MA and London: The Belknap Press of Harvard University Press.

Benjamin, Walter (1999) *The Arcades Project.* Cambridge, MA and London: The Belknap Press of the Harvard University Press.

Benjamin, Walter (1986) 'Theological-Political Fragment' in *Reflections.* New York: Schocken Books: 312 – 313.

Benjamin, Walter (1973) 'Theses on the Philosophy of History' in *Illuminations.* London and Glasgow: Fontana: 255 – 266.

Benjamin, Walter (1968) 'Theses on the Philosophy of History' in *Illuminations: essays and reflections.* New York: Shocken Books: 235 – 264.

Benjamins, Maureen R., Silva, Abigail, Saiyed, Nazia S., and De Maio, Fernando G. (2021) 'Comparison of All-Cause Mortality Rates and Inequities Between Black and White Populations Across the 30 Most Populous US Cities' *JAMA network open* 4(1), e2032086. https://doi.org/10.1001/jamanetworkopen.2020.32086

Benedictow, Ole Joergen (2004) *The Black Death, 1346 – 1353. The Complete History.* London: Boydell Press.

Benedictow, Ole Joergen. (1992) 'Plague in the Late Medieval Nordic Countries' in *Epidemiological Studies.* Oslo: Middelalderforlaget.

Bergen, Richard Angelo (2017) 'A Warp of Horror' *Mythlore* 36(1): 103 – 122.

Berger, Peter L. (1969) *The Social Reality of Religion* London: Faber and Faber.

Berman, Marshall (1982) *All That Is Solid Melts into Air. The Experience of Modernity.* London: Verso.

Blackburn, Robin (2011) *The American Crucible. Slavery, Emancipation and Human Rights.* London and New York: Verso.

Blau, Eve (2006) 'Isotype and Architecture in Red Vienna: The Modern Projects of Otto Neurath and Josef Frank' *Austrian Studies* 14: 227 – 259.

Bloch, Ernst (2000) *The Spirit of Utopia.* Stanford, CA: Stanford University Press.

Bloch, Ernst (1986) *The Principle of Hope.* Cambridge, MA: MIT Press.

Block, Fred, and Somers, Margaret R. (2014) *The Power of Market Fundamentalism: Karl Polanyi's Critique.* Cambridge, MA: Harvard University Press.

Block, Fred, and Somers, Margaret R. (1984) 'Beyond the Economistic Fallacy: The Holistic Social Science of Karl Polanyi' in Theda Skocpol (ed), *Vision and Method in Historical Sociology.* Cambridge: Cambridge University Press: 47 – 84.

Booth, Josh, and Baert, Patrick (2020) *The Dark Side of Podemos? Carl Schmitt and Contemporary Progressive Populism.* London: Routledge.

Bostrom, Nick, and Cirkovic, Milan M. (eds) (2008) *Global Catastrophic Risks.* Oxford: Oxford University Press.

Bourdeaux, Michael, and Popescu, Alexandru (2008) *The Orthodox Church and Communism.* Cambridge: Cambridge University Press.

Bourdieu, Pierre (1991) *The Political Ontology of Martin Heidegger.* Cambridge: Polity Press.

Bowen, Hugh V. (2006) *The Business of Empire: The East India Company and Imperial Britain, 1756–1833*. Cambridge: Cambridge University Press.

Braudel, Ferdinand (1981) *The Structures of Everyday Life. The Limits of the Possible*. Volume 1: *Civilization and Capitalism*. London: William Collins & Co.

Bremer, Thomas (2013) *Cross and Kremlin: A Brief History of the Orthodox Church in Russia*. Grand Rapids, Mich.: William B. Eerdmans Publishing Company.

Bridgeman, Edgar S. (1919) 'The Lisbon Earthquake: a study in religious evaluation' *The American Journal of Theology* 23(4): 500–518.

Bridger, Bobby (2002) *Buffalo Bill and Sitting Bull: Inventing the Wild West*. Austin: University of Texas Press.

Brogan, Hugh (1985) *Longman History of the United States of America*. London: Longman.

Brooke, Geoffrey T.F. (2010) 'Uncertainty, Profit and Entrepreneurial Action: Frank Knight's Contribution Reconsidered' *Journal of the History of Economic Thought* 32(2): 221–235.

Brown, Michael E. (2001) 'The Causes of Internal Conflict' in Michael E. Brown (ed), *Nationalism and Ethnic Conflict*. Cambridge, MA: The MIT Press.

Brunsma, David L., Overfelt, David, and Picon, J. Steen (2008) *The Sociology of Katrina. Perspectives on a Modern Catastrophe*. Lanham, MD: Rowman and Littlefield.

Bryce, Jennifer, Boschi-Pinto, Cynthia, Shibuya, Kenji, and Black, Robert E. (2005) 'WHO Estimates of the Causes of Death in Children' *Lancet* (365): 1147–52.

Buci-Glucksmann, Christine (1994) *Baroque Reason. The Aesthetics of Modernity*. London: Sage.

Buck-Morss, Susan (2021) *Dreamworld and Catastrophe. The Passing of Mass Utopia in East and West*. Cambridge, MA: MIT Press.

Buck-Morss, Susan (2000) 'Hegel and Haiti' *Critical Inquiry* 26(4): 821–865.

Buck-Morss, Susan (1989) *The Dialectics of Seeing: Walter Benjamin and the Arcades Project*. Cambridge, MA: MIT Press.

Burckhardt, Jacob (2002) *History of Greek Culture*. London: Dover.

Burgess, Adam, Wardman, James, and Mythe, Gabe (2018) 'Considering Risk: placing the work of Ulrich Beck in context' *Journal of Risk Research* 21(1): 1–5.

Burt, Jonathan (2006) *Rat*. London: Reaktion Books.

Burton, Robert (1927) *The Anatomy of Melancholy*. London: Chatto & Windus.

Butler, Octavia (1995) *Parable of the Sower*. New York: Warner.

Buttel, Frederick H. (1986) 'Sociology and the Environment: The Winding Road toward Human Ecology' *International Social Science* 38 (3):337–356.

Calhoun, Craig, and Derluguian, Georgi (eds) (2011) *Business as Usual: The Roots of the Global Financial Meltdown*. New York: New York University Press.

Calhoun, Craig, Mendieta, Eduardo, and Van Antwerpen, Jonathan (eds) (2013) *Habermas and Religion*. Cambridge: Polity Press.

Carling, Alan (1993) 'Pessimism of the intellect, optimism of the will' *History of the Human Sciences* 6(2): 115–120.

Carter, David M. (2010) 'The Demos in Greek Tragedy' *Cambridge Classical Journal* 56: 47–94.

Carvalho, de Andre, and Suprinyak, Carlos Eduardo (2022) 'An emigrant economist in the tropics: Nicholas Georgescu-Roegen in Brazilian inflation and development' *Cambridge Journal of Economics* 46: 561–579.

Casanova, José (1994) *Public Religions in the Modern World*. Chicago: University of Chicago Press.

Catton, William R. Jr., and Dunlap, Riley E. (1978) 'Environmental Sociology: A New Paradigm' *American Behavioral Scientist* 24: 15–47.

Chiaruzzi, Michele (2016) *Martin Wight on Fortune and Irony in Politics.* Basingstoke: Palgrave Macmillan.

Child, Brenda J. (2012) *Holding Our World Together. Ojibwe Women and the Survival of Community.* New York: Penguin.

Chinkin, Christine, and Kaldor, Mary (2013) 'The Gender Issue: Beyond Exclusion' *Journal of International Affairs* 67(1): 167–187.

Cohn, Samuel K. (2002) *The Black Death Transformed: Disease and Culture in Early Renaissance Europe.* London and New York: Arnold and Oxford University Press.

Condorcet, Marquis de (2004) [1795] 'Sketch for a Historical Picture of the Progress of the Human Spirit' [transl. by Keith M. Baker] *Daedalus* 133(3): 65–82.

Contreras-Vejar, Yuri, Jen, Joanna Tice, and Turner, Bryan S. (2019) *Regimes of Happiness: Comparative And Historical Studies.* London: Anthem Press.

Cottle, Simon (1998) 'Ulrich Beck, Risk Society, and the Media. A Catastrophic View' *European Journal of Communication* 13(1): 5–32.

Cunha, Ivan Ferreira (2015) 'Utopias and Dystopias as models of social technology' *Principia* 19(3): 363–377.

Cunha, Ivan Ferreira (2013) 'The Utopia of Unified Science: the political struggle of Otto Neurath and the Vienna Circle' *Principia* 17(2): 319–329.

Daly, Herman E. (1996) *Beyond Growth: The Economics of Sustainable Development.* Boston: Beacon Press

Daly, Herman E. (1991) *Steady-State Economics.* Washington, DC: Island Press.

Dannhauser, Werner J. (ed) (1976) *On Jews and Judaism in Crisis. Selected Essays of Gershom Scholem.* New York: Schocken.

Daschuk, James (2013) *Clearing the Plains. Disease, Politics of Starvation and the Loss of Aboriginal Life.* Saskatchewan: University of Regina Press.

Daschuk, James (1992) *The American Holocaust. The Conquest of the New World.* New York: Oxford University Press.

Davis, Fred (1974) *The Yearning for Yesterday: a Sociology of Nostalgia.* New York: Free Press.

Davis, J. C. (1983) *Utopia and the Ideal Society. A Study of English Utopian Writing 1516–1700.* Cambridge: Cambridge University Press.

De Grey, Aubrey, and Rae, Michael (2008) *Ending Aging. The Rejuvenation Breakthroughs that Could Reverse Human Aging in our Lifetime.* New York: St Martin's.

Delanty, Gerard (Ed.) (2021) *Pandemics, Politics, and Society. Critical Perspectives on the Covid-19 Crisis.* Berlin: De Gruyter.

Derrida, Jacques (1994) *Specters of Marx.* New York: Routledge.

Derrida, Jacques (1989) *Specters of Marx: The State of Debt, the Work of Mourning and the New International.* New York: Routledge.

Desroche, Henri (1979) *The Sociology of Hope.* London: Routledge & Kegan Paul.

Diamond, Jared M. (2005) *Collapse. How Societies Choose to Fail or Succeed.* New York: Penguin Books.

Diamond, Jared M. (1999) *Guns, Germs, and Steel: The Fates of Human Societies.* London: W. W. Norton & Company.

Dosdall, Henrik, and Rom-Jensen, Byron Z. (2017) 'Letting Lehman Go: Critique, Social Change, and the Demise of Lehman Brothers' *Historical Social Research* 42(3): 196–217.

Drabek, Thomas E. (2019) *The Sociology of Disaster. Fictional Explorations of Human Experiences.* Abingdon: Routledge.

Dreze, Jeana, and Sen, Amartya (1989) *Hunger and Public Action.* Oxford: Oxford University Press.

Du Bois, William E. (2007) *The Souls of Black Folk.* Oxford: Oxford University Press.

Dumas, Alex, and Turner, Bryan S. (2007) 'The Life Extension Project. A Sociological Critique' *Health Sociology Review* (16): 5 – 17.

Dunbar-Ortiz, Roxanne (2014) *An Indigenous Peoples' History of the United States.* Boston: Beacon Press.

Dynes, Russel R. (2000) 'The Dialogue between Voltaire and Rousseau on the Lisbon Earthquake: The Emergence of a Social Science View' *International Journal of Mass Emergences and Disasters* 1(1): 97 – 115.

Dzingirai, Vupenyu, Bukachi, Salome, Leach, Melissa, Mangwanya, Lindiwe, Scoones, Ian, and Wilkinson, Annie (2017) 'Structural Drivers of Vulnerability to Zoonotic Disease in Africa' *Philosophical Transactions of the Royal Society B.* 372:20160169. https://doi.org/10.1098/rstb.2016.0169.

Edmunds, June, and Turner, Bryan S. (2002) *Generations, Culture and Society.* Buckingham: Open University Press.

Ek, Richard (2006) 'Giorgio Agamben and the Spatialities of the Camp: An Introduction' *Geografoska Annaler: Series B. Human Geography* 88(4): 363 – 386.

Ekeland, Ivar (1988) *Mathematics and the Unexpected.* Chicago: University of Chicago Press.

Elder, Glen H. Jr. (1999) *Children of the Great Depression. Social Change in Life Experience.* Bolder: Westview Press.

Elder, Glen H. Jr. (1974) *Children of the Great Depression. Social Change in Life Experience.* Chicago: University of Chicago Press.

Elias, Norbert (2009) 'Thomas More's critique of the state: with some thoughts on a definition of the concept of utopia' *The Collected Works, Essays 1.* Dublin: UCD Press, vol. 14.

Elliot, Thomas S. (1948) *Notes towards the Definition of Culture.* London: Faber and Faber.

Emanuel, Ezekiel (2014) *The End of Human Life. Medical Ethics in a Liberal Polity.* Boston, MA: Harvard University Press.

Engels, Friedrich (1950) *The Peasant War in Germany.* Cosmo Classics.

Espey, David K., Jim, Melissa A., Cobb, Nathaniel, Bartholomew, Michael, Becker, Tom, Haverkamp, Don, and Plescia, Marcus (2014) 'Leading causes of death and all-cause mortality in American Indians and Alaska Natives' *American Journal Of Public Health* 104(S3): 303 – 311.

Ewert, Ulf C., Roehl, Mathias, and Uhrmacher, Adelinde M. (2007) 'Hunger and Market Dynamics in Pre-modern Communities: insights into the effects of market intervention from a multi-agent model' *Historical Social Research* 32(4): 122 – 150.

Ferry, Luc, and Renaut, Alain (1990) *Heidegger and Modernity.* Chicago: University of Chicago Press.

Fierstein, Daniel (2022) *Social and Political Representations of the COVID-19 Crisis.* Oxon and New York: Routledge.

Finlayson, James G. (2010) '"Bare Life" and Politics in Agamben's Reading of Aristotle' *The Review of Politics* 72: 97 – 126.

Fischer, Lothar (1981) *Otto Dix.* Berlin: Passavia.

Foster, John Bellamy, and Holleman, Hannah (2012) 'Weber and the Environment – classical foundations for a Post-exemptionalist Sociology' *American Journal of Sociology* 117(6): 1625 – 1673.

Foster-Carter, Aidan (1973) 'Neo-Marxist Approaches to Development and Underdevelopment' *Journal of Contemporary Asia* 3: 7 – 33.

Fotheringil, Alice, and Peak, Lori (2015) *The Children of Katrina.* Austin: University of Texas Press.

Foucault, Michel (1977) *Discipline and Punish: The Birth of the Prison*. New York: Vintage.

Frank, Andre G. (1967) *Capitalism and Underdevelopment in Latin America*. New York: Monthly Review.

Freud, Sigmund (2002) *Civilization and its Discontents*. London: Penguin.

Freud, Sigmund (1917) 'Mourning and Melancholia' *The Standard Edition of the Complete Psychology Works of Sigmund Freud*, vol. XIV: 242–251.

Fritz, Charles E. (1961) 'Disaster' in Robert K. Merton and Robert A. Nisbet (eds), *Contemporary Social Problems*. New York: Harcourt, Brace and World: 651–694.

Frow, John (1979) *Time and Commodity Culture*. Oxford: Clarendon Press.

Frye, Northrop (1974) 'The Decline of the West' *Daedalus* 103(1): 1–13.

Furley, William D. (1990) 'Natur und Gewalt – die Gewalt der Natur. Zur Rolle der Natur und der Landschaft bei Thucydides' *Ktema* 15: 173–182.

Galbraith, John K. (1994) *A Journey through Economic Time*. Boston: Houghton Mifflin Co.

Gay, Peter (1969) *The Enlightenment. An Interpretation. The Science of Freedom*. New York: W.W. Norton, vol. 2.

Gay, Peter (1966) *The Enlightenment. An Interpretation. The Rise of Modern Paganism*. New York: Alfred A. Knopf, vol. 1.

Gehlen, Arnold (1988) *Man. His Nature and Place in the World*. New York: Columbia University Press.

Georgescu-Roegen, Nicholas (1986) 'The Entropy Law and the Economic Process in Retrospect' *Eastern Economic Journal* 12(1): 3–25.

Georgescu-Roegen, Nicholas (1975) 'Energy and Economic Myths' *Southern Economics Journal* 41(3): 347–381.

Gerth, Hans, and Mills, C. Wright (eds) (2009) *From Max Weber: Essays in Sociology*. London: Routledge.

Ghosn, Fasten, and Khoury, Amal (2011) 'Lebanon after Civil War: Peace or the Illusion of Peace' *The Middle East Journal* 65(3): 381–397.

Gibbon, Edward (2017) *The Decline and Fall of the Roman Empire*. London: Routledge.

Gibbon, Edward (1978) *Autobiography*. Oxford: Oxford University Press.

Giddens, Anthony (1990) *The Consequences of Modernity*. Cambridge: Polity Press.

Gidley, Mick (1998) *Edward S. Curtis and the North American Indian, Incorporated*. Cambridge: Cambridge University Press.

Giovanni, George di (1995) 'Hegel's "Phenomenology" and the Critique of the Enlightenment. An Essay in Interpretation' *Laval théologique et philosophique* 51(2): 251–270.

Glasgova, Anna, and North, Paul (eds) (2014) *Messianic Thought outside Theology*. Fordham University Press.

Goethe, Johann Wolfgang (2020) *The Sorrows of the Young Werther*. New York: Dover.

Goldmann, Lucien (1973) *The Philosophy of the Enlightenment. The Christian Burgess and the Enlightenment*. London: Routledge & Kegan Paul.

Goldsmith, Oliver (1996) *The Deserted Village*. London: Everyman.

Goldstein, Warren S. (2001) 'Messianism and Marxism: Walter Benjamin and Ernst Bloch's dialectical theories of secularization' *Critical Sociology* 27(2): 26–281.

Goodden, Angelica (2001) *Diderot and the Body*. Oxford: Legenda.

Gowdy, John, and Mesner, Susan (1998) 'The Evolution of Georgescu-Roegen's Bioeconomics' *Review of Social Economy* 56(2): 136–156.

Goytisolo, Juan (2000) *Landscapes of War. From Sarajevo to Chechnya*. San Francisco: City Light Books.

Gramsci, Antonio (2007) *Prison Notebooks*. New York: Columbia University Press, 3 volumes.

Grell, Ole P., and Cunnigham, Andrew (2000) *The Four Horsemen of the Apocalypse. Religion, War, Famine and Death in Reformation Europe.* Cambridge: Cambridge University Press.

Guggenheim, Michael (2014) 'Introduction: disaster as politics – politics as disasters' *The Sociological Review* 62(1): 1–16.

Habermas, Jürgen (2004) 'Religious toleration: the pacemaker for cultural rights' *Philosophy* 79(01): 5–18.

Habermas, Jürgen (1986) 'The New Obscurity' *Philosophy and Social Criticism* 11(2): 1–18.

Habermas, Jürgen (1983) 'The Great Influence' in *Philosophical-Political Profiles.* London: Heinemann: 53–60.

Hall, John R. (2009) *Apocalypse. From Antiquity to the Empire of Modernity.* Cambridge: Polity Press.

Hamalainen, Pekka (2019) *Lakota America. A New History of Indigenous Power.* New Haven: Yale University Press.

Hansen, Lene (2006) *Security as Practice: Discourse Analysis and the Bosnian War.* Abingdon: Routledge.

Harvey, Diana C. (2012) 'A Quiet Suffering: Some Notes on the Sociology of Suffering' *Sociological Forum* 27(2): 527–534.

Hatcher, John (1994) 'England in the Aftermath of the Black Death' *Past & Present* 144(1): 3–35.

Hatcher, John (1977) *Plague, Population, and the English Economy 1348–1530.* London and Basingstoke: The Macmillan Press LTD.

Havens, George R. (1944) 'Voltaire and Rousseau and the "Lettre sur la Providence"' *Modern Languages Association* 59(1): 109–130.

Hayek, Friedrich (2012) *Monetary Theory of the Trade Cycle.* London: Martino Fine Books.

Heidegger, Martin (1977) *The Question Concerning Technology and Other Essays.* New York: Harper & Row.

Heidegger, Martin (1962) *Being and Time.* New York: Harper & Row.

Herring, Alison (2013) 'Sociology of Disaster' in Peter T. Bobrowsky (ed), *Encyclopedia of Natural Hazards* (Encyclopedia of Earth Sciences Series). Dordrecht: Springer Netherlands: 926–936.

Hirschman, Albert O. (1991) *The Rhetoric of Reaction. Perversity, Futility, Jeopardy.* Cambridge: The Belknap Press of Harvard University Press.

Hirschman, Albert O. (1971) *Bias for Hope. Essays on Development and Latin America.* New Haven: Yale University Press.

Hirschman, Albert O. (1968) 'Underdevelopment, Obstacles to the Perception of Change and Leadership' *Daedalus* 97(3): 925–937.

Hirst, David (2010) *Lebanon, Battle Ground of the Middle East.* London: Faber and Faber.

Hodgson, Dennis (2009) 'Malthus's Essay on Population and the American Debate over Slavery' *Comparative Studies in Society and History* 51(4): 742–770.

Hoelzel, Alfred (1979) 'Faust, the Plague and Theodicy' *The German Quarterly* 52(1): 1–17.

Hoff, Derek S. (2012) *The State and the Stork: The Population Debate and Policy in US History.* Chicago: University of Chicago Press.

Hoffman, Wilhelm (1946) *Nach der Katastrophe.* Tübingen und Stuttgart: Rainer Wunderlich Verlag.

Holt, Robert T., Job, Brian L., and Markus, Lawrence (1978) 'Catastrophe Theory and the Study of War' *Journal of Conflict Resolution* 22(2): 171–208.

Homer-Dixon, Thomas F. (1999) *Environment, Scarcity and Violence.* Princeton: Princeton University Press.

Hook, Sydney (1962) *From Hegel to Marx. Studies in the Intellectual Development of Karl Marx.* Michigan: University of Michigan Press.

Hoppe, Andreas (2019) *Catastrophes. Views from Natural And Human Sciences.* London: Routledge.

Horgan, John (2015) *The End of Science. Facing the Limits of Scientific Knowledge in the Twilight of the Scientific Age.* New York: Basic Books.

Horton, Richard (2020) *The Covid-19 Catastrophe. What's Gone Wrong And How To Stop It Happening Again?* Cambridge: Polity Press.

Hufthammer, Anne K., and Walløe, Lars (2013) 'Rats cannot have been intermediate hosts for Yersinia pestis during medieval plague epidemics in Northern Europe' *Journal of Archaeological Science* 40, 1752–1759.

Hughes, H. Stuart (1959) *Consciousness and Society. The Reorientation of European Social Thought 1890–1930.* London: McGibbon & Kee.

Hulliung, Mark (1994) *The Autocritique of Enlightenment. Rousseau and the Philosophes.* Cambridge, MA: Harvard University Press.

Huntington, Samuel P. (1997) *The Clash of Civilizations. Remaking the World Order.* New York: Touchstone.

Illouz, Eva (1997) *Consuming the Romantic Utopia.* Berkeley: University of California Press.

Jackson, Robert H., and Castillo, Edward (1995) *Indians, Franciscans, and Spanish Colonization: The Impact of the Mission System on Californian Indians.* Albuquerque: University of New Mexico Press.

Jacobson, Eric (2001) 'Understanding Walter Benjamin's Theological-Political Fragment' *Jewish Studies Quarterly* 8(3): 205–247.

Jameson, Fredric (2005) *The Desire Called Utopia And Other Science Fiction.* London: Verso.

Joas, Hans (2003) *War and Modernity.* Cambridge: Polity Press.

Judt, Tony (1992) *Past Imperfect. French Intellectuals 1944–1956.* Berkeley: University of California Press.

Kaldor, Mary (2013) 'In Defence of New Wars' *Stability* 2(1): 1–16.

Kaldor, Mary (2003) *Global Civil Society. An Answer to War.* Cambridge: Polity Press.

Kaldor, Mary (1999) *New and Old Wars. Organised Violence in a Global Era.* Cambridge: Polity Press.

Kant, Immanuel (2014) 'What is Enlightenment?' in Marvin Perry (ed), *Sources of the Western Tradition.* Vol. II: *From the Renaissance to the Present, 9th edition.* Boston: Houghton Mifflin: 60–61.

Kant, Immanuel (2006) *Anthropology from a Pragmatic Point of View.* Cambridge: Cambridge University Press.

Kant, Immanuel (1990) *Versuch einiger Betrachtungen über den Optimismus.* Munich: K.G. Saur.

Kautsky, Karl (1927) *Thomas More and his Utopia.* London: AC Black.

Kaye, Howard L. (2019) *Freud as a Social and Cultural Theorist. On Human Nature and the Civilizing Process.* London and New York: Routledge.

Keegan, John (2010) *The American Civil War. A Military History.* London: Vintage.

Kennan, George F. (1979) *The Decline of Bismarck's European Order. Franco-Russian Relations 1875–1890.* Princeton: Princeton University Press.

Kennedy, Paul (1990) *The Rise and Fall of Great Powers.* London: Hyman.

Keynes, John Maynard (1957) *The General Theory of Employment and Money.* London: MacMillan Press and Co. LTD.

Khalid, Adeeb (2007) *Islam after Communism. Religion and Politics in Central Asia.* Berkeley and Los Angeles: University of California Press.

Kipp, Jacob W. (2001) 'Russia's Wars in Chechnya' *The Brown Journal of World Affairs* 8(1): 47–62.

Kirch, Patrick V., and Sahlins, Marshal (1992) *Anahulu. The Anthropological History of the Kingdom of Hawaii*. Chicago and London: University of Chicago Press.

Klein, Kerwin L. (1997) *Fronters of Historical Imagination. Narrating the European Conquest of Native America, 1890–1990*. Berkeley: University of California Press.

Knight, Frank (1921) *Risk, Uncertainty and Profit*. New York: Harper and Row.

Knysh, Alexander (2022) 'Studying Sufism in Russia: From Ideology to Scholarship and Back' *Der Islam 99(1): 187–231*.

Kolakowski, Leszek (1978) *Main Currents of Marxism. Its Origin, Growth and Dissolution*. Oxford: Clarendon Press.

Koselleck, Reinhart (1959) *Critique and Crisis: Enlightenment and the Pathogenesis of Modern Society*. Cambridge, MA: MIT Press.

Krader, Lawrence (1980) 'The Asiatic Mode of Production' *International Journal of Politics* 10(2/3): 99–128.

Kumar, Krishan (2010) 'The Ends of Utopia' *New Literary History* 41(3): 549–569.

Kumar, Krishan (1991) *Utopianism*. Milton Keynes: Open University Press.

Kumar, Krishan (1987) *Utopia and Anti-Utopia*. Oxford: Basil Blackwell.

Kurian, K. Mathew (1974) 'Marxism and Christianity' *Social Scientist* 2(8): 3–21.

Kuspit, Donald (1991) 'Mourning and Melancholia in German Neo-expressionism: the representation of German subjectivity' *The Centennial Review* 35(3): 461–479.

Kuzio, Taras (1998) *Ukraine. State and Nation Building*. London: Routledge.

Lazreg, Marnia (2007) *Torture and the Twilight of Empire. From Algiers to Baghdad*. Princeton, NJ: Princeton University Press.

Lear, Jonathan (2008) *Radical Hope*. Boston, MA: Harvard University Press.

Leibniz, Gottfried W. (2005) [1710] *Theodicy. Essays on the Goodness of God, the Freedom of Man and the Origin of Evil*. La Salle, Illinois: Open Court.

Lemkin, Raphael (1944) *Axis Rule in Occupied Europe: Analysis of Government and Proposals for Redress*. New York: Columbia University Press.

Lepenies, Wolf (1992) *Melancholy and Society*. Cambridge, MA: Harvard University Press.

Leslie, John (1996) *The End of the World. The Science and Ethics of Human Extinction*. London: Routledge.

Levinas, Ruth (1982) 'Dystopian Times? The Impact of the Death of Progress on Utopian Thinking' *Theory, Culture & Society* 1: 53–64.

Linenthal, Edward T. (1995) *Preserving Memory. The Struggle to Create America's Holocaust Museum*. New York: Viking.

Lonitz, Henri (ed) (1999) *The Complete Correspondence 1928–1940/Theodor W. Adorno and Walter Benjamin*. Cambridge, MA: Harvard University Press.

Lorange, Ellen A., Race, Brent L., Sebbane, Florent, and Hinnebusch, B. Joseph (2005) 'Poor vector competence of fleas and the evolution of hypervirulence in Yersinia pestis' *Journal of Infectious Disease* 191(11): 1907–1912.

Luebken, Uwe (2011) 'On the role of natural hazards and catastrophes' *RCC Perspectives* 6: 10–12.

Lurie, Nicole, Keusch, Gerald T., and Dzau, Victor J. (2021) 'Urgent Lessons from COVID-19: why the world needs a standing, co-ordinated system and sustainable financing for global research and development' *Lancet* 397(10280): 1229–1236.

Luttwak, Edward N. (1995) 'Towards post-heroic warfare' *Foreign Affairs* 74(3): 109–122.

Lyotard, Jean-François (1984) *The Postmodern Condition. A Report on Knowledge* Manchester: University of Manchester Press.

Macfarlane, Alan (2018) *Thomas Malthus and the Making of the Modern World*. Cambridge: Cam River Publishers.

Malloy, Michael P. (2014) *Anatomy of a Meltdown. A Dual Financial Biography of the Subprime Mortgage Crisis*. Wolters Kluwer Law and Business.

Malthus, Thomas (2004) *An Essay on Population*. Oxford: Oxford University Press.

Mandel, Ernest (1978) *Late Capitalism*. London: Verso.

Maneschi, Andrea (2006) 'The Filiation of Economic Ideas: Marx, Schumpeter, Georgescu-Roegen' *History of Economic Ideas* 14(2): 105–125.

Mannheim, Karl (1997) *Ideology and Utopia*. London: Routledge.

Mannheim, Karl (1951) *Freedom, Power, and Democratic Planning*. London: Routledge & Kegan Paul.

Marable, Manning (2011) *Malcolm X. A Life of Reinvention*. New York: Viking.

Marazzi, Christian (2007) *The Violence of Financial Capitalism*. Los Angeles, CA: Semiotext(e).

Marcuse, Herbert (1964) *One-dimensional Man. Studies in the Ideology of Advanced Industrial Society*. Boston: Beacon Press.

Marshall, T. H., and Bottomore, Tom (1992) *Citizenship and Social Class*. London: Pluto Press.

Martin, F. X. (1994) *The Course of Irish History*. Dublin: Mercer Press.

Marx, Karl (1970) *Capital. A Critical Analysis of Capitalist Production*. London: Lawrence & Wishart, vol. 1.

Marx, Karl, and Engels, Friedrich (1969) *Manifesto of the Communist Party*. Moscow: Progress Publishers. Part 1: *Bourgeois and Proletariat*: 48–137.

Matsuzato, Kimitaka (2007) 'Muslim Leaders in Russia's Volga-Urals: Self-Perceptions and Relationships with Regional Authorities' *European-Asian Studies* 59(5): 779–805.

Mayumi, Kozo (2001) *The Origins of Ecological Economics*. London: Routledge.

Mazower, Mark (1999) *Dark Continent: Europe's Twentieth Century*. London: Penguin Books.

McCormick, Michael (2003) 'Rats, Communications and Plague. Towards an ecological approach' *Journal of Interdisciplinary History* 34(1): 1–25.

McNeil, William (1976) *Plagues and People*. Garden City, New York: Anchor Press.

Meacham, Jon (2012) *Thomas Jefferson. The Art of Power*. New York: Random House.

Megill, Allan (1985) *Prophets of Extremity. Nietzsche, Heidegger, Foucault, Derrida*. Berkeley: University of California Press.

Meineke, Friedrich (1946) *Die Deutsche Katastrophe: Betrachtungen und Erinnerungen*. Wiesbaden: E. Brockhaus Verlag.

Mennell, Stephen (2007) *The American Civilizing Process*. Cambridge: Polity Press.

Merton, Robert K. (1936) 'The Unintended Consequences of Purposive Action' *American Sociological Review* (1): 894–904.

Moore, John H. (1996) *The Cheyenne*. Oxford: Blackwell.

Mordechai, Lee, and Eisengerg, Merle (2019) 'Rejecting Catastrophe: the case of the Justinian Plague' *Past & Present*: 244 (1): 3–50.

More, Thomas (1961) [1516] *Utopia*. London: Penguin Books.

Morris, Aldon D. (2015) *The Scholar Denied. W.E. Du Bois and the Birth of Modern Sociology* Berkeley: University of California Press.

Morris-Suzuki, Tessa (2017) 'Disaster and Utopia. Looking Back at 3/11' *Japanese* Studies 37(2): 171–190.

Moses, Stephane, and Wiskind, Ora (1989) 'The Theological-Political Model of History in the Thought of Walter Benjamin' *History and Memory* 1(2): 5–33.

Müller-Doohm, Stefan (2005) *Adorno. A Biography*. Cambridge: Polity Press.

Münkler, Herfried (2005) *The New Wars.* Cambridge: Polity Press.

Mulligan, William (2022) 'Erosions, Ruptures and the Ending of International Orders: Putin's Invasion of Ukraine in Historical Perspective' *Society* 59: 259–267.

Myrdal, Gunner (1944) *The American Dilemma. The Negro Problem and Modern Democracy.* NY: Harper & Ros.

Nel, Philip, and Righarts, Marjolein (2008) 'Natural Disasters and the Risk of Violent Civil Conflict' *International Studies Quarterly* 52(1): 159–185.

Nemeth, Elisabeth, and Stadler, Friedrich (eds) (1996) *Encyclopedia and Utopia. The Life and work of Otto Neurath (882–1945)* London: Kluwer Academic Publishers.

Nietzsche, Friedrich (2017) *The Will to Power.* London: Penguin Classics.

Nietzsche, Friedrich (1968) *The Will to Power.* New York: Vintage.

Nivat, Anne (2001) *Chienne de Guerre: A Woman Reporter behind the Lines of the War in Chechnya.* New York: Public Affairs.

Ord, Toby (2020) *The Precipice. Existential Risk and the Future of Humanity.* New York: Hachette.

O'Sullivan, Mary I. (1926) 'Hamlet and Dr. Timothy Bright' *Modern Language Association* 41(3): 667–679.

Palaiologos, Yannis, and Pelagidis, Theodore (2017) 'How to damage an already fragile economy. The rise of populism in Greece' *Georgetown Journal of International Affairs* 18(2): 51–58.

Parsons, Talcott (1991) *The Social System.* London: Routledge.

Phillips, Jerry (2002) 'The Intuition of the Future: Utopia and Catastrophe in Octavia Butler's "Parable of the Sower"' *Novel: A forum on fiction* 35(2/3): 299–311.

Piatote, Beth H. (2013) *Domestic Subjects. Gender, Citizenship and Law in Native American Literature.* New Haven and London: Yale University Press.

Piketty, Thomas (2014) *Capital in the Twenty-first Century.* Cambridge, MA: The Belknap Press of Harvard University Press.

Pinker, Steven (2018) *Enlightenment Now. The Case for Reason, Science, Humanism and Progress.* London: Allen Lane.

Pocock, John G. A. (1999) *Barbarism and Religion. The Enlightenments of Edward Gibbon 1737–1764.* Cambridge: Cambridge University Press.

Poehlmann, Markus (2016) *Der Panzer und die Mechanisierung des Krieges. Eine Deutsche Geschichte 1890 bis 1945.* Paderborn, Germany: Ferdinand Schoeningh.

Polanyi. Karl (1944) *The Great Transformation.* New York: Reinhart.

Politkovskaya, Anna (2007) *A Small Corner of Hell – Dispatches from Chechnya.* Chicago: University of Chicago Press.

Pope, Alexander (2018) *An Essay on Man.* Princeton: Princeton University Press.

Popper, Karl (1957) *The Poverty of Historicism.* London: Routledge and Kegan Paul.

Popper, Karl (1945) *The Open Society and its Enemies.* London: Routledge & Kegan Paul.

Popper-Lynkeus, Josef (1912) *Die Allgemeine Nährpflicht als Lösung der sozialen Frage: eingehend bearbeitet und statisch durchgerechnet: mit einem Nachweis der theoretischen und praktischen Wertlosigkeit der Wirtschaftslehre.* Dresden: Reissner XV1.

Popper-Lynkeus, Josef (1903) *Das Recht zu leben und Die Pflicht zu sterben – Sozialphilosophische Betrachtungen.* Wien-Leipzig: R. Löwit Verlag.

Postpone, Moishe, and Brick, Barbara (1982) 'Critical Pessimism and the Limits of Traditional Marxism' *Theory and Society* 11(2): 617–658.

Radkau, Joachim (2009) *Max Weber. A Biography.* Cambridge: Polity Press.

Rangasami, Amrita (1985) 'Failure of Exchange Entitlements Theory of Famine' *Economic and Political Weekly* 20/41: 1747–1752.

Raposa, Michael L. (1999) *Boredom and the Religious Imagination.* Charlottesville: University of Virginia Press.

Rawls, John (1999) *A Theory of Justice.* Harvard, MA: Harvard University Press.

Reese, Martin (2003) *Our Final Hour. A Scientist's Warning. How Terror, Error, and Environmental Disaster Threaten Humankind's Future in this Century.* New York: Basic Books.

Rieff, Philip (2006) *My Life among the Deathworks. Sacred Order/Social Order.* Charlottesville: University of Virginia Press.

Ritter, Joachim (1982) *Hegel and the French Revolution.* Cambridge, MA and London: MIT Press.

Robertson, Ritchie (2021) *The Enlightenment: The Pursuit of Happiness 1680–1790.* London: Harper & Collins.

Robertson, Roland (1992) *Globalization: Social Theory and Global Culture.* London: Sage.

Robin, Carlotte A. (2018) *Pets, Purity, and Pollution. Understanding the sociology of zoonotic disease transmission.* Thesis submitted to the University of Liverpool for the degree of Doctor of Philosophy.

Rockmore, Tom, and Margolis, Joseph (1992) *The Heidegger Case. On Philosophy and Politics.* Philadelphia: Temple University Press.

Rojek, Chris (2018) 'The long durée of Spengler's thesis of the decline of the West' *Journal of Social Theory* 21(4): 419–434.

Rosenblatt, Helena (2008) *Liberal Values. Benjamin Constant and the Politics of Religion.* Cambridge: Cambridge University Press.

Roth, Günther, and Schluchter, Wolfgang (1979) *Max Weber's Vision of History. Ethics and Methods.* Berkeley: University of California Press.

Rothberg, Michael (1997) 'After Adorno: Culture in the Wake of Catastrophe' *New German Critique* 72(3): 45–81.

Saggers, Sherry, and Gray, Dennis (1998) *Dealing with Alcohol: Indigenous Usage in Australia, New Zealand, and Canada.* Cambridge: Cambridge University Press.

Sarris, Peter (2021) 'New Approaches to the "Plague of Justinian"' *Past & Present* 254: 315–346.

Sarris, Peter (2011) *Empires of Faith. The Fall of Rome to the Rise of Islam 500–700.* Oxford: Oxford University Press.

Sawyer, Malcolm (2013) 'What is Financialization?' *International Journal of Political Economy* 42(4): 5–18.

Schild, Pascale (2022) 'From earthquake victims to citizens: dependencies and precarious claims on the state in Azad Kashmir, Pakistan' *Citizenship Studies* 26(3): 305–321.

Scholem, Gershom (1981) *Walter Benjamin. The Story of a Friendship.* Philadelphia: The Jewish Publication Society.

Schorr, John K. (1987) 'Some Contributions German *Katastrophen-Soziologie* can make to the sociology of disaster' *International Journal of Mass Emergencies and Disasters* 3(2): 115–135.

Schumpeter, Joseph (1942) *Capitalism, Socialism, and Democracy.* New York: Harper & Brothers.

Schumpeter, Joseph (1939) *Business Cycles. A Theoretical, Historical and Statistical Analysis of the Capitalist Process.* New York: McGraw Hill.

Schutz, Alfred (1967) *The Phenomenology of the Social World.* Evanston, Il.: Northwestern University Press.

Scruton, Roger (2012) *Our Church. A Personal History of the Church of England.* London: Atlantic Books.

Segarra, Paulina, and Prasad, Ajnesh (2018) 'How does corporality inform theorizing? Revisiting Hannah Arendt and the Banality of Evil' *Human Studies* 41: 545–563.

Semmler, Willi (2013) 'The Macro Austerity in the European Union' *Social Research* 80(3): 883–914.

Sen, Amartya (2009) *The Idea of Justice*. Cambridge, MA: The Belknap Press of Harvard University Press.

Sen, Amartya (1981) *Poverty and Entitlements*. Oxford: Oxford University Press.

Shaw, Martin (2003) *War and Genocide. Organized Killing in Modern Societies*. Cambridge: Polity Press.

Shippey, Tom A. (2001) *Tolkien. Author of the Century*. London: Harper Collins.

Shreve, Bradley G. (2011) *Red Power Rising. The National Indian Youth Council and the Origins of Native Activism*. Norman: University of Oklahoma Press.

Siddhartha, Anupam, and Joshi, Bharat (2009) 'Blackwater – The Private Military and Security Company' *World Affairs: The Journal of International Issues* 13(3): 106–121.

Skinner, Jordan (2014) 'Thought is the courage of hopelessness: an interview with philosopher Gorgio Agamben' *Comments*, 17 June.

Skocpol, Theda (1979) *States and Social Revolutions. A Comparative Analysis of France, China, and Russia*. Cambridge: Cambridge University Press.

Smil, Vaclav (2008) *Global Catastrophes and Trends. The Next Fifty Years*. Cambridge, MA: MIT Press.

Smith, Jason (2004) '"I am sure that you are more pessimistic than I am" An Interview with Giorgio Agamben' *Rethinking Marxism* 16(2): 116–124.

Somers, Margaret R. (2022) 'Toward a predistributive democracy: Diagnosing oligarchy. dedemocratization, and the deceits of market justice' in Jürgen Mackert, Hannah Wolf and Bryan S. Turner (eds), *The Condition of Democracy*. Volume 1: *Neoliberal Politics and Sociological Perspectives*. London: Routledge: 56–87.

Sorokin, Pitirim (1968) *Man and Society in Calamity: The Effects of War, Revolution, Famine and Pestilence upon Human Mind*. New York: Greenwood Press Publishers.

Speckhard, Anne, and Akhmedova, Khapta (2006) *Democracy and Security* 2(1): 103–156.

Spengler, Oswald (1928) *The Decline of the West*. New York: Alfred A. Knopf.

Spengler, Oswald (1920) *Preußentum und Sozialismus*. Munich: C.H. Beck.

Stamatov, Peter (2013) *The Origins of Global Humanitarianism. Religion, Empires and Advocacy*. Cambridge: Cambridge University Press.

Stanford, David E. (1992) *The American Holocaust. The Conquest of the New World*. New York: Oxford University Press.

Stillinger, Jack (ed) (1971) *Mill. Autobiography*. London: Oxford University Press.

Streeck, Wolfgang (2013) *Zwischen Globalismus und Demokratie. Politische Ökonomie im ausgehenden Neoliberalismus*. Berlin: Suhrkamp.

Swan, Shana, and Stacey, Collino (2022) *Countdown*. New York: Simon and Schuster.

Swingewood, Alan (1970) 'Origins of Sociology: The Case of the Scottish Enlightenment' *British Journal of Sociology* 21(2): 164–180.

Taubes, Jacob (2009) *Occidental Eschatology*. Stanford, California: Stanford University Press.

Taubes, Jacob (2004) *Political Theology of Paul*. Stanford, California: Stanford University Press.

Taylor, Branch (1998) *Pillar of Fire: America in the King Years 1963–1965*. New York: Simon & Schuster.

Tester, Keith (2002) 'Paths in Zygmunt Bauman's Social Thought' *Thesis Eleven* 70(1): 55–71.

Thomas, Scott M. (2001) 'Faith, history, and Martin Wight: the role of religion in the historical sociology of the English school of International Relations' *International Affairs* 77(4): 905–929.

Tierney, Kathleen J. (2019) *Disasters: A Sociological Approach*. Cambridge: Polity Press.

Tierney, Kathleen J. (2007) 'From the margins to the mainstream? Disaster research at the crossroads' *Annual Review of Sociology* 33: 503–525.

Tierney, Kathleen J., Lindell, Michael K., and Perry, Roland (2001) *Facing the Unexpected: Disaster Preparedness and Response in the United States.* Washington, DC: Joseph Hardy Press.

Tinker, George (2003) 'Religion' in Frederick E. Hoxie (ed), *Encyclopedia of North American Indians.* Boston: Houghton Mifflin Co.: 517–541.

Tolkien, J. R. R. (2008) 'On Fairy Stories' in Verlyn Flieger and Douglas A. Anderson (eds), *On Fairy Stories.* London: Harper Collins.

Tolkien, J. R. R. (1954–1955) *Lord of the Rings.* London: George Allen & Unwin, 3 vols.

Tolstoy, Leo (2001) *The Death of Ivan Ilyich.* New York: Penguin Putnam.

Tooze, Adam (2018) *Crashed. How a Decade of Financial Crisis Changed the World.* New York: Viking.

Torpey, John C., and Turner, Bryan S. (2017) 'Demography and social citizenship' in Jürgen Mackert and Bryan S. Turner (eds), *The Transformation of Citizenship.* London: Routledge, vol. 1: 188–203.

Toynbee, Arnold (1972) *Study of History.* London: Oxford University Press and Thames & Hudson, 12 vols.

Traboulsi, Fawwaz (2003) *A Modern History of Lebanon.* London: Pluto Press.

Travers, Tim (1987) *The Killing Ground: The British Army, the Western Front, and the Emergence of Modern Warfare, 1900–1918.* London: Allen & Unwin.

Tribe, Keith (1995) 'Professors Malthus and Jones: political economy at the East India College 1806–1858' *The European Journal of the History of Economic Thought* 2(2): 327–354.

Turner, Bryan S. (2022) 'Vulnerability and existence theory in catastrophic times' *Journal of Classical Sociology* 22(1):90–94.

Turner, Bryan S. (2021) 'Theodicies of the Covid-19 catastrophe' in Michael Ryan (ed) *Covid-19. Volume 1: Global Pandemics, Societal Responses, Ideological Solutions.* Abingdon: Routledge.

Turner, Bryan S. (2015) *Citizenship and Capitalism. The Debate Over Reformism.* London and New York: Routledge.

Turner, Bryan S. (2009a) *Can We Live Forever? A Social and Moral Inquiry.* London: Anthem.

Turner, Bryan S. (2009b) 'Violence, human rights and piety: Cosmopolitanism versus Virtuous Exclusion in response to atrocity' in Thomas Brudholm and Thomas Cushman (eds), *The Religious Responses to Mass Atrocity. Interdisciplinary Perspectives.* Cambridge: Cambridge University Press: 242–263.

Turner, Bryan S. (2006) *Vulnerability and Human Rights.* Pennsylvania: The Pennsylvania State University Press.

Turner, Bryan S. (1987) 'A Note on Nostalgia' *Theory, Culture & Society* 4: 147–156.

Turner, Bryan S. (1986) *Citizenship and Capitalism. The Debate over Reformism.* London: Allen & Unwin.

Turner, Bryan S. (1979) *Marx and the End of Orientalism.* London: Allen & Unwin.

Turner, Bryan S., and Contreras-Vejar, Yuri (2018) 'Happiness' in Bryan S. Turner (ed), *The Wiley Encyclopedia of Social Theory.* Wiley-Blackwell, vol. 3: 1030–1037.

Turner Bryan S., and Dumas, Alex (2016) *Antivieillissement. Vieillir à l'ère des novelles biotechnologies.* Quebec: Les Presses de l'Université Laval.

Turner, Frederick J. (1920) *The Frontier in American History.* New York: H. Holt.

Urdal, Henrik (2006) 'Clash of Generations? Youth Bulges and Political Violence' *International Studies Quarterly* 50(3): 607–629.

Vetter, Linda J. (1997) 'The Strategic and Operational Genius of General Vo Nguyen Giap: a funny thing happened to me on the way to Hanoi' Unclassified Paper to the Naval War College: 1–21.

Vianna Franco, Marco P. (2020) 'The Factual Nature of Resource Flow Accounting in the Calculation in Kind of the "Other Austrian Economics"' OEconomia 10(3): 453–472.

Vierhaus, Rudolf (1988) Germany in the Age of Absolutism. Cambridge: Cambridge University Press.

Vinci, Anthony (2007) '"Like Worms in the Entrails of a Natural Man": A Conceptual Analysis of Warlords' Review of African Political Economy 34(112): 313–331.

Voekel, Pamela (2002) Alone before God. The Religious Origins of Modernity in Mexico. Durham and London: Duke University Press.

Voltaire, Jean-Jacques (1912) Toleration and Other Essays/Poem on the Lisbon Disaster. London: G.P. Putnam's Sons.

Von Friedeburg, Robert (2011) 'Cuius Regio, Eius Religio: The Ambivalent Meanings of State Building in Protestant Germany, 1555–1655' in Howard Louthan, Gary B. Cohen and Franz A. J. Szabo (eds), Diversity and Dissent: Negotiating Religious Difference in Central Europe, 1500–1800. Oxford: Berghahn Books: 73–91.

Vries, Jan de (1976) The European Economy in an Age of Crisis. Cambridge: Cambridge University Press.

Vyronis, Spiros (2005) The Mechanism of Catastrophe. The Turkish Pogrom of September 6–7, 1955, and the Destruction of the Greek Community of Istanbul. New York: Greekworks.

Walters, Philip (1986) 'The Russian Orthodox Church and the Soviet State' The Annals of the American Academy of Political and Social Science 483: 135–145.

Ware, Owen (2006) 'Universality and Historicity- on the sources of religion' Research on Phenomenology. Koninklijke: Brill NV Leiden.

Watts, Michael J. (2004) 'Antinomies of Community: Some Thoughts on Geography, Resources and Empire' Transactions of the Institute of British Geographers 29(2): 195–216.

Watts, Michael J. (1991) 'Entitlements or Empowerment? Famine and Starvation in Africa' Review of African Political Economy 51(July): 9–26.

Watts, Michael J. (1983) Silent Violence: Food, Famine and Peasantry in northern Nigeria. Berkeley and Los Angeles: University of California.

Watts, Michael and Bohle, Hans G. (1993) 'The Space of Vulnerability; the causal structure of hunger and famine' Progress in Human Geography 17(1): 43–67.

Weaver, John C. (2003) The Great Land Rush and the Making of the Modern World 1650–1900. Montreal and Kingston: McGill-Queen's University Press.

Webb, Gary R. (2002) 'Sociology, Disasters, and terrorism: understanding threats of the new millennium' Sociological Focus 35(1): 87–89.

Weber, Max (2009a) 'Politics as a Vocation' in Hans H. Gerth and C. Wright Mills (eds), From Max Weber. Essays in Sociology. Abingdon: Routledge: 77–128.

Weber, Max (2009b) 'Science as a Vocation' in Hans H. Gerth and C. Wright Mills (eds), From Max Weber. Essays in Sociology. Abingdon: Routledge: 129–156.

Weber, Max (2005) 'Remarks on Technology and Culture' Theory Culture & Society 22(4): 23–38.

Weber, Max (1994) Political Writings. Cambridge: Cambridge University Press.

Weber, Max (1981) General Economic History. New Brunswick: Transaction Books.

Weber, Max (1956) The Protestant Ethic and the Spirit of Capitalism. London: Unwin University Books

Welborn, Larry L. (2009) '"Extraction from the Mortal Site": Badiou on the Resurrection in Paul' New Testament Studies 55(3): 295–314.

Wells, Herbert G. (2005) *A Modern Utopia.* London: Penguin

Werckmeister, Otto K. (1996) 'Walter Benjamin's Angel of History, or the Transfiguration of the Revolutionary not the Historian' *Critical Inquiry* 22(2): 239–267.

White, Matthew (2011) *Atrocitology. Humanity's Deadliest Achievements.* Edinburgh: Canongate.

Whitfield, Stephen J. (1981) 'Hannah Arendt and the Banality of Evil' *The History Teacher* 14(4): 469–477.

Whyte, Jessica (2013) *Catastrophe and Redemption: The Political Thought of Giorgio Agamben.* New York: SUNY Press.

Wilder, Craig S. (2013) in *Ebony and Ivy. Race, Slavery, and the Troubled history of America's Universities.* New York: Bloomsbury.

Wilentz, Sean (ed) (2009) *Lincoln.* New York: Plagrave Macmillan.

Wilkinson, Ian (2005) *Suffering: A Sociological Introduction.* Cambridge: Polity Press.

Wilson, Peter (2011) *The Thirty Years War: Europe's Tragedy.* London: Belknap Press.

Wiltgen, Richard J. (1998) 'Marx and Engel's Conception of Malthus. The Heritage of a Critique' *Organisation and Environment* 11(4): 451–460.

Winkler, Heinrich A. (2015) *The Age of Catastrophe 1914–1945.* New Haven: Yale University Press.

Wittstock, Luara W., and Bancroft, Dick (2013) *We Are Still Here! A Photographic History of the American Indian Movement.* St. Paul: Minnesota Historical Society Press.

Wolin, Richard (2001) *Heidegger's Children. Hannah Arendt, Karl Loewith, Hans Jonas and Herbert Marcuse.* Princeton and Oxford: Princeton University Press.

Wood, Ralph C. (2007) 'Tolkien's Augustinian Understanding of Good and Evil: *Why The Lord of the Rings* Is Not Manichean' in Trevor Hart and Ivan Kovacs (eds), *Tree of Tales: Tolkien, Literature, and Theology.* Waco, TX: Baylor UP: 85–102.

Wright, Erik O., Levine, Andrew, and Sober, Elliott (1992) *Restructuring Marxism.* London: Verso.

Wrigley, E. A. (1989) 'The Limits to Growth: Malthus and the Classical Economists' in Michael S. Teitelbaum and Jay M. Winter (eds), *Population and Resources in Western Intellectual Traditions.* Cambridge, MA: Cambridge University Press.

Xenos, Nicholas (1989) *Scarcity and Modernity.* London and New York: Routledge.

Yeo, Richard (2001) *Encyclopaedic Visions. Scientific Dictionaries and Enlightenment Culture.* Cambridge: Cambridge University Press.

Zeeman, E. C. (1976) 'Catastrophe Theory' *Scientific American* 234(4): 65–83.

Ziegler, Philip (1969) *The Black Death.* London: Collins.

Index

https://doi.org/10.1515/9783110772364-010

Erratum to: Chapter 7: The Economics of Catastrophe

published in: Bryan S. Turner, A Theory of Catastrophe, 978-3-11-077223-4

Erratum

Despite careful production of our books, sometimes mistakes happen. We apologize sincerely that the following source was not credited in the original version of this chapter of the book:

Vianna Franco, Marco P. (2020) 'The Factual Nature of Resource Flow Accounting in the Calculation in Kind of the "Other Austrian Economics"' *OEconomia* 10(3): 453–472.

This has now been corrected. The relevant passages on pages 107–109 were updated and the source was added to the reference list.

https://doi.org/10.1515/9783110772364-011. The updated chapters are available at DOI: https://doi.org/10.1515/9783110772364-007 and https://doi.org/10.1515/9783110772364-009.